LUTON LIBRARIES

SCREEN ADAPTATIONS
SHAKESPEARE'S
ROMEO AND JULIET
THE RELATIONSHIP BETWEEN TEXT AND FILM

COURTNEY LEHMANN

methuen |

Methuen Drama

1 3 5 7 9 10 8 6 4 2

First published 2010

Methuen Drama
A & C Black Publishers Limited
36 Soho Square
London W1D 3QY
www.methuendrama.com

A CIP catalogue record for this book is available
from the British Library

ISBN 978 0 7136 7912 0

Typset by Margaret Brain, Wisbech, Cambs

Printed and bound in Great Britain by
CPI Cox & Wyman, Reading, Berkshire

contents

Dedication

In loving memory of Kathy Howlett

Acknowledgements

Special thanks to Deborah Cartmell, Jenny Ridout, Indi Garcha for their indefatigable support of this project. And, as always, I am grateful for the unconditional love of Jim, Lyra, Aquillon, Mom, Dad, Brooke, and Isis.

A note on texts

All excerpts from *Romeo and Juliet* are from *The Oxford Shakespeare Romeo and Juliet*, edited by Jill L. Levenson (Oxford: Oxford University Press, 2008). Citations of Shakespeare's other plays are from *The Oxford Shakespeare: The Tragedies*, Volume III (4 Vols), edited by Stanley Wells, et. al (Oxford and New York: Oxford University Press, 1994).

timeline: cinematic adaptations of *Romeo and Juliet*

··

Credits for key films

West Side Story (1961)

Director	Robert Wise and Jerome Robbins
Writers	Ernest Lehman (Screenplay)
	Arthur Laurents (Book)
Lyrics	Stephen Sondheim
Music	Leonard Bernstein
Choreography	Jerome Robbins

Main cast

Natalie Wood	Maria
Richard Beymer	Tony
Russ Tamblyn	Riff
Rita Moreno	Anita
George Chakiris	Bernardo
Simon Oakland	Schrank
Ned Glass	Doc
William Bramley	Krupke
Tucker Smith	Ice
Tony Mordente	Action
David Winters	A-rab
Eliot Feld	Baby John

Bert Michaels	Snowboy
David Bean	Tiger
Robert Banas	Joyboy
Scooter Teague	Big Deal
Harvey Hohnecker	Mouthpiece
Tommy Abbott	Gee-Tar
Susan Oakes	Anybodys
Gina Trikonis	Graziella
Carole D'Andrea	Velma
Jose De Vega	Chino
Jay Norman	Pepe
Gus Trikonis	Indio
Eddie Verso	Juano
Jaime Rogers	Loco
Larry Roquemore	Rocco
Robert Thompson	Luis
Nick Covacevich	Toro
Rudy Del Campo	Del Campo
Andre Tayir	Chile
Yvonne Othon	Consuelo
Susie Kaye	Rosalia
Joanne Miya	Francisca

Romeo and Juliet (1968)

Director Franco Zeffirelli

Writers Franco Brusati, Masolino D'Amico, and Franco Zeffirelli

Main cast

Leonard Whiting	Romeo
Olivia Hussey	Juliet
John McEnery	Mercutio
Milo O'Shea	Friar Laurence
Pat Heywood	The Nurse
Robert Stephens	The Prince of Verona
Michael York	Tybalt
Bruce Robinson	Benvolio
Paul Hardwick	Lord Capulet
Natasha Parry	Lady Capulet

Antonio Pierfederici	Lord Montague
Esmeralda Ruspoli	Lady Montague
Roberto Bisacco	Paris
Roy Hilder	Peter
Keith Skinner	Balthazar
Dyson Lovell	Sampson
Richard Warwick	Gregory

William Shakespeare's Romeo + Juliet (1996)

Director	Baz Luhrmann
Writers	William Shakespeare, Craig Pearce, and Baz Luhrmann

Main Cast

Leonardo DiCaprio	Romeo
Claire Danes	Juliet
John Leguizamo	Tybalt
Harold Perrineau	Mercutio
Pete Postlethwaite	Father Laurence
Paul Sorvino	Fulgencio Capulet
Brian Dennehy	Ted Montague
Paul Rudd	Dave Paris
Vondie Curtis-Hall	Captain Prince
Miriam Margoyles	The Nurse
Jesse Bradford	Balthasar
M. Emmet Walsh	Apothecary
Zak Orth	Gregory
Jamie Kennedy	Sampson
Dash Mihok	Benvolio
Vincent Laresca	Abra
Carlos Martín Mazo Otálora	Petruchio
Christine Pickles	Caroline Montague
Diane Venora	Gloria Capulet
Pedro Altamirano	Peter
Edwina Moore	Anchorwoman
Quindon Tarver	Choir Boy
Diva	Des'ree
Leontyne Price	Liebestod Vocalist

Other films referred to

10 Things I Hate about You (1999) Directed by Gil Junger for Touchstone Pictures.

1942: A Love Story (1994) Directed by Vidhu Vinad Chopra for Vidhu Vinad Chopra and H. L. Salujah.

A Midsummer Night's Dream (1934) Directed by Max Reinhardt and William Dieterle for MGM.

Ambikapathy (1937) Directed by Ellis Duncan for Salem Shankar Films.

Anjuman (1948) Directed by Akhtar Hussain for Nargis Art.

Beneath the 12-Mile Reef (1953) Directed by Robert D. Webb for Twentieth Century Fox.

Bora Bora (1968) Directed by Ugo Liberatore for Arco Film, Finarco, Franco London Films, and International Film Company.

Bread and Tulips (2000) Directed by Silvio Soldini for Istituto Luce.

Breakfast at Tiffany's (1961) Directed by Blake Edwards for Martin Jurow and Richard Shepherd.

Burlesque on Romeo and Juliet (1902) Directed by George Méliès for Thomas Edison Company.

China Girl (1982) Directed by Abel Ferrara for Great American Films Limited Partnership.

Citizen Kane (1941) Directed by Orson Welles for Mercury Productions and RKO.

Dakan (1996) Directed by Mohamed Camera for Film Du 20ème Créations Cinématographiques.

Di Passaggio (2009) James Kicklighter for Jamesworks Entertainment.

Earth (1998) Directed by Deepa Mehta for Cracking the Earth Films.

Fire (1996) Directed by Deepa Mehta for Kaleidescope India Ltd. and Trial by Fire Films Inc.

Hassan wa Nayima (1959) Directed by Henry Barakat for Abdellah Barakat.

Henry V (1989) Directed by Kenneth Branagh for BBC Films and Renaissance Films.

High School Musical (2006) Directed by Kenny Ortega for Disney Channel, Salty Pictures, and First Street Films.

I Want to Live! (1958) Directed by Robert Wise for United Artists.

Italian for Beginners (2000) Directed by Lone Scherfig for Danmarks Radio.

Josh (2000) Directed by Monsoor Kahn for United Seven Combines.

Judgment at Nuremberg (1961) Directed by Stanley Kramer for United Artists.

La Chinoise (1967) Directed by Jean-Luc Godard for Anouchka Films.

La Dolce Vita (1960) Directed by Federico Fellini for Riama Film.

Letters to Juliet (2010) Directed by Gary Winick for Applehead Pictures.

Los Tarantos (1963) Directed by Francisco Beleta for Tecisa Productions.

Montoyas Y Tarantos (1989) Directed by Vincento Escrivá for Comunicacion Visual Creativa.

Moulin Rouge! (2002) Directed by Baz Luhrmann for Bazmark Films.

My Fair Lady (1964) Directed by George Cukor for Warner Brothers.

My House in Umbria (2003) Directed by Richard Loncraine for Canine Films.

My Shakespeare (2004) Directed by Michael Waldman for Penguin Television.

Never Been Kissed (1999) Directed by Raja Gosnell for Fox 2000.

O (2001) Directed by Tim Blake Nelson for Chickie the Cop.

On the Waterfront (1954) Directed by Elia Kazan for Horizon Pictures and Columbia Pictures.

Playmates (1941) Directed by David Butler for RKO Radio Pictures.

Qayamat Se Qayamat Tak (1988) Directed by Mansoor Khan for Nasir Hussain Films.

Romeo and Juliet (1908) Directed by William V. Ranous for Vitagraph.

Romeo and Juliet (1916) Directed by J. Gordon Edwards for Fox.

Romeo and Juliet (1969) Directed by John W. Noble for Metro.

Romeo and Juliet (1931) Directed by István Kató Kiszly; Producer Unknown.

Romeo and Juliet (1936) Directed by George Cukor for MGM.

Romeo and Juliet (1954) Directed by Renato Castellani for Verona Productions.

Romeo and Juliet (1990) Directed by Armando Acosta for Paul Hespiel.

Romeo and Juliet (Shakespeare: The Animated Tales) (1996) Directed by Efin Gambour for Soyuzmultifilm/Christmas Films.

Romeo and Juliet in Town (1910) Directed by Otis Turner for Selig Polyscope Company.

Romeo e Giuletta (1908) Directed by Mario Caserini for Cines.

Romeo e Giuletta (1911) Directed by Gerolamo Lo Savio for Film d'Arte Italiana.

Satyricon (1969) Directed by Federico Fellini for Les Productions Associés and PEA.

Shakespeare in Love (1998) Directed by John Madden for Universal Pictures.

She's the Man (2006) Directed by Andy Fickman for Dreamworks SKG.

Solomon and Gaenor (1999) Directed by Paul Morrison for APT Films.

Splendor in the Grass (1961) Directed by Elia Kazan for NBI Productions, Newton Productions, and Warner Brothers.

Strictly Ballroom (1992) Directed by Baz Luhrmann for M&A.

Teoroma (1968) Directed by Pier Paolo Pasolini for Aetos Produzioni Cinematografiche and EIA.

The Apartment (1960) Directed by Billy Wilder for The Mirisch Corporation.

The Beach (2000) Directed by Danny Boyle for Figment Films.

The Guilty Generation (1931) Directed by Rowland V. Lee for Columbia Pictures.

The Hustler (1961) Directed by Robert Rossen for Rossen Films and Twentieth Century Fox.

The Indian Romeo and Juliet (1912) Directed by Larry Trimble for Vitagraph.

The Piano (1992) Directed by Jane Campion for The Australian Film Commission.

The Shoes of the Fisherman (1968) Directed by Michael Anderson for MGM.

The Taming of the Shrew (1966) Directed by Franco Zeffirelli for Films Artistici Internazionali.

The Taming of the Shrew (1929) Directed by Sam Taylor for Elton Corporation and Pickford Corporation.

The Twilight Moon Saga: New Moon (2009) Directed by Chris Weitz for Imprint Entertainment.

This is the Sea (1997) Directed by Mary McGuckian for First Look International.

Throne of Blood (1952) Directed by Akira Kurosawa for Shojiro Motoki.

Through a Glass Darkly (1960) Directed by Ingmar Bergman for Svensk Filmindustri.

Titanic (1997) Directed by James Cameron for Twentieth Century Fox, Paramount Pictures, and Lightstorm Entertainment.

To the Last Man (1923) Directed by Victor Fleming for Paramount Pictures.

Torn Apart (1989) Directed by Jack Fisher for Danny Fisher and Jerry Menkin.

Two Women (1960) Directed by Vittorio De Sica for Compagnia Cinematografica Champion, Les Films Marceau, Cocinar, and SGC.

Under the Tuscan Sun (2003) Directed by Audrey Welles for Blue Gardenia Productions, Tatiale Films, Timnick Films, and Touchstone Pictures.

Water (2005) Directed by Deepa Mehta for Deepa Mehta Films.

Television series

Glee

My So-Called Life

The Young and the Restless

PART 1:
Literary contexts

A tale of adaptation

Four hundred years before Baz Luhrmann's 1996 film adaptation of *Romeo + Juliet* debuted at number one, Shakespeare's *Romeo and Juliet* was performed - as the First Quarto informs us - 'with great applause'. Despite its obvious flaws as a 'bad' or unauthorised version of the play (a subject to which I will return in Chapter Two) the 1597 Quarto provides valuable clues about the popularity of *Romeo and Juliet* in its own time, since whoever printed - or, perhaps, even pirated - the text knew that there was a substantial market for it. The fact that within two years, Shakespeare's play had already been the subject of an adaptation, 'Newly corrected, augmented, and amended' in the form of Quarto Two (1599), indicates that *Romeo and Juliet* was still a hot commodity and that a certain proprietary impulse - linked, this time, not to profit based on quantity but to pride in quality - was emerging alongside the attribution 'Shakespeare'.

However, attributing this play to Shakespeare alone cannot be accomplished with a clear conscience, for there are few plays with a more complicated history than *Romeo and Juliet*. In fact, although similar claims have been made on behalf of *Hamlet* and *King Lear*, *Romeo and Juliet* is, arguably, the most textually complex play in the Shakespeare canon - not only because it exists in multiple, discrete versions but also because it is a 'legend play' - that is, a play with a long history as another narrative form, which, in and of itself, is equally mired in centuries of changing cultural expectations and modes of transmission.

Perhaps the most intriguing, little-known truth about the play is that, were it not for Dante, the world's most famous love story might never have come to be. In the Sixth Canto of the *Purgatorio*, Dante – for reasons that remain unknown – yoked the families of the Montecchi and Cappelletti together as enemies, using them as an admonitory example of the consequences of civil strife. Merely three lines of verse, this reference essentially resuscitated names which, according to Olin H. Moore, 'had almost passed from popular recollection' by the end of the thirteenth century, inciting a long series of inquiries into the both the veracity and the meaning of the pairing.[1] Again, as Moore explains, not only had Dante created a set of strange bedfellows by linking what Shakespeare's Prologue would describe as '(t)wo households, both alike in dignity',[2] but also, as Moore concludes, 'Dante referred to them in somewhat cryptic language, as was customary when he assumed the role of high priest. As a consequence, a series of misinterpretations arose, which became crystallised into one of the most famous legends of literature'.[3]

In the interests of clarification, an overview of the two 'households' is in order. Evidence points to the presence of a

---

[1] Olin H. Moore, *The Legend of Romeo and Juliet* (Columbus: Ohio State University Press, 1950), p. 15.

[2] With the exception of *Romeo and Juliet*, all citations of Shakespeare's plays are from *The Oxford Shakespeare: The Tragedies* Volume III (4 Vols), edited by Stanley Wells, et. al (Oxford and New York: Oxford University Press, 1994). All excerpts from *Romeo and Juliet* are from *The Oxford Shakespeare Romeo and Juliet*, edited by Jill L. Levenson (Oxford: Oxford University Press, 2008). The above excerpt is located in the very first line of the Prologue; hereafter cited in the text.

[3] Moore, p. 15.

'Montecchi' family in the twelfth century, after which references construe the name as a political party or faction, for any traces of the Montecchi as a family vanished precipitously by the beginning of the thirteenth century. Interestingly, no chronicles associate the 'Montecchi' and the 'Cappelletti' directly with one another. Moore explains that the Montecchi emerged as 'bourgeois enemies of the noble Veronese house of the Conti'.[4] According to historical records, the first member of the 'Montecchi' household to be referenced was Giovanni Monticulo in 1136. If, however, at the end of the century, the Montecchi, Monticulo, Monticoli, and Montecchio vanished as families, then they enjoyed a renaissance in chronicles, reborn purely as political parties or factions. Citing Rolandino's chronicle, Moore explains that when Azzo Marqui of Este was instated as podesta of Verona in 1207, Ezzelino da Romano was incensed by the preferament proffered to his enemy, and, as Moore relates: 'He therefore called a gathering of his followers – from Verona, Vicenza, and elsewhere – in the castle of Montecchio. This circumstance served as a sort of christening for Ezzelino's followers, who were thenceforth known as Monteccchi'.[5] Located in Vincenza on a 'little mountain' – the Latin translation being 'Monticulus' – this castle 'is the only authentic landmark for the story of the Montagues and the Capulets',[6] despite the fantasy re-creation of Juliet's balcony in the film *Letters to Juliet*. More on that much, much later.

Far more prolific are references to the Cappelletti who were not a family residing in Verona but a faction referred to in conjunction

---

[4] Ibid., p. 3.

[5] Ibid., pp. 4–5. See also Rolandino Patavini, 'Cronica Marchie Trivixane' (c. 1262), *Rerum Italicarum Scriptores*, edited by L.A. Muratori, Città di Castello: Tipi dell'editore S Lapi, 1905.

[6] Ibid., p. 5.

with the politics of Cremona.[7] Appropriately, considering the association with their name, the Cappelletti (also referred to as the Cappellini faction), wore tiny caps as their emblem. The Cappelletti lost a great deal of power throughout the first half of the thirteenth century (to their chief enemies, the Barbarasi), but regained some prestige by 1267, after which they were permitted to return from banishment to Cremona, 'where they seem to have caused a few disturbances worth recording'.[8] Again, Dante is the last of their contemporaries to mention the faction when he does so in the *Purgatorio*. Nevertheless, there is little – if any – compelling evidence to suggest that the Montecchi and the Cappelletti entered into direct conflict with each other, despite Dante's pleas to Albert of Habsburg:

> Vieni a veder Montecchi e Cappelletti,
> Monaldo e Filippeschi, uom senza cura;
> Color già tristi, e questi con sospetti.

Loosely translated from Canto Six of the *Purgatorio*, the passage implores the reader to 'Come see the Cappelletti, callous heart,/ see the Monaldi, the Montecchi ruined,/the Filippeschi fearful of their fate'.[9] What Dante's somewhat cryptic statement appears to invoke is the civil war between the Ghibellines, with whom the Veronese Monticoli were aligned, and the Guelphs, to whom the Cremona-based Cappelletti professed loyalty, during the battle to control Lombardy, which was waged from approximately 1249 to 1266. But there remains no suggestion that the specific factions of

[7] Ibid., p. 9.

[8] Ibid., p. 10.

[9] See Mark Musa's superb translation of Dante's *Purgatorio* (New York and London: Penguin, 1985). Musa translates Canto VI, lines 106–08, p. 60.

the Monticoli and the Cappelletti actually squared off *against each other* in the midst of the larger battle between the Ghibellines and the Guelfs; as Dante implies, this conflict was carried on by the Filippeschi (Guelph) and Monaldo (Ghibelline) factions. Of paramount importance for our purposes is the fact that by the end of the thirteenth century, the Monticoli (or Montecchi, as Dante calls them) and the Cappelletti were little more than incidental names in the long list of the defeated. Indeed, as Olin Moore asserts, 'there appears nevertheless towards the end of the (thirteenth) century to have been a gradually increasing tendency to use this term (Monteculis, Monteclus, etc) as a sort of sobriquet',[10] which may explain the eventual attribution of the names Montecchi (and its variants) and Cappelletti to individual families, long after the civil strife between their respective parties had ended.

From Dante's much disputed passage, a wellspring of comments and commentators emerged, beginning in 1323 with Jacopo della Lanna, who references the Montecchi and the Cappelletti together as factions in Cremona, continuing through 1379, when Benvenuto da Imola became the first to refer to the factions as *families*. It was Francesco da Buti who, in 1380, posited a less-than-amicable relationship between the Montecchi and the Cappelletti. Hence, unlike most legends, which are orally trans-mitted, 'it is notable', as Moore concludes, 'that the commentators' misunderstandings regarding the Montecchi and the Cappelletti were all directly traceable to written sources, rather than to folklore'.[11]

---

[10] Moore, p. 8.
[11] Ibid., p. 20.

Major sources

Though the question as to what constitutes a major and a minor influence is open to debate, I will be limiting major sources only to those stories that have plot lines which closely parallel the story we have come to know as Romeo and Juliet – with one exception: the influence of elements of Boccaccio's *Decameron*, from which a pastiche framework for the Romeo and Juliet story can be pieced together.[12] Boccaccio's tale of Madonna Catalina and Gentil Carisendi, for example, may be classified as a 'separation romance' – replete with parental disapproval of the lovers' union, the 'selling' of the heroine to an unwanted suitor, false report of the death of the heroine, a 'premature' burial – all of which, in turn, are details that Boccaccio himself culls from anonymous continental literature, sung by troubadours or circulated in manuscripts. In fact, the additional detail of the sleeping potion appears all over the *Decameron*, particularly in the story of Fermondo, who takes a potion, collapses into a coma for three days, and is surreptitiously removed from his grave by a dubious duo comprising a monk and abbot of the church. Another critical addition to the legend that may be traced to Boccaccio is the suicide of the lover(s), appearing in the story of Girolamo and Salvestra, which culminates when Girolamo, persuaded that his love no longer desires him, holds his breath and dies; at the public funeral, Salvestra collapses – dead – on his body. Finally, in one other, lesser-known story (that of Ricciardo Manardi), Boccaccio describes the lover arriving at the balcony of his beloved via a ladder – likely the source of the rope ladder incident that will appear in later versions of the legend.

[12] *Il Decamerone di Messer Giovanni Bocacci* (c. 1350–53; rev. 1370–71), edited by Pietro Fanfani (Florence: Successori Le Monnier, 1904).

One such version is the anonymous fifteenth-century novella *Ippolito e Leonora*, which is essentially *Romeo and Juliet* with a happy ending.[13] Like the invented feud of the Capulets and the Montagues, the war between the Bardi and the Buondelmonti is so intense that the captains of each faction maintain a retinue of approximately three hundred men. At a feast, Ippolito Buondelmonte, who is eighteen, falls in love with Leonora Bardi, who is fifteen at the time. Later, she will loudly lament the hostilities that beset the two families, much like Juliet does at her balcony in the aftermath of the Capulet ball. Meanwhile, also similar to Act One of Shakespeare's play, Ippolito becomes weak and melancholy from his love affliction; at last his mother threatens to disown him if he will not reveal the cause, and he tells her the truth. Though she is disappointed by her son's news, Signora dei Buondelmonti arranges a meeting between the two lovers, with the help of the mother superior of the local convent, who happens to be Leonora's aunt and, therefore, a willing party to her happiness. Hidden behind a curtain in Leonora's room, Ippolito, having promised to perform nothing untoward, overhears Leonora utter her love for him. At this, he emerges from behind the curtain and terrifies her, but offers his dagger for her to kill him with, should she be untrusting of his motives. They confirm their mutual love and, before arranging a proper consummation (with the help of a rope ladder), Leonora insists on a *per verba* 'spousal', or, essentially, a promise of marriage which, in the Renaissance, was legally binding. Nevertheless, en route to Leonora's room, Ippolito is spotted and apprehended for attempted theft. Not wanting to indict Leonora's honour in any way, Ippolito staunchly refuses to answer any of the questions posed by the authorities, and his execution is

---

[13] A synopsis of this story is provided by Moore, pp. 29–33.

precipitously arranged. Permitted to pass by the Bardi house one more time to apologise, Ippolito does so only to find Leonora descending the ladder and exclaiming that she will not have her lover killed. The two youths appear before the fathers of their respective houses; Leonora explains that she and Ippolito are wife and husband and that he was simply undertaking a conjugal visit. The story ends with the two families reconciled and Ippolito's doom revoked.

Although many of Boccaccio's own sources are themselves culled from classical literature (Ovid's *Pyramus and Thisbe* being an obvious contender), I will proceed to examine the undulating chronology from which *Romeo and Juliet* evolved.

Masuccio

Masuccio Salernitano's 'Thirty-Third-Novel' from *Il Novelino*, composed in the mid-fifteenth century, is believed to be the first printed version of the legend which spawned the series of imitations that would lead to Shakespeare's variation on the Romeo and Juliet theme.[14] This short story features two lovers named Mariotto Mignanelli and Giannozza Saraceni, as well as an Augustine Friar who willingly marries the lovers in secret. But Masuccio's version is less compelling as a tale of tragic love than it is a critique of the corrupt clergy and the lasciviousness of women. The scheming Friar, who takes a bribe to perform the lovers' forbidden marriage, self-evidently embodies the former, while Giannozza becomes a sexual aggressor, as the character who asks Mariotto to marry him so that

[14] Masuccio Salernitano, 'The Thirty-Third-Novel,' from *Il Novellino* (1475), in *Romeo & Juliet: Original Text of Masuccio Salernitano, Luigi Da Porto, Matteo Bandello, William Shakespeare*, edited by Adolph Caso, translated by Maurice Jonas (Boston: Dante University of America Foundation, 1992), pp. 15–22.

they might partake of love's 'sweetest fruits'.[15] Moreover, it is implied that the Friar is unusually and, it would seem, inappropriately attached to Romeo, though the details of their relationship have to be read between-the-lines. Nevertheless, there are several other elements that are common to the Romeo and Juliet legend more generally, including the protagonist's banishment and the female lover driven to drink a sleeping potion by a father intent on marrying her to another man. Consequently, as in Shakespeare's play, miscommunication leads Mariotto to learn that Giannozza is dead, for her letter to him is never delivered; her messenger is slain by Corsairs as he sails to Alexandria to confirm the plan. Meanwhile, Mariotto, 'with great joy, hastened to his *predetermined death'*,[16] returning to her sepulcher in Siena, in order to lie with her in her grave; but, alas, Mariotto is apprehended by a host of friars who claim that he's a grave robber. He is executed for his deed at the same time that Giannozza, *dressed as a monk*, travels with her accomplice-friar to Alexandria, where she presumes that Mariotto dwells. When she learns that he has left for Siena, devastated by her "death," she dresses again in men's clothes and returns to Siena to learn that Mariotto was beheaded only three days prior. Of her own volition, she decides to enter a convent, wherein her life – due to her grief and her refusal of food and sleep – is greatly foreshortened. Worthy of note is that this is the first text to suggest the legendary or 'predetermined' nature of the lovers' tragic destiny.

[15] Quoted in Caso, p. 17.

[16] Quoted in Caso, p. 20, emphasis mine.

Da Porto

It was Luigi Da Porto who first named the lovers in Masuccio's story 'Romeo and Juliet', that is, 'Giulietta e Romeo', and it was Da Porto who was responsible for the play's setting in Verona.[17] It is critical, however, to peruse Da Porto's dedicatory epistle before reading the story he composes, for in and of itself, the letter attests to the problems of transmission that have forever plagued the legend of Romeo and Juliet. Da Porto mentions that he was traveling with an archer who, 'like all those who come from Verona . . . was a very great talker'.[18] It is this archer, later identified as Pellegrino da Verona, who relates the story of star-crossed love. When he begins, however, the archer acknowledges that his source is an 'old chronicle', which was evidently narrated to him, because, he explains before starting, 'I will relate the story to you as I have heard it without the least alteration'.[19] So, too, in his opening dedication to 'the most beautiful and gracious Lady Lucina Savorgnano', Da Porto himself admits that although he has 'heard the same story many times', he will, by committing it to writing, pay the 'debt of honor which I owe to you . . . .'[20] Hence, from Da Porto's archer, who is relaying – ostensibly verbatim – the story as he has heard it, we receive the following tale of 'Giulietta e Romeo'. Da Porto, if we can attribute the tale to him for writing it down, adapts the story and provides us with many of the details upon which Shakespeare would later draw, using Masuccio

[17] Luigi Da Porto, *Istoria novellamente ritrovata di due nobili amanti, con la loro pietosa morte, intervenuta già nella citta di Verona nel tempo del Signor Bartolommeo della Scala* (1530), in *Romeo & Juliet: Original Text of Masuccio Salernitano, Luigi Da Porto, Matteo Bandello, William Shakespeare*, edited by Adolph Caso, translated by Maurice Jonas (Boston: Dante University of America Foundation, 1992), pp. 23–52.

[18] Quoted in Caso, p. 25.

[19] Quoted in Caso, p. 26.

[20] Quoted in Caso, p. 24.

before him and, most certainly, plot devices from Ovid's *Pyramus and Thisbe* and, even, *Pygmalion*.[21]

Indeed, nearly every major and, even, minor character who appears in Shakespeare's play is referenced in Da Porto's story, beginning with the Prince. The first major event is the Cappelletti ball, where It Is not so much Romeo who Is enamored wIth GIulIetta (for he is anxiously seeking out his present – not future – love) as Giulietta is infatuated with Romeo. When he lowers his mask, Romeo catches the attention of everyone, who collectively watch in wonder as he reveals himself to be decked out like a nymph; in the following description, Romeo is virtually androgynous, for the 'beauty of his appearance in everyone's opinion surpassed that of all the lovely ladies present'.[22] It is during the last dance that the character of Marcuccio is introduced, but all that is said of him is that 'his hands were always freezing'.[23] Also at this time Giulietta takes Romeo's hand, and the greeting of Shakespeare's Romeo, 'If I profane with my unworthiest hand/This holy shrine' (I.v.92–93), may very well have been inspired by Da Porto's Romeo exclaiming: 'If by my hand I warm yours, your beautiful eyes have inflamed my heart'.[24] After this initial encounter, Romeo and Giulietta are left to admire each other from afar, until one night, Romeo ascends the balcony walls and Giulietta – for propriety's sake – having refused to allow him entry into her bedchamber, asks Romeo, 'Who is freezing from the snow outside, what would you have me do?'.[25]

---

[21] See Books Four and Ten, respectively, of Ovid's *Metamorphoses* (8 AD), in *The Oxford World Classics* edition, translated by A.D. Melville (Oxford and New York: Oxford University Press, 1998).

[22] Quoted in Caso, p. 27.

[23] Quoted in Caso, p. 27.

[24] Quoted in Caso, p. 28.

[25] Quoted in Caso, p. 30.

Easily, we can recall that Shakespeare will embellish this simple question with the more pointed words: 'What satisfaction canst thou have tonight?' (2.1.169). When Da Porto's Romeo indicates that he wishes to 'converse' with her (slang for sexual consummation), Giulietta becomes indignant, and refuses to grant him his wish until they become properly married.

Appropriately, Friar Lorenzo fulfills this duty. Romeo and Giulietta enjoy each other for several days until the feud breaks out once again; Romeo kills 'Tebaldo' and is thereafter banished to Mantua. Although, provocatively, Giulietta offers to cut off her hair and follow him as a servant, Romeo declines her offer; thus, Giulietta is left longing for a swift death. Giulietta's sorrow increases exponentially when her mother, believing her daughter to be in love, suggests to Giulietta's father that she be married, explaining that their daughter 'is not the sort of merchandise to keep to long in the house . . . .'[26] It is not the Count Paris but the Count of Ladrone who is picked by her father, and the news that Giulietta rejects his choice enrages him – a scene that Shakespeare also integrates into the play. Shrewdly, just as she will do in Shakespeare's version, Juliet asks her mother's permission to attend confession, thereby pleasing her mother while permitting the Friar to arrive at his desperate solution to Juliet's predicament. The Friar asks if, once having taken the potion and feigned death, she will be afraid of lying near her recently-departed cousin Tebaldo, and she bravely informs him that she would pass through the 'infernal regions' themselves to be with her Romeo. Shakespeare, of course, permits Juliet seventeen lines of speculation as to what will happen should she encounter Tybalt's corpse while in the Capulet crypt (4.3.40–56). As in Shakespeare's version, however, the other friar, who is charged with briefing Romeo on life in Verona, does not

[26] Quoted in Caso, p. 34.

succeed in delivering the letter, and Pietro, the servant, tells him in person that Giulietta is dead. A scene employed in many opera versions, as well as Baz Lurhmann's film adaptation, Romeo enters Giulietta's tomb and takes the poison; Giulietta awakes while Romeo is still alive, believing herself – initially – to be in the arms of Friar Lorenzo. Olin Moore observes at this juncture that, based on 'the dramatic substitution of Romeo for Friar Lorenzo, Da Porto accomplishes the double purpose of welding Masuccio's narrative with the Pygmalion theme, and of emphasising the churchman's weakness of character'.[27] Significantly, before Romeo dies, he offers an encomium to Giulietta's 'eyes', 'mouth', and 'bosom', much like Shakespeare's Romeo, who will stare at his 'dead' love and exclaim: 'Eyes look your last/Arms take your last embrace! And lips, O you/The doors of breath, seal with a righteous kiss/A dateless bargain to engrossing death' (5.3.112–114).

A major difference between Da Porto and Shakespeare, Giulietta – in the former account – holds her breath in order to die, after the Friar indicates that he will convey her to a nunnery. The Friar does his best to honour Romeo and Giulietta's last wish that they be permitted to lay together for eternity, but, other meddling friars with whom Friar Lorenzo has fallen out, report his actions to the authorities. In so doing, 'Da Porto gives us an early hint of Friar Lorenzo's future conduct by introducing him as a sort of necromancer, bound to Romeo by confidential relations, yet careful of his reputation in the community'.[28] Nevertheless, granted the opportunity to relay the tragedy to the Prince, Friar Lorenzo tells all, and the Prince is so moved by the tale that he orders the bodies to be laid out on the church carpet (a tableau that Zeffirelli will repeat in his 1968 film, where the lovers are similarly displayed in the church

[27] Moore, p. 54.
[28] Ibid., p. 57.

entryway), where the parents of the children make amends and commission a monument for the two lovers, vowing to bury their strife with their children's death. As we shall see, Baz Luhrmann not only depicts the lovers' death in an exquisitely lit Catholic church, but also shows Juliet awaking just as Romeo takes the poison.

Bandello

Similar to Da Porto's version, in Bandello's 'Romeo and Giuletta',[29] Romeo – 'a youth of twenty or thereabouts' – is identified at the Capelletti ball as 'the handsomest and most courteous (youth) in all Verona'.[30] Bandello generally elaborates on the developments that Da Porto before him merely touches on; for example, Bandello goes to great lengths to establish Romeo's love for another woman – so much so that Romeo's good friend (whom Shakespeare will call Benvolio) becomes desperately concerned about Romeo's condition, and convinces him to go to the ball where he will meet another great lady – naturally, our heroine, Giulietta. Like Da Porto, Romeo is situated in the final dance on one side of Juliet, with Marcuccio on the other. Expanding somewhat on this character, Bandello not only explains that Marcuccio has desperately cold hands, but also that he never fails, through his great wit, 'to set the company laughing'.[31] Shakespeare builds considerably upon this hint, converting Mercutio into a hot-tempered, lusty young man, who takes it upon himself to make Romeo 'sociable' – that is,

[29] Matteo Bandello, 'La sfortunata morte di dui infelicissimi amanti che l'uno di veleno e l'altro di dolore morirono, con vari accidenti', Le Novelle (c.1554), in Romeo & Juliet: Original Text of Masuccio Salernitano, Luigi Da Porto, Matteo Bandello, William Shakespeare, edited by Adolph Caso, translated by Percy Pinkerton (Boston: Dante University of America Foundation, 1992), pp. 53–88.

[30] Quoted in Caso, p. 55.

[31] Quoted in Caso, p. 58.

pointing him in the direction of sexual experience – through his wit and bawdy promptings. Bandello might be said to be the first to employ conspicuous foreshadowing of Romeo and Giulietta's ill-fated end, by referring to Romeo, for example, as someone who 'drank in draughts of the luscious poison of love' and, shortly thereafter, as one who 'had become deeply impregnated with love's subtle poison'.[32] Bandello is also the first to introduce the character of the Nurse, with whom Shakespeare deals quite roundly. As in Da Porto, the lusty Romeo devises a plan to enter Giulietta's bedchamber where, he claims, he may 'show (her) the magnitude of (his) love'.[33] Here, too, Giulietta demands that only marriage will make any their mutual desire legitimate, a bargain to which Romeo eagerly agrees. Although Bandello introduces the new' element by which Romeo ascends to Giulietta's chamber – the rope ladder – this prop, as we have seen, comes from Boccaccio. Prefiguring Shakespeare's play, both the Nurse and Romeo's servant, Pietro (Balthazar), are accomplices to Romeo and Giulietta's clandestine affair.

Bandello is also the first to be sexually explicit about the 'delicious dalliance' of which Romeo and Giulietta partake. Meeting in a garden, they '(i)n mutual kisses' find themselves in the throes of 'infinite, unspeakable delight. Withdrawing to a corner of the garden where there was a bench, they then and there con-summated the marriage'.[34] Shakespeare is much less candid, as he modestly describes the lovers only in their waking or *aubade* scene the morning after, when they exchange quips about the 'nightingale' versus the 'lark'. Similarily, while Da Porto's time frame spans the pre-Lent 'Carnivale' period through Easter, Bandello's

[32] Quoted in Caso, p. 57, p. 59.

[33] Quoted in Caso, p. 61.

[34] Quoted in Caso, p. 65.

period is less specific, but also ranges across several weeks, beginning during an unspecified period of sundry entertainments and elegant balls and ending at Easter time.

As in Da Porto, there is a fight that ruins the Friar's plans of making peace between the two factions. Departing from his immediate source, however, Bandello has Romeo attempt to keep the peace, killing Tebaldo purely in self-defence (Marcuccio is not present), whereas Da Porto has Romeo inflamed by Tebaldo to the point of murdering him intentionally. These different interpretations, as we shall see in Chapter Two, are reiterated in Quarto 2 and Quarto 1, respectively. When Giulietta receives news of Romeo's banishment, she weeps incessantly 'not for the loss of her cousin, but because all hope had vanished of the alliance',[35] suggesting that her love for Romeo also has a shrewd social purpose, motivated, in part, by her desire for reconciliation between the families. In both Da Porto's and Bandello's versions, Giulietta offers to escape with Romeo disguised as his page, but Romeo refuses this indignity to her person – tragically, as it turns out – in both versions.

At this point, Bandello alters slightly Giulietta's chosen suitor's name from Count Ladrone to Count Paris Di Lodrone, enabling Bandello to show Juliet's wit when she informs her confessor, Fra Lorenzo, that the Count ought to be called 'ladrone' (or 'thief', as he is in Da Porto) rather than Lodrone, 'since he would steal the property of another'.[36] Both Da Porto's and Bandello's accounts contain Old Capulet's outrage at his daughter's refusal to marry his chosen suitor, after which, Giulietta conspires with Fra Lorenzo in concocting the sleeping potion plan. Significantly, Bandello is the first to introduce Giulietta's hysterical speculation over what will happen in the crypt, where she fears seeing Tebaldo, 'with all the blood streaming from a

[35] Quoted in Caso, p. 67.
[36] Quoted in Caso, p. 72.

gash in his throat. . . . Her every hair stood on end'; Fra Lorenzo has
planted this fear in her mind, however, when he asks her, in a way
that can't help but strike the modern reader as amusing: 'Say, now,
my daughter, shall you not be afraid of your cousin Tebaldo, who lies
in the vault where you will be placed? By this time, he must stink
horribly'.[37] Nevertheless, Giulietta takes the potion and, in the
morning, her Nurse will attempt to rouse her by calling Giulietta a
'slug-a-bed'[38] – precisely the term that the Nurse will use in
Shakespeare's play. Bandello also introduces the idea that the letter
explaining Fra Lorenzo's plan to Romeo never arrives, due to an
outbreak of the plague; hence, Romeo learns of Giulietta's 'death'
and hastens, with Pietro, to the tomb. An addition from Bandello that
reappears in Shakespeare is Romeo's decision to relate all of the
recent events in a letter to his father, a letter that doubles as his will,
for it also indicates that Pietro should be taken care of, as well as the
poor. Here, as in Da Porto, Giulietta awakens just as Romeo takes the
poison; however, Bandello gives them an hour or so to love and
grieve in equal measure. Romeo even apologises to Tybalt, just as he
will in Shakespeare's play, before the snakewater kills him.
Importantly, Bandello's portrait of Fra Lorenzo issues a corrective to
Da Porto's version, removing any hint of an inappropriately intimate
relationship with Romeo, along with the charges of necromancy and
grave-robbing brought forth by the Watch. Likewise, Fra Lorenzo
offers to dispose of Giulietta in a nunnery, but she preempts his
suggestion when she spontaneously expires with grief. The prose tale
ends with the governor's decision to bury both lovers in a common
tomb and, as Bandello concludes – surprisingly inauspiciously – 'this
caused a peace to be made between the Montecchi and
Capelletti, though it did not last very long'.[39]

[37] Quoted in Caso, p. 75, p. 77.
[38] Quoted in Caso, p. 78.
[39] Quoted in Caso, p. 88.

Brooke

Although Arthur Brooke became the first person to adapt the Romeo and Juliet legend into verse, ironically, perhaps the most interesting feature of his 3020 line poem 'The Tragicall Historye of Romeus and Juliet' is its letter 'To The Reader', which, given its publication in 1562 – only four years into Elizabeth's still-contested reign – suggests a subtle strain of anti-Catholic propaganda, as Brooke describes a

> couple of unfortunate lovers, thrilling themselves to unhonest desire,
> neglecting the authoritie and advise of parents and frendes, conferring
> their principall counsels with drunken gossyppes, and *superstitious friers*
> (*the naturally fitte instruments of unchastitie*), attempting all adventures of
> perryll, for th(')attanynyng of their wished lust, *using auricular confession*
> (*the key of whoredom, and treason*), for furtherance of theyr purpose. . . . [40]

Another critical piece of information we receive from Brooke is his reference to a precedent-setting or 'Ur' theatrical version of *Romeo and Juliet*, of which no trace has ever been unearthed. Issuing a

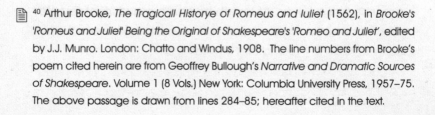

[40] Arthur Brooke, *The Tragicall Historye of Romeus and Iuliet* (1562), in *Brooke's 'Romeus and Juliet' Being the Original of Shakespeare's 'Romeo and Juliet'*, edited by J.J. Munro. London: Chatto and Windus, 1908. The line numbers from Brooke's poem cited herein are from Geoffrey Bullough's *Narrative and Dramatic Sources of Shakespeare*. Volume 1 (8 Vols.) New York: Columbia University Press, 1957–75. The above passage is drawn from lines 284–85; hereafter cited in the text.

caveat, Brooke informs the reader that he has persevered with his poetic adaptation despite having seen a far superior stage version, hoping that the reader will pardon the fact that 'I saw the same arguyment lately set forth on stage with more commendation, then I can looke for: (being there much better set forth then I have or can dooe). . . .' (285).

Although Brooke's long poem is considered Shakespeare's primary source, the work ultimately adds very little to the details discussed above. However, it is interesting to note that Brooke is the first to reference the story's past history as a legend, suggesting that his 'Tragicall Historye' is history indeed: 'No legend lye I tell' (39), Brooke asserts, for he proceeds to invoke *actual witnesses* of the civil strife between the feuding families as his primary source of information, explaining that 'scarce yet theyr eyes be drye/That did behold the grisly sight, with wet and weping eye' (39–40). Nearly three decades before the English public stage became a form of early modern journalism, Brooke uses poetry as a form of 'eye-witness' reporting.

As in the preceding versions, Romeus is introduced as a figure whose beauty exceeds that of women, but he does not go so far (as Da Porto does) to feminise him as a 'nymph'. Rather, he is one 'With which the heavens him had and nature so bedect/That Ladies thought the fairest dames were fowle in his respect' (177–78). More interesting is the introduction of Juliet, which may be the source of the play's preoccupation with rape – a point to which I will return in Chapter Three. Romeus's first glimpse of Juliet is described as follows: 'At length he saw a mayd, right fayre of perfect shape/Which Theseus, or Paris would have chosen to their rape . . . .' (197–98).

Arguably it is the character of the Nurse in Brooke's poem that makes the strongest impression upon Shakespeare's conception of the play. Although Brooke describes a deep friendship between the Nurse and Juliet, he rarely passes up an opportunity to take a misogynistic jab at the Nurse's unenviable role as a gossip and 'prater', adding that her status as a widow predisposes her not just to superfluous chatter but also to damaging untruths, explaining that 'boldly do they chat . . . when no man checkes theyr lies' (666). Shakespeare, it should be observed, does not indict the Nurse as a liar; he does, however, make her quite the 'prater'. In fact, Brooke's version of the Nurse's story about rearing Juliet is adopted – and adapted – by Shakespeare in Act One, scene three, undoubtedly inspired by the following lines:

> A pretty babe (quod she), it was when it was yong,
> Lord how it could full pretely have prated with its tong,
> A thousand times and more I laid her on my lappe,
> And clapt her on the buttocke soft and kist where I did clappe,
> And gladder then was I of such a kisse forsooth,
> Then I had been to have a kisse of some olde lechers mouth.
> And thus of Juliets youth began this prating noorse. (653–659)

In a more charitable vein, Brooke provides further backstory upon which Shakespeare will rely, adding the detail that Juliet's lone confidante once served as her 'wet nurse': 'This olde dame in her youth, had nurst her with her mylke,/With slender needle taught her sow, and how to spin with silke' (345–46). (Significantly, at least two film adaptations show Juliet doing handiwork as she awaits the Nurse's news from Romeo.)

Like Bandello before him, Brooke also employs conspicuous foreshadowing devices. For example, even prior to the lovers' first meeting, the inauspicious nature of the relationship is suggested in Brooke's description of Romeus's affliction with love-at-first-sight. At this moment, Romeus not only forgets his 'former love' – the character that Shakespeare will reinvent as 'Rosaline' – but also 'forgets himselfe' as 'he swalloweth downe loves sweet empoysonde bait' (215). Indeed, Romeus will quite literally die for love by swallowing poison; meanwhile, Brooke – relentlessly compelled to complete his couplet – adds: 'How surely are the wareles wrapt by those that lye in wayte?' (215, 219). Given Shakespeare's approach to Juliet as an outspoken figure who is easily 'half the wooer' in the transactions that occur throughout the balcony scene, one cannot help but wonder if, in Brooke's explicitly moralising version, Juliet is more explicitly positioned as a *femme fatale* who 'lies in wait' for Romeus, aggressively angling for his attention. Turning, once again, to inauspicious insinuations, Brooke proceeds not merely to imply but actually to spell out Romeus's death at the hands of an infectious, opportunistic love when, upon Romeus's first sight of Juliet, Brooke ruefully exclaims: 'So is the poyson spred throughout his bones and vaines/That in a while (alas the while) it hasteth deadly paines' (221–22).

In keeping with earlier treatments of the legend, Brooke's Juliet insists on being Romeus's 'lawfull wedded wife' (426) before the relationship can proceed any further, and hopes that their union will end the strife between the two households. Continuing his use of nautical imagery and allusions to angling – the early modern term for fishing – Brooke describes the pending consummation of the lovers as follows:

> The seas are quite appeased, and thou by happy starre
> Art comme in sight of quiet haven and, now the wrackfull barre
> Is hid with swelling tyde, boldly thou mayst resort
> Unto thy wedded ladies bed, thy long desyred port. (801–4)

Although some of the more significant differences between Quartos 1 and 2 will be discussed in the following chapter, it seems very likely that Brooke's rather indiscrete reference to Juliet's in-tact hymen – 'And now the virgins fort hath warlike Romeus got,/In which as yet no breache was made by force of canon shot' (921–22) – influences Juliet's oddly violent characterisation of her love for Romeo in the so-called 'bad quarto' of Shakespeare's play: 'Love's heralds should be thoughts,/And run more swift, than hasty powder fired,/Doth hurry from the fearful Canon's mouth' (Q1, 2.5.4–6).

Brooke's consistently sanctimonious tone may stem from the fact that, like others before him, Romeus and Juliet's courtship – and, more specifically in Brooke, their clandestine conjugal visits – occur over a period of several months (from Christmas to Easter) as opposed to mere days in Shakespeare's play. In fact, the poem's argument makes it clear from the very beginning that 'Three months he (Romeus) doth enjoy his cheefe delight' (Argument 5), setting the stage for the poem's narrative tone, which is at once punitive and prudish, but always titillating in its tattling. Appropriately, the end of Lent – the day after Easter – is the fateful point at which Tybalt seeks out mischief with the Montague clan; although Romeus tries to part the combatants, he is unsuccessful. Tybalt's ensuing reply to Romeus's demand for peace will be converted by Shakespeare into both the written and spoken challenge that Tybalt addresses to Romeo in the play. In Brooke's version, the saucy youth chides Romeus for his glib naivete: 'No, coward, traytor boy (quoth he) straight way I mind to try/Whether thy sugred talke, and tong so smothely fylde,/Against the force of this my swerd shall serve thee for a shylde' (1116–18). In the play, following Romeo's litany of brotherly compliments to his new-found kinsman, the stunned Tybalt exclaims: 'Boy, this shall not excuse the injuries/That thou hast done me, therefore, turn and draw' (3.1.65–66). Distinct from Shakespeare's play, in Brooke's poem, Romeus acts out of self-defence, striking Tybalt in the throat, a death blow that mimics the one dealt by Bandello's more ruthless Romeo. It is also worth noting that, as in earlier versions of the legend, Mercutio is not present as the fight's *agent provocateur*; he is, rather, a figure who barely receives mention at the Capulet ball as someone who has very cold hands (261–62). Mercutio is not introduced into the fight until Shakespeare ingeniously weaves all the elements of his predecessors' work together.

When Romeus subsequently receives the Prince's doom of banishment, the young lover devolves into a kind of madman, tearing his hair and clothing much as Shakespeare's Romeo does (1291–92). It is here that Shakespeare's borrowings from Brooke are most apparent, for Shakespeare's Romeo quite specifically echoes Romeus's outrage and antics (3.3). Moreover, Friar Laurence's tirade against Romeo bespeaks a tangible affinity with the words spoken by Fryer Lawrence (alternately spelled as 'fryer' and 'fryre'), who upbraids Romeus for his 'womanish' behavior: 'Art thou (quoth he) a man? Thy shape saith so thou art:/Thy crying and weping eyes, denote a womans hart' (1353–54). Similarly, Friar Laurence exclaims, indignantly, to Romeo: 'Art thou a man? Thy form cries out thou art./Thy tears are womanish . . . .' (3.3 108–9). Clearly, Shakespeare outright steals from Brooke at this juncture; hence, it is peculiar that, when Brooke proleptically composes a line that sounds quintessentially 'Shakespearean', namely, the Friar's counsel to Romeus – 'Unto a valiant hart there is no banishment,/All countreys are his native soyle beneath the firmament' (1043–44) – Shakespeare disregards this poetic prompt. In fact, at certain points it almost seems as though Shakespeare is at war with Brooke, mimicking the internal feud around which the legend turns while also positing a proprietary impulse toward his play. For example, Fryre Lawrence tells Romeus that once he undertakes the work of restoring his good name and mitigating hostilities between the warring households, then Juliet 'With *doubled honor* shall she call thee home within a whyle' (1448, emphasis mine). For Shakespeare, such a statement is evidently not dramatic enough, for his Friar promises that once Romeo leaves for Mantua, he will

> find a time
> To blaze your marriage, reconcile your friends,
> Beg pardon of the Prince and call thee back,
> *With twenty hundred thousand times more joy*
> Than thou wentst forth in lamentation.
>   (3.3.149–53, emphasis mine).

Shakespeare's decision to exaggerate – exponentially – the joy with which Romeo will be greeted suggests the extent to which Shakespeare is competing with Brooke to establish playwriting, like poetry, as a legitimate lyrical form in its own right, rather than just a strictly commercial enterprise.

Like his predecessors, Brooke includes as one solution to the lovers' unexpected predicament Juliet's offer of cross-dressing, making Shakespeare one of the most prominent purveyors of the legend who does not reference this possibility – even though, as in other versions – Romeo vehemently rejects the notion. Indeed, after Juliet raises the point in Brooke's tale, Romeus is quick to dismiss her plan. Overly sure of himself and tragically blinded by love to pragmatism, Romeus tells her: 'From Verone will I cary thee, into a forein lande,/Not in mans weede disguised, or as one scarcely knowne,/But as my wife and onely feere, in garment of thyne owne' (1680–82). Subsequently, Juliet is left with no choice but to return home to bewail her existence and Romeus's absence; in fact, she cries so much that, just as Old Capulet will exclaim in Shakespeare's play 'How now? A conduit, girl? What, still in tears?' (3.5.129). Brooke is similarly driven to exaggerate Juliet's grief as she empties her 'payned hart by conduits of the eyne' (1805). Hence, in Brooke's poem, when Juliet's father wishes to cheer her up by seeing her married at the tender age of sixteen, Juliet refuses. Like Old Capulet, Juliet's father has laboured to make a fortuitous match for his daughter according to her degree, is outraged by his seemingly insolent and stubborn child. After a long and nasty rant, he promises instead to wed her to a *jail* that shall not fail to make her wish 'a thousand times a day' for 'sodayn death' (1981).

When Juliet goes to the Friar in search of some solution to her predicament of forswearing her marriage to Romeus, Friar Lawrence repeatedly reassures Juliet of Romeus's plan to sweep her off her feet and away from Verona, often referring to Romeus as 'thy knight' (2092; 2163; 3020). Oddly enough, this is a detail that not Shakespeare but Luhrmann will, somehow, take up in his 1996 adaptation, choosing to dress Romeo as a knight in shining armor at the Capulet ball. Subsequently, when Juliet takes the potion, Shakespeare follows Brooke in representing Juliet on the eve of her 'death' as a brave young girl who requests that her nurse leave her to lie alone (2331); similarly, though not nearly as long as her fearful speculation in Shakespeare's play, Juliet pauses momentarily in Brooke's version to consider the fearful sight of looking upon the grisly 'carkas of Tybalt' (2380). Meanwhile, the Friar's letters to Romeus miscarry when 'frier John' is stopped and confined because another, local brother of his order has died of the plague in Mantua; and no one believes that this newcomer is an out-of-towner who couldn't have possibly been exposed to the victim. Romeus, predictably, finds out from his 'man' that Juliet is 'dead' and purchases illegal poison from a poor apothecary for 'fiftie crownes of gold' (2577). Resolute, Romeus exclaims to the apothecary: 'What by no friendship could be got, with money should be bought' (2572) – a line that is reminiscent of Romeo's diatribe on the evils of gold (5.2.80–83). Hence, when Romeus arrives in the tomb, it is not the Friar but Romeus himself around whom intimations of necrophilia swirl. Indeed, Brooke informs us that, as Romeo stands over Juliet's body: 'He waterd her with teares, and then an hundred times her kyst . . . /But no way could his greedy eyes be filled with her sight. His fearfull handes he layd upon her stomacke cold,/And on them divers parts beside, the woeful wight did hold' (2634; 36–38).

Romeus proceeds to apologise to Tybalt for robbing him of his youth, and, unlike the preceding versions, Juliet wakes one hour *after* Romeus has died, and the Friar is their to escort her to 'somme religious house' (2717) where she shall spend the remainder of her days – an offer she refuses. As in Shakespeare's play, both the Friar and Balthazar flee when they hear a noise; Juliet draws Romeus's dagger while holding his body in her arms and, after a long speech, she presumably stabs herself. Brooke appears to be tongue-tied at this point: 'She grones, she stretcheth out her limbes, she shuttes her eyes,/And from her corps the sprite doth flye. What should I say? she dyes' (2791–92). Although Brooke is credited with converting the instrument of Juliet's death to a dagger, as we shall see below, Boaistuau, just three years earlier, had made the very same emendation. Subsequently, arraigned before Prince Escalus, the Friar confesses to his role in the tragedy, recounting the story of Romeus and Juliet's love. Balthazar, Romeus's man, confirms all with a letter. Unlike Shakespeare's play, in Brooke's version, the punishment meted out by Escalus shows the explicit morality tale embedded in the poem. The nurse is banished for concealing the marriage and the apothecary is hanged for selling Romeus the poison. The Friar, though absolved for his involvement, goes to a hermitage and dies after five years of misery, guilt, and shame (3004).

Finally, it certainly is worth noting that Shakespeare's last lines, 'For never was a tale of more woe/Than this of Juliet and her Romeo' (5.3.309–10) resemble those of a student trying to hide plagiarism, for Brooke's couplet reads: 'There is no monument more worthy of the sight,/Then is the tombe of Juliet, and Romeus her knight' (3019–20).

Minor tales of 'adaptation'

Adrien Sevin

Although all of the preceding narratives have been 'adaptations' of major sources dealing with the legend of Romeo and Juliet, what distinguishes those minor sources mentioned below is their effort – much like that a filmmaker would undertake – to *transpose* the legend into a discrete place, time, or culture. Hence, the Frenchman Sevin, a contemporary of Rabelais, creates a story surprisingly similar to the legend, but moves his characters to a Greek setting in which Romeo is named Halquadrich, Juliet is Burglipha, Tybalt is changed to Burglipha's brother (and named Bruhachin), while Balthazar the servant is Bostruch.[41] Importantly, there is no fight between the families until Bruhachin becomes jealous of the two *eleven year-old lovers*. Bruhachin forbids Halquadrich from visiting Burglipha – whose last name, amusingly for English speakers, is 'Humdrum'. Naturally, Halquadrich challenges the upstart brother to a duel, and kills him in the very room in which he and his sister are

---

[41] Adrien Sevin, 'Le Philocope de messire Iehan Boccace Florentin', Paris, 1542. Cf. H. Hauvette, 'Une variante française de la légende de Roméo et Juliette', *Revue de littérature comparée* I, 3 (1921), pp. 329–37.

getting dressed – a rather strange, potentially incestuous, detail. Burglipha labels Halquadrich a traitor, causing him to swoon, and Burglipha then seeks the advice of an elderly priest. Informing him that she will take her life if he refuses to help her, Burglipha is warned by the priest that her parents will never allow her to wed her brother's murderer. Eventually, the priest gives her the sleeping potion, and promises to ferry her body onto a boat headed for Halquadrich's castle. As in the legend, everything goes wrong; the Balthazar character (Bostruch) reports Burglipha's 'death' to Halquadrich, and he decides to kill himself, visiting an apothecary who gives him a stick of poison. (Importantly, though long attributed to Brooke, the apothecary scene is Clizia's invention, as we will see below.) Hence, when Halquadrich arrives to pay homage to his love, he eats, coincidentally, only *half* of the poison; Burglipha awakes to find him dying on her behalf, and, after kissing and talking with him at length, she begs to eat the other half of the poison. She does, she dies, and the two share a beautiful tomb for eternity.

Clizia

Contrary to common wisdom, Olin Moore asserts that 'the first important imitator of Luigi Da Porto' was not Matteo Bandello but, rather, 'was Cavaliere Gerardi (or Gherardo) Boldieri, (who) adopted the feminine pseudonym of "Clizia"'.[42] Clizia's adaptation is the first novella of the story to employ verse. Unlike earlier versions of the legend in which Juliet's speech is more voluminous and her character more aggressive, Clizia's adaptation makes a conscious effort to balance Romeo's lines with those of his lover, Giulia.[43]

[42] Moore, p. 67.

[43] Clizia, 'L'infelice Amore de' due fedelissimi amanti Giulia e Romeo scritto in ottava rima da Clizia, nobile Veronese ad Ardeo suo' (1553), in Alessandro Torri's *Giulietta e Romeo* (Pisa, 1831), pp. 149–93.

Indeed, Romeo is given several important speeches, including one that Shakespeare appears to recall in the balcony scene. In Clizia's tale, Romeo says to Giulia that the more he looks into her eyes, the less he is himself, or, 'Romeo', a line that Shakespeare echoes when Romeo exclaims: 'Call me but love, and I'll be new baptized./ Henceforth I never will be Romeo' (2.1.92–93). Also, although Bandello is given credit for embellishing the battle scene that leads to Romeo's banishment, it is Clizia, rather, who first represents Romeo attempting to make peace with Tebaldo; however, upon losing his closest friend (the Mercutio character), Romeo is driven to kill Tebaldo impulsively. Clizia is also intent on establishing a closer relationship between Tebaldo and Giulia, which, in the wake of his death, will become the source of a stronger mother–daughter bond. (Again, in Luhrmann's film, there is the suggestion of an overly close relationship between Tybalt and Lady Capulet, who mourns excessively for his death.) It is also Clizia's invention to show Giulia feigning sorrow for Tebaldo's death in order to cover her agony over Romeo's banishment. Easily overlooked is Clizia's introduction of the word 'sleepyhead' – which Bandello converts, one year later, into 'slug-a-bed' – to describe the motionless Giulia when the Nurse bids her rise, the morning after Giulia has taken the potion. Finally, the representation of the Friar in this novella is something of a compromise formation, falling somewhere between Bandello and Da Porto – the latter plainly bent on making the Friar's perverse tendencies evident. Here, in Clizia's adaptation, Romeo and the Friar have an 'intimate' relationship, but there is no suggestion that anything untoward happens; moreover, the Friar is spared public charges of necrophilia and robbing the dead. Lastly, in contrast to all the other written versions before him, Clizia writes in verse (often *ottava rima*), and, hence, may be responsible for inspiring Brooke's version.

Boaistuau

Three years before Brooke published his influential poem, Pierre Boaistuau's *Histoires tragiques* were published, containing yet another adaptation of the legend.[44] Perhaps the most noteworthy aspect of Boaistuau's version is the turnabout it performs in relation to Frer Laurens, converting him back to the far more suspicious character of Da Porto's version – a curious change, since Bandello, not Da Porto, is acknowledged as Boaistuau's primary source. An exceedingly minor innovation, however, also proves instructive when examining a film like Baz Luhrmann's *William Shakespeare's Romeo + Juliet*. For example, when Rhomeo learns of Juliette's fate, he cries, but then washes his face so that his sorrow will not be obvious; in Luhrmann's film, at the Capulet ball, Romeo plunges his head into a sink in order to clear his vision from the ecstasy pill he has received from Mercutio. Like Clizia, Boaistuau makes Juliet a more passive character (when her father rails at her, she weeps complacently, rather than speaking her mind). Moreover, she is more chaste than either Shakespeare's verbally aggressive character or the Italian Giuliettas before her, for the Italians, at least in the sixteenth century, were apparently more permissive of the latter kind of heroine than the French. Finally, an omission is the only other significant deviation from the preceding versions of the legend; regrettably for his readers, Boaistuau eliminates the moving final words of the two dying lovers.

---

[44] Pierre Boaistuau, *XVIII Histoires extraictes des oeuvres italiennes de Bandel, et mises en langue françoise* . . . (1559). Les six premières par Pierre Boisteau, surnommé Launay, natif de Bretaigne. Les douze suiuans par Franc, de Belle Forest, Comingeois (Lyon, 1578), pp. 37–77.

Although it is true that, when considering Shakespeare's sources for *Romeo and Juliet*, scholars and critics tend to rely too heavily on Arthur Brooke, neglecting the vast amount of information that may have found its way into Shakespeare's imagination through other figures, there is universal agreement that 'the play, considered in relation to its source(s), is one of the dramatist's most brilliant transformations.'[45]

[45] Frank Kermode, *Romeo and Juliet* in *The Riverside Shakespeare*, 2nd Edition, edited by G. Blakemore Evans (Boston and New York: Houghton Mifflin, 1997), pp. 1101–03.

The 'bad', the 'good', and the ugly: the complex text(s) of Shakespeare's *Romeo and Juliet*

Q1 vs Q2 (and 3 and 4)

Although the literal pretext(s) of Shakespeare's play are intriguing in their own right, when it comes to the battle to authenticate the play itself, one could easily imagine a film emerging . . . Picture this: the scene is set in a frenetic, early modern literary marketplace that preceded the protections of copyright, leading to a dog-eat-dog world in which printers treat popular manuscripts on a competitive, first-come, first-served basis, with no regard to proprietary rights, merely to profit. So it goes that the first or 'bad' Quarto of *Romeo and Juliet* (1597) came into existence, at least according to one theory. Indeed, the notion that the first printed version of Shakespeare's play derived from literary piracy – stolen by jealous, bit-part players in search of fast cash – and was poorly reconstructed from memory (a practice known as 'memorial reconstruction') not only subscribes to a romantic historiography but also explains the alleged inferiority of Q1 as 'non-Shakespearean', safeguarding the Bard's sacred place in the pantheon of dramatic literature. Adding to the intrigue, as one prominent bibliographic scholar contends, is the drama surrounding the actual publication of Q1 which – somewhat unusual for its time – is claimed by two printers. According to H.R. Hoppe, John Danter, whose imprimatur appears on the first four pages of the document, had his print shop raided for printing without the authority of the Stationer's Register between early February and late March, 1597.[1] Henceforth, Edward Allde printed the remainder of the manuscript. The logic behind Hoppe's surmise is fairly straightforward: the first printer, Danter, indicates on the title page that the play was performed by 'the right Ho-/nourable the L. of Hunsdon/his Seruants'; however, as of mid-March, Shakespeare's Company no longer went by that name, so to some degree it makes sense that the 'bad' Quarto printing of *Romeo and Juliet* began with Danter and ended with Allde, who serendipitously benefited from the demise of Danter's enterprise.

The 'bad'

If only it were that simple – and, I might add – that exciting. As appealing as Hoppe's theory is, it has been subject to heated debate and, since the early 1980s, largely overruled. But this territory is too important to tread upon lightly; how do we make sense of the publication of Q1, let alone Q2? As Jill Levenson describes it in her Oxford edition of *Romeo and Juliet*, the theory of piracy-by-memorial reconstruction 'has become a modern orthodoxy'; however, she adds, this is 'the theory which raises the most . . . secondary questions'.[2] For example, Peter W.M. Blayney explains that there is no doubt that a practice best described as 'memorial reconstruction' existed, given the fact that friends – even high-

[1] Harry R. Hoppe, *The Bad Quarto of 'Romeo and Juliet': A Bibliographical and Textual Study*, Cornell Studies in English, 36 (Ithaca: New York, 1948), pp. 12–15.
[2] Levenson, p. 117.

ranking patrons – of an acting company often desired transcripts of the play-as-performed, which had to be penned from either a prompter's copy (often difficult to get one's hands on) or, more likely, from an actor's memory, which meant that 'those parts of the performance he had least opportunity to observe might prove extremely difficult to reconstruct and might emerge noticeably garbled'.[3] Blayney concludes that 'we have been too busy chasing imaginary pirates to listen' to such banal explanations for the existence of so-called 'Bad' Quartos like the 1597 *Romeo and Juliet*.[4] Indeed, the basis for the argument *against* piracy by actors or 'reporters' looking to increase their cash flow is a matter of simple economics: not only were playbooks *not* in high demand (hence, a publisher acquiring such a manuscript frequently risked not recovering his costs), but also, as Blayney estimates, plays sold to publishers garnered approximately 30 shillings – in essence, pocket change.

Debunking another contemporary orthodoxy that early modern print and performance were mutually exclusive media, Lukas Erne shows evidence of a consistent pattern of publication for the first twelve plays that Shakespeare penned for the Lord Chamberlain's Men. Erne contends that a 'new play . . . did not need extra publicity', but, '(o)n the other hand, selling a manuscript to a publisher may have been a way of securing *free promotion for a revival* when a playbook would have been sold in bookshops and advertised with title pages put up on posts throughout London'.[5]

[3] Blayney, Peter. 'The Publication of Playbooks'. *A New History of Early English Drama*, edited by John D. Cox and David Scott Kastan (New York: Columbia University Press, 1997), p. 394.

[4] Ibid.

[5] Lukas Erne, 'Shakespeare and the Publication of His Plays', *Shakespeare Quarterly* 53.1 (Spring 2002): p. 14, emphasis mine.

Hence, the pattern of publication that Erne presents shows that prior to 1600, a Shakespeare play appeared in print approximately two years after it was first performed – a statement which also suggests that plays (at least the Shakespearean plays in the Lord Chamberlain's Men's repertory) may have been revived every two-to-three years. This appears to be precisely the case with Q1 of *Romeo and Juliet*, which was printed for sale in 1597, roughly two years after it was initially performed; that the 1597 printing of the 'Bad Quarto' was intended to serve as publicity for a revival is suggested not by Henslowe's Diary but from John Marston's 1598 *The Scourge of Villanie*, wherein a conversation reveals that 'Iuliet and Romeo' was then playing at The Curtain.[6]

Since the publication of the Arden, Oxford, and many other editions of *Romeo and Juliet*, more recent studies have emerged that inflect the debate over the value of 'bad' quartos with new intellectual energy. One such study is an essay by Lene Petersen that likens the practices employed in the transmission of folk ballads to those that led to the production of 'bad' quartos. According to Petersen, plays such as *Romeo and Juliet* and *Hamlet* (both of which exist in multiple versions), exhibit striking affinities with orally-transmitted narratives such as folk songs, similarities that include 'omission, repetition, formulae, telescoping, transposition and addition across (discrete narratives)'.[7] Though this essay deserves much more attention than space allows, the most important contribution that Petersen makes to the ongoing debate over the origin and value of Q1 is her assertion of the role that the audience plays in the 'authorship' of both folk ballads and, even 'bad'

---

[6] Ibid, p. 15.

[7] Lene Petersen, 'De-composition in Popular Elizabethan Playtexts: A Revalidation of the Multiple Versions of *Romeo and Juliet* and *Hamlet*', *Oral Tradition* 23.1 (March 2008): p. 122.

quartos. Essentially, the form that a ballad takes is based on the disposition of the audience; if the audience is restless, then the song with be shortened, whereas if they are receptive, then the performer may augment his story, 'savoring each descriptive passage'.[8] Similarly, if, as it is generally presumed, the 'bad' quartos trace their lineage to performance, then 'they may very likely reflect audience participation, expectations, and, above all, receptiveness to the degree that play length and structure have been gradually adjusted in response to circumstances similar to those' that affect the transmission of folk songs and tales.[9] Though Petersen's claims are based on an extremely complex parallel analysis of the *Romeo and Juliet* and *Hamlet* quartos, a straight-forward example of the similarities between the folk ballad and early quartos is their tendency toward narrative front-loading, characterised by 'verbally tighter initial acts, . . . with variation (between "good" and "bad" quartos) increasing in the middle and final acts . . . .'[10] This is certainly true of *Romeo and Juliet*, wherein, for example, Act Five has Capulet announcing the death of both his wife *and* Benvolio, a decision which, according to Petersen's argument, is informed by the balladic structure of 'heightened symmetry and patterning', reinforcing, in turn, the theme of the 'tragedy of the young' around which the play revolves. Petersen ends her rigorous analysis with the following, provocative conclusion:

[8] Albert B. Lord. *The Singer of Tales*, 2nd edition, edited by Stephen Mitchell and Gregory Nagy (Cambridge, MA: Harvard University Press. 2000), p. 17.

[9] Petersen, p. 143.

[10] Ibid.

I would like to argue that the textual stylistic variance between the two 'bad' Quarto cases discussed here indicates different stages in dramatic transmission in the tradition of each particular play, the presumption being that the more marked the above 'balladic' parameters, the more intense the transmission history behind the version. On these premises, Q1 Romeo would be ranked as less orally/memorially influenced, that is, less traditionalised than Q1 Hamlet. Or in less neutral terms Q1 Romeo would qualify as a rather 'good' 'bad' text.[11]

The 'good'

Then there is Quarto 2 (1599), which, according to 'modern orthodoxy', appears to have derived from the author's original documents as a corrective to Q1. Nevertheless, this 'Newly corrected, augmented, and/amended' version contains occasional cross-references to Q1, where – so the story goes – the autograph copy must have been illegible. Erne and Levenson find this argument untenable. For Levenson, the 'question that does remain is whether a playwright or redactor would have had more than fifteen hundred changes (from Q1) . . . some of the variants quite minor and not all of them improvements.'[12] Erne actually conjectures that the Lord Chamberlain's Men sold the manuscript that would become Q2 to publisher Cuthbert Burby before Danter began to publish his edition (Q1) which, significantly, Danter had licensed but did not enter in the Stationer's Register. Erne bases his evidence on the print history of Love's Labor's Lost (which Burby had published as a 'Newly corrected and augmented' version in 1598, suggesting that he had actually acquired the manuscript

---

[11] Ibid., p. 144.

[12] Levenson, p. 121.

significantly earlier) and *Hamlet* – whose 'good' Quarto (Q2) was, as the Stationer's Register entry attests, in the hands of its publisher in 1602 – prior to the publication of the 'bad' Quarto in 1603. Recent scholarship agrees that Quarto 2 appears to be based both on the author's holograph and interventions that point to printing house practices rather than stage performances.

Is it possible that Q2 points to the practice of authorial revision? Though this theory, too, has proven attractive to scholars intent on constructing Shakespeare as a conscientious predecessor to the proprietary author of the eighteenth century, the extent to which Q2 appears to be reliant on a copy *independent* of both Shakespeare's 'foule papers' *and* Q1 makes such a determination unlikely. The truth is, although we now know more than ever before about the relationship between Shakespeare's early Quartos and Renaissance printing practices, we are still building castles in the sand and 'chasing imaginary pirates' when it comes to determining the exact provenance of such texts.

Indeed, just as there has been – from Newtonian gravity to today's 'super string theory' – a quest in physics to produce a 'unified field theory' that explains the workings of the cosmos based on a single principle, so, too, Shakespearean textual studies have long sought a unified explanation for how playtexts came to be – and, more curiously – not to be. Hence, one final 'modern orthodoxy' is worth exploring before moving into a discussion of the actual content of the Quartos themselves. Referring to the most influential work in all of Shakespearean textual studies, namely, W.W. Greg's *Dramatic Documents from the Elizabethan Playhouses: Stage Plots, Actors' Parts, Prompt Books.*[13] Paul Werstine observes

[13] W.W. Greg, *Dramatic Documents from the Elizabethan Playhouses: Stage Plots, Actors' Parts, Prompt Books* (Oxford: Oxford University Press, 1931).

that Greg's work remains the hallmark of a 'general theory' of Shakespearean production.[14] For Greg, extant manuscripts from the early modern era fall into categories which, by now, are familiar to us: either they are 'fowle papers', which trace their existence to the fabled authorial hand itself, or 'prompt books', which, according to Werstine's paraphrase of Greg's idealising rhetoric, refer to 'a unique manuscript inscribed in a single hand and a single ink to include not only the playtext but also the theatrical annotations'. Werstine proceeds to explain the stakes of such assertions:

> By providing what purports to be a general theory of the production ('fowle papers') and reproduction ('prompt books') of early modern drama and by conveniently listing the allegedly distinctive features of each of his idea categories, Greg empowered generations of editors to carry out their task without ever having to engage the fierce particularities of extant manuscripts.[15]

Referring not to Levenson's edition of *Romeo and Juliet* but rather to Wells' and Taylor's *Complete Works*,[16] Werstine goes so far as to claim that '(e)ven the recent Oxford edition, for all its pretensions to having subverted editorial tradition, is uncritically enthralled by Greg's general theory'.[17]

---

[14] Paul Werstine, 'Plays in Manuscript', *A New History of Early English Drama*, edited by John D. Cox and David Scott Kastan (New York: Columbia University Press, 1997), p. 492.

[15] Ibid., p. 492, p. 495.

[16] *The Complete Works: Original-Spelling Edition*, edited by Stanley Wells, Gary Taylor, John Jowett, and William Montgomery, Oxford: Oxford University Press, 1986.

[17] Ibid.

The ugly

While acknowledging the extraordinary debt that Shakespearean scholarship owes to Greg, Werstine takes issue with the presumed linearity and limitations of such a taxonomy, which obfuscates the 'irreducible historical messiness of the actual manuscripts' and, in turn, 'disrputs the conceptual tidiness, the orderliness of classification, and the economy of hypothesis that Greg so successfully championed'.[18] Hence, Werstine concludes with an entreaty to appreciate '(e)ach dramatic manuscript . . . in its uniqueness as the matrix of a variety of possible scholarly narratives about the inscription of early modern drama'.[19] As the saying goes, however, 'what is one man's trash is another man's treasure'; accordingly, what Werstine considers alluringly ugly – the 'irreducible historical messiness' of early modern playtexts – Jonathan Goldberg finds sexy. Writing in response to the publication of Brian Gibbons's *The Arden 3 Shakespeare Romeo and Juliet*, an edition that takes unprecedented liberties with the balcony scene (a point to which I shall return), Goldberg calls a spade a spade by interjecting the possibility that perhaps what is most irreducible about the Shakespearean text is the *desire* that others cathect into it – be they established scholars, casual readers, or, even, aspiring filmmakers.[20] For Goldberg, every attempt to reconcile or 'fix' the undulating utterances of *Romeo and Juliet*'s texts is a kind of murder, marking the difference between the characters' 'multiple

 [18] Werstine, p. 482.

[19] Ibid., pp. 494–95.

[20] Brian Gibbons, ed. *The Arden Shakespeare Romeo and Juliet*, 2nd edition, London: Methuen, 1980; 1997. See also Jonathan Goldberg's '"What? In a name that which we call a Rose", The Desired Texts of *Romeo and Juliet*', *Crisis in Editing: Texts of the English Renaissance*, edited by Randall McLeod (New York: AMS Press, 1988), p. 192.

textual desire and (their) singular textual devastation'.[21]

Goldberg uses for his example what we might think of as the bibliographic history of the balcony scene. In Q1, Juliet's lines read:

Iul: Tis but thy name that is mine enemie.
       Whats *Mountague*? It is nor hand nor foote,
       Nor arme, nor face, nor any other part.
       Whats in a name? That which we call a Rose
       By any other name would smell as sweet:
       So *Romeo* would, were he not *Romeo* cald,
       Retaine the diuine perfection he owes:
       Without that title *Romeo* part thy name,
       And for that name which is no part of thee,
       Take all I haue.

Q2 reads as follows, with the changes in bold:

Iu.   Tis but thy name that is mine enemie:
       Thou are thy selfe, though not a Mountague,
       Whats *Mountague*? it is nor hand nor foote,
       Nor arme, nor face, **o be some other name**
       Belonging to a man.
       Whats in a **name that** which we call a Rose
       By any other **word** would smell as sweet:
       So *Romeo* would, we**ne** he not *Romeo* cald,
       Retaine the **deare** perfection **which** he owes:
       Without that tytle *Romeo* **doffe** thy name,
       And for **thy** name which is no part of thee,
       Take all **my selfe.**

Gibbons's edition, to which Goldberg strongly objects in its desire to establish a 'unified field theory' of the play's incorrigible multiplicities, not only creates a composite of Q1 and Q2, but adds an authorial flourish of its own, reversing the order of Juliet's plea to be 'some other name' and the phrase 'Belonging to a man':

> Juliet. 'Tis but thy name that is my enemy:
> Thou are thy selfe, though not a Montague.
> What's Montague? It is nor hand nor foot,
> Nor arm nor face nor any other part
> Belonging to a man. O be some other name.
> What's in a name? That which we call a Rose
> By any other word would smell as sweet;
> So Romeo would, were he not Romeo call'd,
> Retaine the dear perfection which he owes:
> Without that title. *Romeo*, doff thy name,
> And for that name, which is no part of thee,
> Take all myself.

This type of composite text, according to Goldberg's psychoanalytic theory, is driven by an editorial endgame of 'fort da!' in which the hope is that, in combining texts and supplying changes where the texts are incomplete or aesthetically unappealing, the lost object – that is, the whole text and nothing but the text – will be restored to its (phantasmatic) original plenitude. Hence, for Goldberg, the very profession of editing is inseparable from the most primary forms and expressions of desire.

It is fascinating to note that, dare we throw Q3 into the mix, the balcony scene changes again. The plausible explanation here is that an 's' is mistaken for a question mark and vice versa, as the text reads: 'What? in a name's that which we call a Rofe'; despite its awkwardness and seemingly obvious error, this is precisely the version of the line that appears in the First Folio (1623). For this and other reasons, Goldberg explains the relationship between Q1 and Q2 in terms which, for our purposes, make the most sense: 'It (Q2) is a selection from or an anthology of a number of productions of *Romeo and Juliets*, one of which was close to the performance represented by Q1, close enough to allow Q2 to use Q1 as its authority at some points'. He thus concludes that '(t)here never was a final *Romeo and Juliet*, a single authoritative or authorial version of the play. There were only versions, from the start'.[22]

Just when we thought things couldn't get any more compli-cated, we arrive at Q4 – one of two plays (the other is Q4 of *Hamlet*) among 'the sixty-three separate quarto editions of Shakespeare's plays printed before 1640 . . . (that) were issued without title-page dates'.[23] Using evidence from paper stock, R. Carter Hailey painstakingly conjectures that the Q4 *Romeo and Juliet* was printed in 1623, very likely shortly after the Folio itself. The critical stake in positing a firm date for Q4 is determining the extent to which one text influences another; Q4, for example, has long been considered to be heavily influenced by the printing of the First Folio in 1623, when, in fact, it appears as though both the Folio and Q4 were printed from 'separately marked-up copies of Q3'.[24] Significantly, Hailey's supposition brings us full cycle, by indicating that 'the Q4 printer appears to have occasionally consulted Q1 where the F1 printer did not'.[25] (385). And, just as profit and publicity seem to be

---

[22] Goldberg, p. 186, p. 189.

[23] R. Carter Hailey, 'The Dating Game: New Evidence for the Dates of Q4 *Romeo and Juliet* and Q4 *Hamlet*', *Shakespeare Quarterly* 58.3 (2007): p. 367.

[24] Ibid., p. 385.

[25] Ibid.

the motives behind the printing of Q1, so, too, the peculiar publication of the Q4 *Romeo and Juliet* alongside the First Folio suggests that 'some publishers anticipated that the publication of a high-profile collected edition of Shakespeare's plays would actually increase the market for their more affordable quarto editions'.[26]

Though talk of watermarks, frontispieces, matching paper stocks, and the Stationer's Register may sound dry at best to students, exploring the actual, substantive differences between competing versions of *Romeo and Juliet* – specifically, Q1 and Q2 – provides students with a unique form of empowerment, as they are able to imitate the work of editors themselves. In the undergraduate classroom, I routinely teach both texts, asking students to make arguments for *which reading* of a given line or scene is optimal according to their vision of the play.

Act 1: Q1 vs. Q2

An early example of a significant difference between Q1 and Q2 is Mercutio's introduction of Queen Mab. In Q1 he tells us that 'This is that Mab that makes maids lie on their backs' (1.4.92), whereas in Q2 (and, incidentally, F1), Mercutio exclaims that 'This is the hag, when maids lie on their backs, that . . . (1.4.69). The difference in agency is striking; in Q1 Mab *forces* maids into a compromising, 'sluttish' position. whereas Q2 is considerably more ambiguous: 'This is the hag, when maids lie on their backs . . .' (1.4.90). Are the maids in Q2 lying down to sleep and, perchance, to dream of Queen Mab, or to engage in sexual intercourse with an interloper? Given Mercutio's predisposition toward obscene punning and his preoccupation with sex, either reading is viable, though Q1 is, perhaps, the more intriguing of the two, making Mab into a diminutive dominatrix.

Act 2: Q1 vs. Q2

In this Act, Romeo and Juliet have their famous 'balcony scene'. In 2.2, there are minor differences in Romeo and Juliet's dialogue; however, once we get to their exchange beginning at line 149 or so (quoted so memorably in *Shakespeare in Love*), Q1 and Q2 part ways. Q1 leaves out the 'exchange of vows' dialogue between the young lovers, thus altering the impact of the scene. Does the absence of vows compromise the romantic arc of the scene, suggesting Juliet's further hesitation at the thought of her 'rash contract'? Finally, while waiting for news of Romeo's plan, Juliet exclaims in Q1: 'Love's heralds should be thoughts,/And run more swift, than hasty powder fired,/Doth hurry from the fearful Canon's mouth' (2.4.4–6). This more violent use of metaphor actually complements Romeo's desperate entreaty to the apothecary in Q2:

> Let me have
> A dram of poison, such soon-speeding gear
> As will disperse itself through all the veins,
> That the life-weary taker may fall dead,
> And that the trunk may be discharged of breath
> *As violently as hasty powder fired*
> *Doth hurry from the fatal cannon's womb.*27
> (5.1.59–65, emphasis mine)

27 In this particular passage, Q2 has clearly taken its cues from Q1, which reads: "Give me a dram of some such speeding gear/As will dispatch the weary taker's life/As suddenly as powder being fired/From forth a cannon's mouth" (5.1.43–46).

In Q2, the implied violence of Juliet's 'Canon' image in Q1 is exchanged for an expression of rich natural beauty: "Love's heralds should be thoughts,/Which ten times faster glides than the sun's beams,/Driving back shadows over louering hills" (2.4.4–6). Some of the most impassioned arguments have emerged from this comparison, as support for the passages tends to be divided nearly in half. Q1 captures the impetuousness of Romeo and Juliet's love, alluding to the feud and foreshadowing their fatal end; Q2, by contrast, suggests a more mature, thoughtful Juliet who radiates her love for Romeo like the sun itself, even though she must be careful to keep it hidden among the shadows.

Act 3: Q1 vs. Q2

In Act Three, Q1 and Q2 also contain provocative differences, not the least of which occurs in the fight scene when, after Mercutio is fatally wounded, Romeo explains to him in Q1: "I *did* all for the best" (3.1.59) whereas in Q2 Romeo states: "I *thought* all for the best" (3.1.104). The difference here between decisive action and uncertain speculation is provocative. What does Q1's version of this scene convey about Romeo and Mercutio's relationship, as well as about Romeo's own sense of his role in the play/fray?

With respect to Juliet, we find that, as in Act 2, her lines in Q1 are radically reduced in 3.2. Yet, the lengthy speech Juliet utters in Q2 assumes somewhat perverse undertones. For example, in anticipation of Romeo's conjugal visit, Juliet proclaims:

> Come gentle night, come loving black browed night,
> Give me my Romeo, and when I shall die,
> Take him and cut him out in little stars,
> And he will make the face of heaven so fine,

That all the world will be in love with night
And pay no worship to the garish sun. (20–25)

It is strange that Juliet is preoccupied – on her wedding night – with thoughts of her own death and visions of Romeo's mutilation. Then again, in the Renaissance, thoughts of sex and death were curiously intertwined, as the pun on 'to die' (to achieve orgasm) encapsulates. The more important question is: does the scene read better without Juliet's morbid musings, or, conversely, do her reflections contribute to her own development as a character and, for that matter, complement the violence that Romeo himself has just committed against Tybalt? Significantly, Q4 reads when '*he* shall die' rather than 'when *I* shall die'; referring to this interesting substitution, Brian Gibbons claims in his Arden 3 edition that Q4 'lacks the element of tragic premonition of their shared fate expressed in Q2'.[28] Might this position be complicated by considering Juliet's unwitting confirmation that her love for Romeo is indeed 'star-crossed', based on her assertion that 1) Romeo *will* die, and, 2) he will become immortalised by the stars, which, in effect, he has always already been? Moreover, the reading 'when *he* shall die' is consonant with Juliet's ominous reply to Romeo's 'I would I were thy bird', to which she responds, 'Sweet, so would I/Yet I should kill thee with too much cherishing' (2.2.228–29).

Act 4: Q1 vs. Q2

Once again, the key difference between Q1 and Q2 revolves around Juliet's lines, or lack thereof. In Q1, 4.3 deletes much of Juliet's hysterical speculation about waking up in the tomb of her ancestors. Yet, it might be argued that less is more in this case,

[28] Gibbons, no. 21, p. 170.

allowing the audience to fill in her frightful speculation – rather than reading the below selection of lines from Q2 that leave little to the imagination:

> O if I wake, shall I not be distraught,
> Environèd with all these hideous fears,
> And madly play with my forefathers' joints?
> And pluck the mangled Tybalt from his shroud,
> And in this rage with some great kinsman's bone,
> As with a club, dash out my desp'rate brains? (4.3.48–53)

In an interesting way, this last line anticipates Lady Macbeth's speculation:

> I have given suck, and know
> How tender 'tis to love the babe that milks me.
> I would, while it was smiling in my face,
> Have plucked my nipple from its boneless gums
> *And dashed the brains out,* had I so sworn
> As you have done to this. (*Macbeth* 1.7.54–59)

Before moving on to Act Five, it is important to note one easily missed departure in Q1, wherein Juliet foreshadows her own death with Romeo's knife:

> Must I of force be married to the County?
> This shall forbid it. – Knife, lie thou there. – (4.3.14–15).

The ambiguous use of 'this', which could refer either to the potion or to the knife, is intriguing to say the least, for it gives us a stronger sense of Juliet's resolve to die rather than be forsworn.

Act Five: Q1 vs. Q2

In thinking about the differences between Q1 and Q2 in Act Five, a potentially stark discrepancy emerges in the characterisation of the Friar. In all adaptations of Shakespeare's play, theatre and film directors have to make a decision about his moral fortitude: after all, isn't it a bit suspicious that a figure who has forsworn bodily desire should so readily become a pander to it? Often, the Friar is depicted as well-intentioned rather than devious; Q1, however, follows the Italianate tradition in rendering him a more ambiguous character. For example, in his lengthy speech attempting to set the record straight, the Friar in Q1 appears to lie about his role in the body toll at the play's conclusion, exclaiming: 'What after happened, touching Paris' death,/Or Romeo's, is to me unknown at all' (5.3.179–80). If we read further, we find that he doesn't even take responsibility for Juliet's death, knowing full-well that he is, albeit inadvertently, responsible for all three deaths at the end of the play (Paris, Romeo, and Juliet). Is he a priest impersonator, attempting to wipe out the younger, hard-to-hold generation? Would *Romeo and Juliet* be a better play if we believed that the young lovers were 'set up' for tragedy by a conniving priest, or do we need to believe that their fates were circumscribed by the stars?

We can see a subtle but damning difference between Q1 and Q2 in 5.3 when, upon realising that his plan has backfired, the Friar bluntly informs Juliet: 'I will provide for you in some close Nunnery' (108). In Q2, Friar Laurence says to Juliet: 'Come, I'll dispose of thee /Among a sisterhood of holy nuns' (156–57). To a Renaissance audience, the word 'nunnery' could also mean 'whorehouse' (a slander most famously deployed by Hamlet in his 'get thee to a nunnery' speech to Ophelia). Juliet, having been 'ruined' by Romeo while being betrothed to another man, would easily qualify as a 'whore' (frankly, she could potentially qualify as such for being so outspoken a character, even without any lascivious actions to back up her words). Might the Friar in Q1 be trying to cover his tracks and dispose of Juliet where he feels she really belongs? Clearly, Q2's Friar takes pains to eliminate the 'whorish' implications of the word 'nunnery' by referring to a 'Sisterhood of holy Nuns', imitating the damage control that dates back to Bandello, who sought to exonerate the Friar and, by extension, the Catholic Church at large, from charges of corruption intimated by Masuccio and Da Porto.

Date of composition

Considering the multiple extant versions of Shakespeare's *Romeo and Juliet*, determining the actual date of 'the play's' composition seems to be something of a moot point. Nevertheless, exploring the types of evidence and approaches that scholars adopt in seeking to locate *Romeo and Juliet* within the broader trajectory of Shakespeare's career is instructive. Brian Gibbons, for example, asserts that although the case has been made for a date of composition as early as 1591, speculation that the play was written and performed between 1595 and spring of 1596 – at the very latest – is the most accurate time period for those seeking to understand the play in its historical context.[29] The primary basis for such determinations is the Nurse's allusion to the earthquake which, she recalls, occurred eleven years ago (1.3.23); the problem lies with the fact that there were three earthquakes, both near Verona and in England in the 1580s, which make all three dates plausible. However, scholars typically rule out the earliest date (1591) since, setting aside the obvious differences in content, *Romeo and Juliet*

[29] Gibbons, p. 26.

has little in common with the *Henry VI* plays (c. 1591–94), both in terms of style and language.

If, based on the earthquake allusion, the latest date of composition for *Romeo and Juliet* is 1596, then the earliest date, Gibbons claims, is 1593, based on several (not entirely convincing) poetic allusions to John Eliot's *Ortho-Epia* of 1593. More compelling is the comparison with Shakespeare's own coterminous works. For instance, *Two Gentlemen of Verona* (1593–94) refers in several places to Arthur Brooke's *The Tragicall Historye of Romeus and Juliet* which, as we recall, is Shakespeare's principal source for *Romeo and Juliet*. Commonalities such as the Verona setting, the use of a rope ladder, the character of Friar Laurence, and an impulsive flight to Mantua (in this case, Silvia's self-banishment in pursuit of Proteus) – make *Two Gentlemen* a bit like *Romeo and Juliet* with a happy ending. Something of a transitional play, *Romeo and Juliet* lacks the simplistic language and the patently unbelievable ending of *Two Gentlemen*, but it does not quite achieve the aesthetic grandeur and complexity of the plays composed shortly after 1596, such as *The Merchant of Venice* (c. 1597). Hence, Gibbons concludes that the best indication of the play's date, which he places between 1594–5, is the 'shared lyrical feeling' between *Romeo and Juliet*, *Love's Labour's Lost*, *A Midsummer Night's Dream*, and *Richard II*, all of which may be traced to the period 1594–96.[30]

Others argue according to different grounds. Examining stage properties, Andrew Gurr suggests that the play is best situated prior to 1594, a date that positions *Romeo and Juliet* among the 'large plays' that required considerable accommodations for proper staging. Instead of battle scenes or spectacle, as in the *Henry VI*

[30] Ibid., p. 27.

plays or Marlowe's more demanding work, *Romeo and Juliet* uniquely required a balcony, a rope ladder leading up into a bedroom, and a view into the conjugal chamber itself.[31] Others, like Robert Babcock and E.P. Kuhl, place the play closer to 1596, citing Mercutio's references to Spanish blades and ambuscados in his Queen Mab speech, as possible allusions to the Spanish takeover of Cadiz in June of 1596.[32] Convinced that Vincentio Saviolo's fencing manual, titled *Practise* (1595), set the outer limit for Shakespeare's composition of the play, Joan Ozark Holmer argues persuasively for a composition of no later than 1595, due to the strong correspondences between Saviolo's popular publication and the play's preoccupation with Italian dueling rhetoric.[33] By contrast, the inventor of the Shaxicon database, Donald W. Foster, believes the opposite to be the case: that, if anything, *Romeo and Juliet* influenced Saviolo's use of the phrase 'worm's meat' (from Mercutio's death speech). Moreover, Foster contends that – based on his concordance of rare words that occur in major literary works of the 1590s – Q1 was written in 1592–3, Q2 between 1594–7, and both quartos were potentially revised after 1594.[34] Adding intrigue to inquiry, still others have speculated that Shakespeare wrote *Romeo and Juliet* around 1594 with his patron, the Earl of Southampton, in mind. Indeed, the Earl was known to have been protecting Sir Charles and Sir Henry Danvers, who were accused of

[31] Andrew Gurr, *Playgoing in Shakespeare's London*, Second Edition (Cambridge: Cambridge University Press, 2002), p. 122.

[32] Robert Babcock, '*Romeo and Juliet*, 1, iv, 86: An Emendation', *PQ* 8 (1929), pp. 407–8. See also E.P. Kuhl, '*Romeo and Juliet*, I, IV, 84F', *PQ* 9 (1930), pp. 307–8.

[33] Joan Ozark Holmer, '"Draw, if you be men": Saviolo's Significance for *Romeo and Juliet*', *Shakespeare Quarterly* 45.2 (Summer 1994): pp. 163–89. See also Vincentio Saviolo, *His Practise* (London: printed by Thomas Scarlet, 1595).

[34] Levenson, p. 102.

killing Sir Henry Long 'in a family feud', as Jill Levensen describes it, apropos of the irascible conflict between the Capulets and the Montagues.[35]

Speculation about a 'shared lyrical feeling' is quite generous when compared to what the venerable Dr Samuel Johnson refers to as *Romeo and Juliet*'s many pathos-inducing phrases – or 'pathetic strains' – which, Johnson laments, are 'polluted with some unexpected depravations'.[36] Surely Johnson is referring in part to *Romeo and Juliet*'s use and abuse of Petrarchan conceits, which were all the rage in Elizabeth's court during the 1580s and 90s – a time when the Queen fashioned her own royal persona as an unattainable mistress, denying all suitors while controlling the amorous fates of her favorites – and responding violently to any who crossed her will. It is no wonder, therefore, that Shakespeare has Romeo employ the full battery of Petrarchan paradoxes in his first speaking appearance. In Act One, for example, Romeo is incapable of uttering little more than dolorous 'depravations' of Petrarch:

> Where shall we dine? O me! What a fray was here?
> Yet tell me not, for I have heard it all:
> Here's much to do with hate, but more with love.
> Why then, O brawling love, O loving hate,
> O anything, of nothing first created;
> O heavy lightness, serious vanity,
> Misshapen chaos of well-seeming forms,
> Feather of lead, bright smoke, cold fire, sick health,
> Still-waking sleep, that is not what it is:

---

[35] Ibid., p. 100.
[36] Johnson, quoted in Kermode, p. 1101.

This love feel I, that feel no love in this.
Dost thou not laugh? (1.1.169–79)

Although Romeo begins the play as a literary parrot – and a bad one at that – he matures into a rather stunning *poet*. Read as a kind of literary *bildungsroman*, Romeo's language becomes far more interesting once Juliet becomes his mentor. For whereas Romeo starts out uttering nonsense (above) and then graduates, in the balcony scene, to learning how to release himself from the clutches of disingenuous metaphors – such as 'Lady, by yonder blessèd moon I vow,/That tips with silver all these fruit-tree tops' – Juliet has always been capable of recognising the power of abstraction. Hence, Juliet's language moves away from referentiality toward linguistic autonomy, as her famous speech 'What's in a name? That which we call a rose/By any other word would smell as sweet' epitomises (2.1.86–87). She therefore admonishes Romeo when he attempts to 'swear by the moon, th'inconstant moon' and, ultimately, demands that he abandon the speech act altogether: 'Do not swear at all . . .' (2.1.152, 155). Romeo must learn, quite literally, to speak for himself.

By Act Three, in the *aubade* scene, Romeo has made significant progress, for rather than using language as an instrument of reactionary hyperbole, he begins to employ it rationally, for empirical purposes, while demonstrating a burgeoning lyricism:

It was the lark, the herald of the morn;
No nightingale. Look, love, what envious streaks
Do lace the severing clouds in yonder east.
Night's candles are burnt out, and jocund day
Stands tiptoe on the misty mountaintops.
I must be gone and live, or stay and die. (3.5.6–11)

It is in Act Five, however, that Romeo shows a true facility with and, oddly enough, freedom from language, which culminates in his final, fatal effort to divorce his body from the tragic referentiality of his name. Returning, significantly, to the topos of Petrarchanism through the conceit of the blazon, Romeo turns it on its head, as he anatomises *himself*:

> Ah, dear Juliet,
> Why art thou yet so fair? Shall I believe
> That unsubstantial death is amorous,
> And that the lean abhorrèd monster keeps
> Thee here in dark to be his paramour?
> For fear of that I still will stay with thee
> And never from this pallet of dim night
> Depart again. Here, here will I remain . . . .
> O, here
> Will I set up my everlasting rest
> And shake the yoke of inauspicious stars
> From this world-wearied flesh. *Eyes, look your last!*
> *Arms, take your last embrace! And, lips, O you*
> *The doors of breath, seal with a righteous kiss*
> *A dateless bargain to engrossing death.*
> (5.3.101–115, emphasis mine)

Inscribing his poetic signature on his very flesh, Romeo's language has evolved into a shape and form that is his alone; and, by the end of this most tragic – and, simultaneously, clichéd – of love stories, this is no small consolation.

'What more in the name of love?' Issues for adaptation

One man come in the name of love
One man come and go
One man come here to justify
One man to overthrow
In the name of love!
One man in the name of love
In the name of love!
What more? In the name of love!

U2[1]

'These violent delights have violent ends . . .' warns the Friar, as he prepares Romeo to wed Juliet, advising him to 'love moderately; long love doth so' (2.5.9, 14). But anyone who has ever been caught up in the tumultuous pangs of young love knows that this sensation is the very antithesis of reason, and that moderation, therefore, has no place where love is experienced as limitless. The play of *Romeo and Juliet* epitomises this unique, all-consuming and, above all, violent love that must, perforce, extinguish itself – yet another admonitory point made by the Friar, as he engages two lovers who

---

[1] U2, 'In the Name of Love'/'Pride', *The Unforgettable Fire*, 1994.

will 'in their triumphs die, like fire and powder/Which as they kiss consume' (2.5.10–11).

The title of this chapter is derived from the U2 song 'In the name of love' (also known as 'Pride'), which describes the life and death of Martin Luther King, Jr. The refrain incredulously asks: 'what more' could one possibly offer than one's life – for another, or for a cause – 'in the name of love'? But love alone – for another, or for a cause – isn't enough, because the hero of the song pays with his life, as do Romeo and Juliet. Indeed, despite the fact that *Romeo and Juliet* has achieved iconic status as a phrase that is synonymous with not just any love but, rather, '*true* love', the play is marked by surprising eruptions of violence that belie its generic status as a love story. Invoking a Tina Turner song in her essay, '"What's love got to do with it?" Reading the liberal humanist romance in *Antony and Cleopatra*', Linda Charnes observes that '(a)s a speech act, this song is a critical "intervention": a disruptive response to a narrative that precedes and exceeds it'.[2] *Romeo and Juliet* is nothing if not a play that at once precedes and exceeds itself, as both its legendary prehistory and its textual effervescence – its eruption into multiple versions – alone suggest. So, too, considerations of the play's historical context cannot ignore the fact that, when Shakespeare was writing *Romeo and Juliet*, the culture around him was in desperate need of an 'intervention' to arrest the violence being played out in every conceivable corner of the English landscape. Apprentices were rioting in London, rumours abounded that a second Spanish Armada was being assembled, and a scarcity of grain led to widespread social unrest and even public

[2] Linda Charnes, '"What's Love Got to Do With It?" Reading the Liberal Humanist Romance in Shakespeare's *Antony and Cleopatra*', *Textual Practice* 6, no. 1 (1992): p. 1.

protests. In short, England was being threatened from both within and outside of its geographical borders. In this context, it is not surprising that Shakespeare's play depicts Verona as ripe for rebellion, opening with images of 'mutiny' and 'civil blood(shed)', wrought by the 'ancient grudge' between the Capulets and the Montagues (Prologue 3–4). Though for a short time Romeo and Juliet strive to balance their families' long-standing hatred with their newfound love for each other, this precarious equilibrium proves unsustainable in the wake of Tybalt's murder of Mercutio, after which a *rapprochement* between these opposing forces can be achieved only through Romeo and Juliet's death, resonating as their final 'intervention' in the name of love.

In her essay on *Antony and Cleopatra*, Charnes explores romantic love as 'the most pervasive and effective – yet least deconstructed – of all ideological apparatuses: one of the most effective smokescreens available in the politics of cultural production'.[3] She contends that in the context of romantic narratives, among which *Romeo and Juliet* would surely be at the top of the list, 'love is regarded as "content" rather than as something that influences our reception of other elements'; instead, Charnes 'propose(s) that we look at love as a genre, or in Bourdieu's terms, a restructuring structure . . . whose coercive influence is camouflaged by its very obviousness'.[4] The issue of how 'love' functions as a smokescreen in *Romeo and Juliet* has not been examined as such precisely because, as Charnes argues of Shakespeare's work in general, this play has been 'girded with (and ultimately hypostasised by) the status, dignity and decorum of canonical drama'.[5] The first question we might consider asking,

[3] Ibid.

[4] Ibid.

[5] Ibid., p. 2.

then, with respect to *Romeo and Juliet*, is what does 'love' conceal in the name of *hate*?

Xenophobia

The play's setting in 'fair Verona', by all accounts an exquisite, walled Renaissance city, is an important issue for adaptation, since not every adaptor has chosen to take the Prologue at its word. (Baz Luhrmann, for instance, interprets 'fair' as 'foul', shooting on location in the polluted and politically corrupt corporate centre of Mexico City.) In fact, in Shakespeare's day, this unsavoury vision is similar to how Robert Ascham, famously known as Elizabeth I's tutor and sententious adviser, felt about the seemingly obligatory travel of young Englishmen to Italy. For the English, Italy was a place where would-be gentlemen sojourned to improve their Classical education and knowledge of foreign 'tongues' – in both literary and literal respects – since Italian women were considered to be innately promiscuous, going so far as to prostitute their bodies to the gaze of the masses by performing as actresses on stage. England, of course, banned female actresses (and, yet, by comparison, the English practice of men dressing as and impersonating women in the theatre seems far more risqué). In any case, for Ascham, England's hot-blooded neighbour to the south was 'marvelous dangerous' to English youth, despite being the former bastion of Classical learning: 'Virtue once made that country mistress over all the world. Vice now maketh that country slave to them, that before, were glad to serve it'.[6] Indeed,

[6] Robert Ascham, 'The Schoolmaster, or Plain and Perfect Way of Teaching Children the Latin Tongue' (London, 1570), p. 23–28; reprinted in *Romeo and Juliet: Texts and Contexts*, edited by Dympna Callaghan (Boston: Bedford/St Martin's, 2003), p. 168.

Ascham's assertion of England's superiority to Italy stems principally from his investment in the 'one true faith' – Protestantism and, more specifically, the Church of England – as opposed to the papists who lead the way 'to Circe's court'. Unable to resist 'all the Siren songs of Italy', gullible English sojourners all too quickly 'become devils in life and condition'.[7]

Perhaps the most fascinating aspect of Ascham's critique is his concern that one need not go to the proverbial mountain to be corrupted, for the mountain comes to (English)men in the form of Italian books-in-translation. So concerned is Ascham by the power of Italian stories – from Petrarch's love poetry to Saviolo's fencing manual – that he exclaims with tangible indignity:

> These be the enchantments of Circe, brought
> out of Italy, to mar men's manners in England,
> which, by example of ill life, but more by precepts
> of some books, of late translated out of Italian
> into English, (and) sold in every shop in London . . . .
> Ten sermons of Paul's Cross do not so much good
> for moving men to true bearing, as one of those
> books do harm, with enticing one to ill living.
> Yea, I say farther, those books tend not so much
> to corrupt honest living, as they do to subvert
> true religion. More papists be made, by your
> merry books of Italy, than by your earnest books
> of Louvain.[8]

One cannot help but wonder, given Ascham's outrage at the act of translation, why Shakespeare decided to adapt the quintessen-

[7] Ibid., pp. 168–70.
[8] Ibid., p. 170.

tially Italian story of *Romeo and Juliet* in the midst of such obvious xenophobia. Why, for instance, wouldn't this act be considered seditious? Moreover, unlike Brooke's cautionary tale, which condemns the two lovers and the Friar for their lechery and treachery, respectively, Shakespeare is more inclined to 'enchant' us with his lyrical poetry as well as enable audiences to identify with the plight of the titular heroes and their tale of human tragedy. Perhaps the only way that Shakespeare is able to stage such a compelling 'love' story is because the play ends in a kind of petit genocide, in which the only children – and heirs – of two incorrigible Italian patriarchs kill themselves, eradicating two lines of the Italian aristocracy with one efficient strike. Undeniably, then, there is an implicit *cultural* violence in *Romeo and Juliet* that demands recognition; we might go so far as to say that Shakespeare, an English poet, quietly performs a *coup d'état* on his Italian setting, by sapping it of the noble blood that gives it life. Through the play's conclusion, in other words, a myopic tale of tragic love becomes a 'smokescreen' for the widespread reality of ethnic antagonisms, which have historically occurred along a 'north-south' trajectory, effectively naturalising – in geography itself – the enmity between England and its southern European neighbours (Italy played second fiddle only to arch-rival Spain). Hence, as a play that engages in what Clifford Geertz has famously termed 'deep play', *Romeo and Juliet* – examined in light of the unspeakable, nationalistic desires buried in the darkness of the Capulet vault – does more than deliver an exotic, 'Italianate' change of scenery for its staid English audience; far more ambitiously, its agenda is nothing less than to 'Anglicise' a country of non-believers.[9]

---

[9] See Clifford Geertz's *The Interpretation of Cultures*, especially 'Deep Play: Notes on a Balinese Cockfight', New York: Basic Books, 1977.

Class uprisings

'For now these hot days in the mad blood stirring' (3.1.4), exclaims Benvolio at the beginning of the scene that will claim Mercutio's life. As Benvolio's line implies, Italian summers were predictably hot; but there was something particularly unique about the *English* summer that this line, by extension, simultaneously invokes. For in June of 1595 – a time when *Romeo and Juliet* was likely being performed in London – the heat and madness reached a fevered pitch, as twelve of the thirteen riots recorded that year occurred between June 6 and June 29.[10]

Consonant with Charnes's assertion that the concept of 'love' as a transhistorical, transcendent phenomenon has been dangerously under-interrogated, Chris Fitter argues that because *Romeo and Juliet* is the quintessential 'romance narrative', its political subtext has rarely been excavated.[11] Those who are willing to break with interpretive tradition, however, will find that Shakespeare is, once again, using both love and Italy as 'smokescreens' to contest and, on some level, contain the outrage that was seeping into the streets of London. And it is precisely this rhetorical shell game that enables a more subversive political agenda to be voiced. Indeed, Fitter offers the startling suggestion that the play is not only speaking directly to the 'London commoners at that particular historical juncture' but also encoding therein a narrative of 'political protest'.[12] Without question, the

[10] Roger B. Manning, *Village Revolts: Social Protest and Popular Disturbances 1509–1640* (Oxford: Oxford University Press), 1988, p. 208.

[11] Chris Fitter, '"The quarrel is between our masters and us their men": *Romeo and Juliet*, Dearth, and the London Riots', *English Literary Renaissance* 30 (2000), p. 155.

[12] Ibid., p. 156.

massive grain shortage and failed harvests disproportionately affected 'the poorer sorte',[13] as one 1595 tract makes plain – a fact supported by the sundry other anonymous 'Complaintes' that found their way into the Stationer's Register. In a nutshell, then, Fitter speculates that *Romeo and Juliet*'s prevailing 'food motif(s)' – coupled with its 'scenic juxtapositions' of the fertile Veronese setting alongside images of 'hunger with careless patrician feasting' – are some of the ways in which the play draws attention to the dire state of affairs at home.[14]

What is at stake in Fitter's reading – one that filmmakers have tapped into from *West Side Story* to Baz Lurhmann's *Romeo + Juliet* and, even, to a certain extent, *Shakespeare in Love* – is social justice. This problem in *Romeo and Juliet* is, for Fitter, easily summarised in three-fold terms: 'class-generated violence', 'officially allocated class culpability', and 'differential class punishment'.[15] During the long, hot summer of 1595, the citizens of London engaged in peaceful demonstrations to demand market regulation for sustenance-based products – grain, for example – which was being exported to foreign countries to profit the Crown while the lower classes were starving. In 1596, Lord Burghley, keenly aware of the crisis, introduced a commandment calling for the 'Restraint of Eating' so that the poor might benefit from greater charity. In *Romeo and Juliet*, however, Capulet is depicted as a figure driven by greed, excess, and conspicuous consumption; not only does he furnish several feasts throughout the course of the drama, but also, he is outfitted with lines that flaunt 'restraint',

---

[13] Quoted in R.B. Outhwaite, *Dearth, Public Policy and Social Disturbance in England, 1550–1800* (Cambridge, Cambridge University Press), p. 28.

[14] Fitter, p. 159.

[15] Ibid., p. 165.

impulsively ordering one of his servants to 'go hire me twenty cunning cooks' to celebrate Paris's pending marriage to Juliet (4.2.2). As for charity, Capulet's sensibilities do not lean in this direction; for example, when Juliet resists her father's chosen suitor, he screams: '(H)ang! Beg! Starve! Die in the streets' (3.5.192) – a reminder of those who were, in fact, engaged in any and, even, all of these unsavory exploits. Capulet's words would surely have reminded Shakespeare's audience of the aftermath of the Apprentice's Insurrection of June 29, 1595, when five such figures were made an example of, publicly hanged, drawn, and quartered. The failure to recognise in Juliet's plight that of the disenfranchised London citizenry is to 'depoliticize(e) interpretation of the play' in the interests of 'honoring a "transcendent" love'.[16]

Quite remarkably, at the same time that the lower classes were making their grievances known as well as demonstrating their outrage against the torture and wrongful death or imprisonment of their fellow protestors, the aristocracy engaged in the fashionable and deadly pastime of dueling and gang violence, made popular not only by the publication of Vincentio Saviolo's fencing manual in 1595, but also by the invention of the rapier – a weapon which, unlike the relatively heavy, blunt sword and buckler, could kill in an instant. Fitter explains that the combination of the code of honour (punctilio), which made even the most trivial insults worthy of contest, along with introduction of the rapier, created a culture of dueling with an extremely high mortality rate. Furthermore, the only significant action that Elizabeth I took to stop the bleeding – like the Prince in *Romeo and Juliet*, who merely 'winked at (the) discords' of the well-to-do households (5.3.294) – was to limit the length of the rapier to 'one yarde and halfe a quarter of the blade at the

---

[16] Ibid., p. 179.

uttermost'.[17] In other words, the historical period in England known retrospectively as 'the Golden Age' was, in Romeo's confused poetic motif, a literal hotbed of 'brawling love' and 'loving hate' (1.1.172), wherein 'a poor man was hanged for stealing food for his necessities and a luxurious courtier . . . could be pardoned after killing the second or third man'.[18] Indeed, Elizabeth's 1594 'Proclamation Prohibiting Unlawful Assembly under Martial Law' reveals this class bias in its opening sentence, which is directed not at the aristocracy but at the 'unlawful great assemblies of multitudes of a popular sort of base condition. . . .'[19] The fear of social class miscegenation is so great that Elizabeth herself refers to these potential 'multitudes' as 'compounded of sundry sorts of base people', as if they could spontaneously – or alchemically – beget more such aspiring rabble-rousers, whom the Queen refers to with great disdain, adding to her list of suspects 'some known apprentices such as are of base manual occupation, and some others wandering idle persons of condition of beggars and vagabonds, and some colouring their wandering by the name of soldiers returned from war' – all of whom, under the new Proclamation, could be 'without delay . . . execute(d) upon the gallows by order of martial law'.[20]

That Italy figures heavily in this alternative reading of *Romeo and Juliet* is evident in the English fascination with the Italian rhetoric and style of the duello that Shakespeare features in the battle

[17] Elizabeth I, quoted in Charles Edelman, *Brawl Ridiculous: Swordfighting in Shakespeare's Plays* (Manchester: Manchester University Press, 1992), p. 174.

[18] Lawrence Stone, *The Crisis of the Aristocracy 1558–1641* (Oxford: Oxford University Press, 1965), p. 120.

[19] Queen Elizabeth I, 'Proclamation Prohibiting Unlawful Assembly under Martial Law' [20 June 1591]; reprinted in Callaghan, p. 233.

[20] Quoted in Callaghan, p. 233.

between Mercutio and Tybalt. Prior to the fight, Mercutio makes fun of the highly-affectatious style of dueling that Tybalt adopts, citing his *passado*, *punto*, *reverso*, and *hay* as examples of the newfangled Italian style of fencing which, in this context, resonates as both a geopolitical insult and a personal one (2.3.24–25). When Benvolio suggests they move their violent leisure elsewhere, it is because the citizens' gaze is upon them in the public light of the piazza (3.1.52). Indeed, what too often goes unnoticed is the fact that the 'base', 'poorer', or 'popular sort' in *Romeo and Juliet* are precisely the ones keeping the peace. Earlier, in the opening brawl, Benvolio utters another warning, but it comes too late, as the citizens have entered to arrest the miscreants, crying: 'Clubs, bills and partisans! Strike! Beat them down! Down with the Capulets! Down with the Montagues!' (1.1.32). In this play, the common citizenry of Verona – not the aristocrats – are the lawful and legitimate keepers of the peace. Thus, as Fitter concludes: 'Shakespeare's treatment of violence and punishment assumes the aspect of a populist counter-indictment', as '*Romeo and Juliet* lays the blame for "mutiny" and civil bloodshed, even by the lower classes, at the door of urban nobility, and contrasts a citizen activism of laudable responsibility, rebuking specifically the catastrophic effects of a royal double standard in punishment of bloody disorders'.[21]

Gender, consent, crime

After the actual combatants have been taken into account, the second-largest group of casualties of any war – though rarely acknowledged as such – comprises women who have been victims of rape, a category of violence that has everything to do

[21] Fitter, pp. 164–65.

with claims to power, place, and privilege. Complementing the above discussion of Italy, Stephen Watson and Stephen Dickey audaciously observe that 'according to Shakespearean drama, Italy's the right place for rape'.[22] Whether or not one agrees with this bold statement, one would hardly expect *Romeo and Juliet* – as opposed to, say, *Titus Andronicus* – to be the principal basis for this argument. Nevertheless, as in the above cases, the more closely we examine the text, the more prevalent allusions to rape become. Although there are no actual sexual assaults performed in the play (only *West Side Story* will be bold enough to include an attempted rape scene), the rampant linguistic, cognitive, and cultural preoccupation with rape creates an ominous environment of *anticipatory* violence – as if, once the curtain falls, real chaos will ensue. Thus, here again, we see how unconditional love becomes a 'smokescreen' for its antithesis, which, in this case, are non-consensual acts of violence against women and, to a lesser degree, men.

To begin, knowing that Juliet is not quite fourteen 'assures the criminality of the match by Elizabethan standards, which also means that neither the Nurse nor the Friar – both of whom will lack the courage to defend the couple in other moments of crisis – could support Juliet's claim of marriage without risking jail'.[23] In his tract titled *The Countroy Justice*, published in 1618, Michael Dalton observes that the 'taking away of a maide under sixteene yeares of age, without the consent of her parents or governors, of contracting marriage with her, or deflowering her, is no felony, but yet shall be punished with long imprisonment, withoute baile, or with

[22] Robert N. Watson and Stephen Dickey, 'Wherefore Art Thou Tereu? Juliet and the Legacy of Rape', *Renaissance Quarterly* 58 (2005), p. 142.
[23] Watson and Dickey, pp. 139–140.

grievous fine'.[24] Though our perception is that, as a rule, women in the Renaissance were married as girls, most women were, in fact, married in their twenties. Nevertheless, there were others, like Henry Swinburne, who argued in his 'Treatise of Spousals' (widely circulated in manuscript in 1600) that marriage is best performed when women are of a 'ripe age', specifically, twelve years old, and when men were fourteen; the logic behind his claim is that

> at these years the man and the woman are not only presumed to be of discretion, and able to discern betwixt good and evil, and what is for their profit and disprofit; but also to have natural and corporal ability to perform the duty of marriage, and in that respect are termed *puberes*, as it were plants, now sending forth buds and flowers, apparent testimonies of inward sap, and immediate messengers of approaching fruit. And albeit this age may seem over-tender . . . the Almighty hath naturally disposed and enabled to increase and multiply . . . all creatures.[25]

Such was the relatively new doctrine of Protestant marriage, a subject that is violently at odds – in the literal sense of the term – with the obviously Catholic intonation and setting of *Romeo and Juliet*, a point to which I will return below.

Though it has been argued that Romeo treads a thin line between rapture and rape – particularly given the ambiguity of his entreaty – 'O wilt thou leave me so unsatisfied?' (2.1.168) ('O' suggests the 'O'-sounds of orgasm), there is no question that Paris is

---

[24] Michael Dalton, *The Countrey Justice* (London: 1618), p. 248.

[25] Henry Swinburne, *A Treatise of Spousals* (1600), printed in 1686. The above excerpt is from Section IX. Of Ripe or Lawful Age for Marriage, reprinted in Callaghan, p. 288.

a figure who would be considered by many to be a rapist, were he to consummate his marriage to the unwilling Juliet. Note that Shakespeare's contemporary, Cyril Tourneur, argues in *The Atheist's Tragedie*: 'Why what is't but a rape to force a wench/To marry, since it forces her to lie with him she would not?'.[26] If we move from examining contemporary literature to exploring literary allusion, this argument becomes more persuasive, for Paris is, of course, the name of the man who forcibly abducted (raped?) Helen, stealing her away from Menelaus to begin the Trojan War. Indeed, despite its designation as the greatest love story of all time, *Romeo and Juliet* speaks in a language that is deeply-inflected with misogynistic violence. A glance at the opening scene, for example, reveals Sampson and Gregory engaging in wordplay that all too quickly displaces the object of civil strife from the bodies of men to women:

Gregory: That shows thee a weak slave, for the weakest goes to the wall.

Sampson: 'Tis true, and therefore women being the weaker vessels are ever thrust to the wall: therefore I will push Montague's men from the wall and thrust his maids to the wall.

Gregory: The quarrel is between our masters and us their men.

Sampson: 'Tis all one, I will show myself a tyrant: when I have fought with the men, I will be civil with the maids, I will cut off their heads.

Gregory: The heads of maids?

Sampson: Ay, the heads of the maids, or their maidenheads, take it in what sense thou wilt. (1.1.14–25)

---

[26] Cyril Tourneur. *The Atheist's Tragedie* (1611), edited by Irving Ribner (Cambridge, MA: Harvard University Press, 1964), 1.4.129–31.

What begins as a show of courtesy (it was customary for men to allow women to take the wall-side of street as a display of protection) ends with an ultimatum that predestines women either to a real or a social death, as the choice between killing – cutting off their heads with rapiers – and rape, which would 'cut off' their maidenheads (hymens), swiftly becomes their only conceivable fates, should these Montague women be so unlucky as to encounter a Capulet 'sword'. Watson and Dickey reiterate this sentiment in considering Juliet's double-betrothal:

> Furthermore, in the fights over Juliet Shakespeare conflates the two main ways Renaissance women were denied subjectivity and choice in the process of courtship: by their treatment as objects of exchange and competition among men, and by deprivation of their consent in their choice of spouses – though this was a problem for men also – and in their sexual relations with those spouses.[27]

Mercutio, too, is famous for his violent references to even presumably consentual sex. Functioning as Romeo's sexual 'conjurer' (2.1.16), Mercutio instructs his student as follows: 'If love be rough with you, be rough with love/Prick love for pricking and you beat love down' (1.4.27–28). Subsequently, in a borderline pornographic remark, Mercutio vividly imagines Romeo spending the night with a woman whose 'open-arse' is the perfect fit for his 'poperin' (pop-her-in) pear (2.2.38). Not even the Friar himself is immune to the cultural sensibility that conflates violent sword play with sex; for upon seeing Romeo up so early in the morning after the Capulet ball, Friar Laurence exclaims: 'then here I hit it right –/Our Romeo

---

[27] Watson and Dickey, p. 146.

hath not been in bed to-night' (2.2.41–42). Unbeknownst to the good Friar, his remark singles out women as the target through which men score a 'hit', that is, a touch or point in fencing with obvious sexual implications. Hence, this ubiquitous wordplay and innuendo establishes Verona's culture of misogynistic violence as typical, leading Watson and Dickey to conclude that: 'Though Romeo's covert activities beneath Juliet's window may not seem especially sinister on their own, there is something lurking out there with him: a cumulative culture of sexual extortion from which Juliet will have to extricate her love story'.[28] But based on the words we hear from Juliet's own mouth, extricating a love story may prove impossible; after all, it is she who alludes to the rape of Philomel when, during the morning after her marital consummation, she exclaims:

> Wilt thou be gone? It is not yet near day.
> It was the nightingale, and not the lark,
> That pierc'd the fearful hollow of thine ear;
> Nightly she sings on yond pomegranate tree.
> Believe me, love, it was the nightingale. (3.5.1–5)

This allusion to Tereus's rape of Philomel from Ovid's *Metamorphoses* would not be lost on Renaissance ears, as the following excerpt from John Lyly's play *Campaspe* suggests:[29]

> What Bird so sings and yet does wail?
>> O 'tis the Ravish'd Nightingale.
>> Jug, jug, jug, jug, Tereu, she cries,
>> And still her woes at midnight rise.

[28] Ibid., p. 127.

[29] Ovid, *Metamorphoses*, translated by Charles Martin (New York: W.W. Norton, 2004).

> Brave prick-song! Who is't now we hear?
>> None but the lark so shrill and clear.
> Now at heaven's gate she claps her wings,
>> The morn not waking till she sings.[30]

Of all people, the gentleman poet John Lyly cannot resist a bawdy reference to the Nightingale's 'Brave prick-song', so common was the notion of 'prick(ing) love for pricking' in order to 'beat love' – and women – 'down'. It is from examples such as those cited above that Watson and Dickey form the radical conclusion that in *Romeo and Juliet*, the specter of rape is a veritable *lingua franca*: 'Rape is thus the threat encompassing and permeating the physical actions, the psychological tensions, and the classical allusions of what is widely deemed the *ultimate love story*.'[31]

Religion

Literally invoking the notion of the smokescreen, Karl Marx famously observed that 'religion is the opium of the people'.[32] More so in its screen incarnations does Romeo and Juliet confront the uses and abuses of religion than in its play form. Nevertheless, as a play written for a Protestant audience about Catholic lovers who, against Canon law, commit violence upon themselves that culminates in their double suicide, Shakespeare had to tread cautiously. After all, in order for the play to be successful, the audience had to sympathise with Romeo and Juliet – the same

[30] John Lyly, *Campaspe* (1583), edited by G.K. Hunter (Manchester: Manchester University Press, 1991). 5.1.35–42

[31] Watson and Dickey, p. 148.

[32] See Marx's *Critique of Hegel's Philosophy of Right* (1843), edited by Joseph O'Malley (Cambridge: Cambridge University Press, 1977), p. 131.

figures who, in one of their earliest exchanges, pose as 'saints' and 'pilgrims' who pray by kissing. Though the Catholic and Protestant tensions within the play have been scarcely addressed in scholarship, Paul Siegel ventures one opinion as to how Shakespeare walked the line, arguing that *Romeo and Juliet* – with its structure of 'sin', punishment, and implicit moralism – plays a significant role in 'anticipat(ing) *Pamela, Charlotte Temple*, and the modern Hollywood Biblical "epics", in which the audience is invited to sin vicariously with the pagans while being edified by the pious sentiments of the Christians'.[33] According to Siegel, the play creates a 'subtle blend' of 'passionate love' and the 'Christian moralistic condemnation of it . . . .'[34] I would argue more specifically that Shakespeare accomplishes this compromise-formation by harping on the 'Catholic' nature of Romeo and Juliet's love, which is epitomised by Juliet's request that Romeo 'swear by (his) gracious self,/Which is the god of my idolatry' (2.1.156-57). For an Elizabethan, Protestant audience, such a reference to the sin of idol worship would damn Romeo and Juliet from the beginning. So how, then, does Shakespeare achieve a balanced perspective through which his audience is able to sympathise with the forlorn lovers?

Siegel argues that it is only through a rapprochement between Pagan and Christian doctrines of love that Shakespeare is able to make Cupid – the god of love – 'one' with God's love, thus enabling Romeo and Juliet to die in exaltation. Yet, Siegel adds, their apotheosis 'does not, however, cause us to forget the tragic fact of death of the two young people who have so deeply engaged our sympathies. For the glorification of the love of Romeo and Juliet involves a basic acceptance of this world, that

---

[33] Paul Siegel, *Shakespeare Quarterly* 12.4 (Autumn 1961), p. 373.

[34] Ibid., p. 372

acceptance which is necessary if suffering and death are to be tragically meaningful'.[35] Whether or not we agree with Siegel's perspective on the reconciliation of Christian and Pagan notions of love, he makes a useful point about 'acceptance', which was rapidly finding its way into the otherwise sin-obsessed discourse of militant Elizabethan Protestantism. The fact that one of its greatest spokesmen, Sir Philip Sydney, permits his character Erona, who believes her lover to be dead, 'to send her soule . . . to be maried in the eternall church with him', suggests the shifting sentiment whereby love, sex, and Godly devotion could be reconciled without the fear that earthly idolatry would purchase damnation.[36] Eventually, then, it was the burgeoning Protestant and, more specifically, Puritannical view that sex in marriage – the only sex Romeo and Juliet have – is an expression of God's desire for people to 'be fruitful and multiply', which would have permitted Shakespeare's lovers to escape an infernal eternity.

In touching on this complex and contestatory issue in *Romeo and Juliet*, Shakespeare surely could be said to anticipate one 'Biblical "epic"' in particular: John Milton's *Paradise Lost*. Indeed, it was not until three quarters of a century later that Milton would boldly confront the theological and ontological question: 'was there sex in Paradise?' While ending some arguments, Milton's words began others, but there can be little doubt that his 'attempt to justify the ways of God to man' retroactively absolves both Romeo and Juliet from the taint of sin once and for all, as the narrator of *Paradise Lost* proclaims:

---

[35] Ibid., p. 392.

[36] *Sir Philip Sidney: Selected Prose and Poetry*, edited by Robert Kimbrough (Madison: Wisconsin University Press, 1983), p. 398.

Whatever Hypocrites austerely talk
Of purity and place and innocence,
Defaming as impure what God declares
Pure, and commands to some, leaves free to all.
Our Maker bids increase, who bids abstain
But our Destoyer, foe to God and Man?
Hail wedded love, mysterious Law, true source
Of human offspring, sole propriety
In Paradise of all things common else.[37]

For Milton, religion is not a smokescreen but a stage, wherein the faithful perform their love of God with their eyes wide open. Indeed, it is no surprise that Milton originally envisioned *Paradise Lost* as a play, only changing his mind when he feared that Satan might steal the show. Centuries later, filmmakers continue to grapple with the implications of sex, sin, and salvation in *Romeo and Juliet*, focusing their adaptations on both the physical representation and ideological ramifications of the extreme violence – and violations – contained in the play. As we shall see, some will venture purgatory to do so, going so far as to over-rule the Catholic doctrine forbidding suicide by boldly ushering the dead lovers swiftly into Heaven – before the Devil can drag them down.

37 John Milton, *Paradise Lost in John Milton: Complete Poems and Major Prose*, edited by Merritt Y. Hughes (New York: Macmillan, 1957), Book IV, lines 744–53.

PART 2:

From text to screen

A brief history of *Romeo and Juliet* on screen

As we have established, Brooke's *Tragicall Historye* is Shakespeare's principal source – and the Bard follows him quite precisely. The marvel of Shakespeare's play is that he telescopes Brooke's tragedy, which occurs over several months, into several days. The principal challenge of the play thus becomes persuading audiences that Romeo and Juliet truly cannot live without each other, having known each other for less than a week. While such telescoping is particularly conducive to both the pacing and technology of cinematic narration, it is arguably *more* difficult to make Romeo and Juliet's romance believable on screen. Whereas page and stage tend to leave more to the individual imagination, film pre-selects and, hence, pre-determines the spectator's point-of-view. In other words, to a much greater degree than other media, traditional cinematic narration actually conditions viewers to forgo fantasies of their own making in favour of those constructed by the camera. Given that the average film length is less than 'two hours' traffic of our stage' (Prologue 12), the camera that takes on *Romeo and Juliet* must perform a yeoman's work to insure that the reality of 'love' lingers – from 'first sight' – to forever.

If, as Stephen Watson and Stephen Dickey explain, the Renaissance stage created a 'heavily allusive artistic culture,' then Shakespeare's plays embody a broader effort not only to reveal the day-to-day 'workings of the human mind' but also to 'navigat(e) through the internal and external complexities of human experience by a layering of allusions, stories of varying degrees of proximity and vividness, most of them indirectly inherited, that tell us what to want and what to fear'.[1] Filmmakers arguably work through even more richly allusive material, since they traffic in words and spectacle, as well as the history of cinematic representation itself, eliciting memories of other films through a network of associations derived from a given film's style, casting choices, and mise-en-scène. Although the following chapters focus on the three most famous adaptations of *Romeo and Juliet*: the Shakespearean spinoff better known as *West Side Story* (1961), Zeffirelli's 'flower child' version of 1968, and Baz Luhrmann's 1996 blockbuster, it is important to establish – as we have with the text(s) – the broader history of *Romeo and Juliet* films.

Perhaps it should not surprise us that from its earliest moments on screen, *Romeo and Juliet* was being adapted in ways that advanced the craft of cinema itself, forcing the camera to accommodate the extraordinary vicissitudes of emotion contained in the play by creating novel filming techniques. Fittingly, in the race to release the first screen adaptations, the Italians won, as Mario Caserini's Cines production appeared in 1908, and was swiftly followed by adaptations from the UK and the US, respectively. Of the three films released in 1908, there is no question that the US-made Vitagraph production set the standard. Pre-figuring Baz Luhrmann's inventive cinematic vocabulary, this production, starring Florence Turner, employs seventeen different camera angles, cross-cutting as well as location shooting and off-camera editing – all for a film that lasts less than fifteen minutes. Similarly, one wonders if

[1] Watson and Dickey, p. 146.

Luhrmann knew of Gerolamo Lo Savio's twenty-five minute adaptation of 1911, for this film – shot on location in the streets of Verona – is the first to depict Juliet waking while Romeo is still in his death throes, which is precisely the gambit to which Luhrmann will return. Unlike cinematic adaptations of other Shakespeare plays, *Romeo and Juliet* immediately inspired spinoffs which were, remarkably, occurring in tandem with these early adaptations. Although little is known of the 1902 film titled *Burlesque on Romeo and Juliet*, two spinoffs of note appeared less than ten years later: *Romeo and Juliet in Town* (Otis Turner 1910), which focuses on Juliet Brown and Romeo Smith as two lovers torn apart by their feuding families, and *The Indian Romeo and Juliet* (Larry Trimble 1912), another silent, Vitagraph one-reeler that tells the story of the star crossed lovers from the perspective of Native American tribal warfare.

Of course, all of the above films are short, silent productions – a point that seems particularly ironic in the case of our most loquacious playwright – indeed, a contradiction in terms, for how can anyone conceive of a 'silent' Shakespeare? As the hundreds upon hundreds of silent Shakespeare films attest, the more important point is that cinema could not be conceived of apart from Shakespeare – above all other possible candidates for the translation of 'literature' into film – during the pre-sound era. Moreover, among the plays themselves, Robert Hamilton Ball notes that '*Romeo and Juliet* was clearly the most popular subject for Shakespeare film . . .', adding that early cinema in particular found in Shakespeare a means of 'draw(ing) and hold(ing) audiences who found pleasure in the relatively new experience of watching moving images on a screen'.[2] Kenneth Rothwell has famously

---

[2] Robert Hamilton Ball, *Shakespeare on Silent Film: A Strange Eventful History* (New York: Theatre Arts Books, 1968), p. 235, p. 29.

observed that Shakespeare – particularly with respect to the Vitagraph Series – served to elevate the status of early cinema by investing it with artistic legitimacy, so powerful was the 'enormous cultural capital' that the Bard possessed.[3] And though the limitations of silent film were staggering compared to the kind of technologies that would emerge within three decades of cinema's birth, the stalwart champions of this new 'electric theater' – among them, the US's first and foremost critic of filmed Shakespeare, Stephen W. Bush – argued vehemently that 'there is no play of Shakespeare that cannot be retold in moving images'.[4] And the rest is silence or, better put, history.

Well, not exactly, for in 1916, two of the great studios, Metro and Fox, went head-to-head with their first feature-length productions of *Romeo and Juliet* in celebration of Shakespeare's 300th birthday. Though both films are now lost, they represent a crucial moment in the rise of cinema as we know it; the fact that the two studios fought for the first release date and the best quality picture tells us that the then-emergent film industry was beginning to think of itself as a contender with other forms of popular entertainment, indeed, an art form in its own right, rather than a poor imitation of theatre. Fox beat Metro to the punch and to the quality mark by featuring the handsome Francis X. Bushman in the part of Romeo. (Bushman's performance proved far superior to Fox's Romeo, Harry Hilliard, a musical comedy star who was cast chiefly because he looked like Bushman.) Not surprisingly, *Romeo and Juliet* proved to be Hilliard's first – and only – film. Uncannily balancing the Metro production's male talent was Fox's casting of the famous 'vamp'

[3] Kenneth Rothwell, *A History of Shakespeare on Screen: A Century of Film and Television* (Cambridge: Cambridge University Press, 1999), p. 12.
[4] Stephen W. Bush, *Motion Picture World* 5 Dec. 1908, pp. 446–47.

actress Theda Bara as Juliet, whose pathos-drenched performance topped Metro's Beverly Bayne by a country mile. In other respects, however, the films were well-matched: Metro boasted a budget of $250,000 and a cast of 600, while Fox countered by advertising a cast of 2500 persons. As the October release date drew nigh, the new-sprung grudge between the studios intensified. Metro warned the public: 'Don't be misled. There is one and only one Special Production de Luxe of Shakespeare's Love Story of the Ages . . . Don't be misled by inferior imitations of a masterpiece'.[5] Indeed, there can be no doubt from extant accounts of the films that Metro was superior to the Fox production. No detail was ignored, as Ball observes, '(c)ontrary to the usual practice, the cast learned Shakespeare's lines and spoke them in the film'.[6] A production that was incomparably long – two and a quarter hours – the Metro *Romeo and Juliet* was warmly received by critics and audiences alike, as one review from *Moving Picture World* attests: 'Of the twelve thousand inches of film devoted to the portrayal . . . not a single one is superfluous'.[7] George F. Blaisdell concludes his rave review in terms that will draw a knowing chuckle from contemporary cinephiles, who have made similar claims about Shakespeare's gift as a 'filmmaker': 'It has demonstrated that Shakespeare dead three hundred years penned in his youth lines that stamp him as the greatest title builder in the world of to-day'.[7] Indeed, the reviews were in, and the consensus was that the motion picture had, for the first time in history, rendered Shakespeare immortal.

---

[5] Quoted in Ball, p. 236.

[6] Quoted in Ball, p. 237.

[7] George F. Blaisdell, quoted in Ball, p. 238.

The reception of the Fox *Romeo and Juliet* was less enthusiastic, though Theda Bara's performance was universally commended – particularly given that, both before and after this film, she had been known exclusively as a classic *femme fatale* or 'vamp'. Hence, as Juliet, she became a 'femme fatale' of a different order, playing the part of a classic tragic heroine that she embraced to the fullest. In an article written by Bara herself, she rationalised the excess of emotion – and eroticism – she felt the part required; having given 'the character a great deal of study', she 'discovered that Juliet lived in a period of passionate abandon. Italy, in the days of *Romeo and Juliet*, was no place for a Sunday-school girl'.[9] But Bara was forced to carry the production on her shoulders, for according to all accounts, Metro trumped Fox – beating the rival studio to the release date and, as indicated above, surpassing it in quality. Perhaps this explains why, in contrast to the Metro production, which made only one significant alteration to the text (Rosaline actually appears on screen), Fox was more daring, devoting an entire scene to a Da Porto-style ending in which Juliet awakes to find Romeo alive, but poisoned, and they perform a drawn-out but nevertheless heart-wrenching conclusion that culminates in Juliet's suicide when, at last, 'the potent poison o'ercrows (Romeo's) spirit' (*Hamlet* 5.2.305). There was some consolation in the fact that the Fox production actually fared better on the international scene, as it was booked into venues ranging from the Stratford Shakespeare Festival to Sydney, where the film was said to have commanded as much as two shillings for admission – no small sum in 1916.

By far the most interesting early sound version of *Romeo and Juliet* also happens to be the first known Hungarian adaptation,

[8] Ibid.
[9] Theda Bara, quoted in Ball p. 240.

István Kató's animated short film (1931) created entirely in silhouette. The film literalises, in surprisingly subtle ways, the tensions built into the play between 'day', which is invariably associated with death, and 'night' which, for Romeo and Juliet, is the province of life and love. Though historians would likely rather ignore MGM's lavish 1936 adaptation, directed by George Kukor, the film – despite its failure at the box office and in posterity – is of historical importance as the first feature length effort to adapt *Romeo and Juliet* as a 'high period' film. Assembled with the care it takes to synchronise the tiny gears of a watch, this *Romeo and Juliet* combined the best talent of its day. From its acclaimed director and Tchaikovskian score to its all-star cast, multi-million dollar financing, distinguished screenwriter (Talbot Jennings) and, above all, its visionary producer Irving Thalberg – the watchmaker who oversaw every aspect of the film – *Romeo and Juliet* seemed predestined to make history as the Hollywood studio system's first 'legitimate' Shakespearean masterpiece of the sound era. From Thalberg's purist perspective, earlier adaptations did not qualify as truly 'Shakespearean': the Pickford/Fairbanks *Taming of the Shrew* (1929), for example, relied too heavily on interpolated dialogue; likewise, the Reinhardt/Dieterle (1935) *Midsummer Night's Dream* compromised its status by casting contract actors who had no classical training, such as James Cagney and Mickey Rooney. By contrast, Thalberg dispatched agents to Verona to photograph the scenery, his crew studied paintings by the Renaissance masters – specifically, Botticelli, Bellini, Carpaccio, and Gozzoli – and academics from Harvard and Cornell were brought in as advisors. Indeed, Thalberg's film *did* make history – not as a blockbuster but, rather, as a bust – losing nearly one million dollars. The main problem with the adaptation was not its $2 million dollar mise-en-scene but its principals: Norma Shearer played Juliet at thirty-seven while Leslie

Howard played Romeo at forty-two (the fifty-five year-old John Barrymore supplied the role of Mercutio while Basil Rathbone performed Tybalt at forty-four). In short, the film was a geriatric adaptation of Shakespeare's tale of teenage lovers; despite the garish sets, gorgeous costumes, and Tchaikovskian musical accompaniment, nothing could turn back time for these would-be youngsters.

Cukor and Jennings retained just under fifty percent of the play for the screenplay – possibly the most of any adaptation of *Romeo and Juliet* – and interpolated several scenes (as is a commonplace among contemporary adaptations) involving Friar John, while reducing Friar Laurence's part. Agnes de Mille choreographed the lengthy Capulet Ball sequence, wherein she includes a vision of Rosaline patently resisting Romeo's charms, expanding upon Metro's introduction of Rosaline in its 1916 adaptation. The overall failure of *Romeo and Juliet* is believed to have contributed to the untimely death of Irving Thalberg, the film's producer and Shearer's husband. Nevertheless, the production is significant on a number of levels, particularly as the first Shakespeare film to be accompanied by a 'tie-in' book, replete with scholarly commentary from William Strunk Jr, better known for his famous grammar book, *The Elements of Style*. In fact, despite all its disappointments, the film received four major Oscar nominations: Best Picture, Best Actor, Best Actress, and Best Art Direction. Moreover, this Cukor-Thalberg vehicle left an indelible impression on other directors. Renato Castellani's *Romeo and Juliet*, for example, demonstrates knowledge of its filmic predecessor in the Capulet Ball scene, wherein Juliet, as in the Cukor-Thalberg production, willingly dances with Paris as someone with whom she is politely familiar. Similarly, Baz Luhrmann's 1996 version not only represents Juliet's reluctant but deferential dance with Paris as a display of filial duty, but also directly references the Cukor-Thalberg film in its depiction of the balcony scene. Considered one of the most original renderings of this famous exchange, the balcony scene in Luhrmann's *Romeo + Juliet* features a swimming pool as the central medium of Romeo's courtship; however, the Cukor-Thalberg adaptation – made six decades earlier – is the first to employ a pool as a key signifier of the architectural and social limits that Romeo 'o'er perches' in his pursuit of Juliet. Hence, even if the 1936 adaptation failed to impress audiences, It left its mark on future *auteurs*.

What could have been the first great film of *Romeo and Juliet* is Renato Castellani's 1954 adaptation. Deeply influenced by the post-war, Italian neo-realist movement, Castellani's style has been characterised as 'realismo rosa' (soft or 'pink' neorealism). This style maintains the raw quality of Italian neorealism while also mitigating the genre's ironic, deliberately painful juxtapositions of narrative understatement with bold visual contrasts, typically featuring Italy's war-ravaged landscape. Soft neorealism is indeed the ideal description of Castellani's *Romeo and Juliet*, for despite being shot in Technicolor, the film employs a palette of exquisitely muted colors, as the mollifying sepia tones and a combination of celadon, ochre, and antique rose hues persuade the audience that they have stepped into a faded Renaissance painting. The focus is rarely turned away from the principals, as Castellani fought to assert Romeo's sense of isolation; hence, Mercutio and Friar Laurence – not to mention the Nurse – are virtually non-existent in the film. Visual interpolations abound in this adaptation; one of the more poignant ones occurs when the angry Montague pulls his banished son from his mother's final embrace; another interpolation shows Juliet and the Nurse amidst a handful of women, patiently passing their lives away sewing – drawing attention to the fate feared most by Renaissance girls – becoming a 'spinster'. Though described by one critic as 'a sumptuous travelogue' rather than a film, Castellani's exquisitely composed adaptation won the *Grand Prix* at the Venice Film Festival.

Unfortunately, the hideously-dubbed soundtrack unwittingly makes the film resemble a Renaissance period version of a classic kung fu parody. Were it not for the lack of synchronisation that leads to comical miscues such as the brawling Capulet's taunt 'what, drawn – ?' *before* Benvolio draws his sword, this film would likely receive the recognition it deserves as one of the most aesthetically sophisticated Shakespeare adaptations ever created. Yet it would be remiss not to note that Castellani's film is also distinguished by its bold and frequently-cited opening gambit, in which Sir John Gielgud impersonates William Shakespeare himself. With a readily identifiable voice and distinguished face, Gielgud-as-'Shakespeare' thrusts the audience into the playful milieu of the 'neo': the only respite they will receive from the realism – howsoever 'softly' rendered – that relentlessly reminds them of the war-torn lives that Castellani's art imitates.

In the decades before, during, and after Castellani's adaptation, three somewhat unlikely *Romeo and Juliet* films were made: a loose adaptation from India, titled *Anjuman* (Akhtar Hussein 1948), the 1959 Egyptian film *Hassan and Naima*, which transposes *Romeo and Juliet* into Islamic culture, and the Oscar-nominated *Los Tarantos* (Francisco Rovira Beleta 1963) a Spanish, flamenco-style adaptation that followed on the heels of *West Side Story*'s success. Although the film is based on *La historia de los Tarantos* by Alfredo Mañas, this story of feuding gypsy factions is, in and of itself, an adaptation of Shakespeare's play – the major difference being that, in the end, Rafael and Juana are killed by the Paris figure, Curro. Hence, what is particularly interesting is the extent to which films such as this and the 1989 re-make *Montoyas Y Tarantos*

(Vincente Escrivá) hint at the textual polyvocality that characterises Shakespeare's own adaptation of the legendary love story.

Beleta's film is important not just as one of the first Spanish-language adaptations of *Romeo and Juliet*, but also as a political statement during Franco's dictatorship, at which time the Catalonian language – and sundry other expressions of its culture – was officially banned. Indeed, Beleta's decision to adapt Mañas's story of Catalon Gypsies (and, thus, a marginalised group within another marginalised group) at this historical juncture cannot help but be interpreted as an act of social justice and cultural reclamation. This message is an embedded one, to be sure, as the film largely becomes a vehicle (and, as it turned out, swan song) for the legendary Flamenco dancer Carmen Amaya. Employing both black-and-white and colour sequences to create a sense of heightened realism, Beleta's adaptation takes place, significantly, in the now non-existent district of Somorrostro, in Barcelona. Like Shakespeare's feuding aristocrats, the Catalonian Gypsies are `a community defined by a kinship network and a territory' and, therefore, it is no surprise that the Romeo and Juliet characters meet at a wedding, where precisely such ties are celebrated.[10] Interestingly, though, as ethnographer David Lagunas Arias points out, Gypsy weddings are marked by a unique division of social space in which `single and married women occupy the central stage at the ball', while `men remain in the outer edge of the space . . . .'[11] On a practical level, this arrangement allows for the virtuoso performances of Amaya to take center stage, while also facilitating Rafael's initial infatuation with Juana. Their love-at-first sight meeting is, much like the one featured in Baz Luhrmann's film,

[10] David Lagunas Arias, *Romani Studies* 5, Vol. 12, No. 1 (2000), p. 51.
[11] Ibid., p. 42.

a wordless cacophony of gazes and clapping; moreover, the lovers' first exchange culminates in an underwater kiss – a scene to which Luhrmann is indebted in several instances. On another level, the culturally-specific negotiation of the ritualised wedding space enables Beleta to take liberties with Shakespeare that highlight the film's Catalonian Gypsy context. For example, in dances and at weddings in particular, it is the mothers 'who exercise control and meta-languages halfway between the men and the other women'.[12] Hence, *Los Tarantos* differs from Shakespeare's play in its augmented treatment of one mother in particular – Rafael's mother Angustias – who intercedes on behalf of the lovers but, of course, to no avail. Similar to the pathological paternalism embodied by the figure of Old Capulet in Shakespeare's play, the patriarchal structure of Catalonian Gypsy culture makes it all too easy for Juana's father, Rosendo, to overrule Angustias's hopes for the couple, on the grounds that their households are, in fact, historic enemies.

The inevitable tragedy begins to unfold with the introduction of the Paris/Tybalt figure (Curro), who slays Rafael's friend, Mojigondo (Mercutio), not long after Mojigondo has performed what will be (unbeknownst to him) his last dance – the equivalent of Mercutio's Queen Mab performance in this Flamenco transposition. Taking the ethnic tensions and Latin-American machismo to a higher level than perhaps even *West Side Story* before it, Beleta's adaptation is implicitly more violent than Shakespeare's play; Curro, for example, physically abuses Juana out of jealousy, creating the sense of urgency that leads the lovers to consummate their relationship before they marry (Rafael and Juana intend to elope the next day). Given that the two have been covertly communicating with each other through pigeon messengers, their murder by Curro –

[12] Ibid.

who finds them hiding in the crammed pigeon coop – serves as a rustic parallel to the suffocating Capulet mausoleum. In retribution, Juana's brother Sancho kills Curro. The film concludes with the remaining family members grieving together, as an indication to the audience that their 'ancient grudge' has been, with their children, laid to rest. The final tableau shows the children from the two families holding hands, as they walk with the carrier pigeon down the beach. If Beleta's film is an unacknowledged source in Lurhmann's film, then Doug Lanier argues that *Los Tarantos* is, in turn, undeniably influenced by *West Side Story*, contending that 'the look of the villains, the use of music and dancing, the urban barrio milieu, and several specific shots . . .' are all indebted to the earlier film.[13]

As noted at the beginning of this chapter, *Romeo and Juliet* and cinematic innovation have historically gone hand-in-hand. Armando Acosta's 1990 adaptation is no exception, for it features only a solitary 'live' actor, with the remainder of the cast supplied by cats. The voices of the cats, however, are provided by a host of superluminary stars, including Francesca Annis as Juliet, Vanessa Redgrave as Lady Capulet, Ben Kingsly as Capulet, and Maggie Smith as Rosalyne. John Hurt cross dresses to play a bag-lady-turned-boat-lady in keeping with the film's setting in Venice, famous for its feral cats. (Feral cats were also brought in from New York and Ghent, perhaps for a more multicultural look and sound.) Below, John Hurt-the-boat-woman shares his thoughts on the production:

Armando Acosta was the American director. He had all sorts of people in Belgium who had all given up their salaries, I didn't know this at the time, and they decided to do a production

[13] Douglas Lanier, 'Film Spin-Offs and Citations', in *Shakespeares after Shakespeare: An Encyclopedia of the Bard in Mass Media Culture*, Vol. 1 (2 Vols.) (Westport, Connecticut and London: Greenwood Press, 2007), p. 275.

almost entirely with cats. And he would go on at great length saying: 'You just want to watch that cat. It is so stunning, the cat that is playing Juliet.' And I thought, I've got to go in for this ride. This can't be anything but interesting. I didn't ask him why he wanted me to be a boat-woman. I think he felt that I had some great and deep spirituality that was going to fill the role. And obviously he felt that I was going to have some great affinity with cats, too. When one actually jumped off the boat and into the canal and wasn't able to swim, he found there was a very deep significance in this. I did suggest to him that it was not a good idea. It was a fairly extraordinary film.[14]

Extraordinary indeed, for Acosta spared no time – or expense – in seeing what many viewed as a 'pipe dream' through to reality. The score features the music of Sergei Prokofiev and Emanuel Verdi's music for *Romeo and Juliet*, and was performed by the London Symphony Orchestra under the conduction of Barry Wordsworth and Andre Previn. Not surprisingly, Acosta is reported to have spent nearly five thousand hours in the cutting room to create the final, two-hour product from more than two hundred hours of footage.

Running the gamut from silent film to cel animation, *Romeo and Juliet* has also been adapted for the children's series: *Shakespeare: The Animated Tales*. In several of the *Tales*, unique forms of animation are employed; one features stop-action photography using large-scale wooden puppets, while the other involves painting on glass – the fascinating effect of which is a visual palimpsest – as each scene carries something of the preceding one with it.

14 'Interview', *The Guardian*, Thursday, April 27 2000, http://www.guardian.co.uk/film /2000/apr/27/guardianinterviewsatbfisouthbank1#article_continue (last accessed 11/08/09).

However, *Romeo and Juliet* was to be approached traditionally from all angles, as the time-worn technique cel animation carried the day and a controversial sequence was edited out of the final film. Indeed, this adaptation initially contained 'sexual content', as a consummation scene was, for a time, initially part of the production, courtesy of the production team's more risqué Russian animators. However, their more prudish British co-producers insisted that the scene be removed; the compromise struck between the 'rival households' was to include the post-consummation scene, featuring its famous lark/nightingale *aubade*.

Some scholars have alleged that *Romeo and Juliet* is the most filmed play of all time. One of the major issues in determining which movies genuinely qualify as adaptations is determining the extent to which a given film is inherently 'Shakespearean' – a quality that does not necessarily demand the use of Shakespeare's language – as Akira Kurosawa's *Throne of Blood* has so brilliantly demonstrated. Indeed, what is it about *West Side Story* that makes it qualify as Shakespearean, while the 1941 musical film *Playmates* (David Butler) – a story about Romeo the swing musician and Juliet the opera singer (whose father respects classical music exclusively) – continually slips under the radar of Shakespearean film anthologies, dictionaries, and encyclopedias?

The answer to such questions will always be idiosyncratic; certainly, every film whose plotline contains forbidden love and feuding families will not make the cut. But it is worth noting that, in and of itself, there are more than 230 known spinoffs and citations of *Romeo and Juliet*, with the vast majority of them hinging on both of these themes, while often duplicating other Shakespearean characters and subplots. Those with 'happy endings' clearly belong to the category of spinoff rather than adaptation; but what do we do with those films which adopt Shakespeare's play for a different genre, retaining virtually the entire plot but not Shakespeare's language? Were it not for the tendency to spin Shakespeare's play in the direction of a 'happy ending', many of the early *Romeo and Juliet*-inspired westerns and gangster films, such as *To the Last Man* and *The Guilty Generation*, respectively, would rank as adaptations. Other important productions – those that mark important junctures in the film history or, as discussed at the beginning of this chapter, technological innovation – are worthy of mention. The 1937 film *Ambikapathy* is one of the earliest-known South Asian period films. Set in 1083, the film features the a forbidden love affair between Ambikapathy, the son of a great poet, and the princess Amaravathy; naturally, the princess's father does not approve of her pauper-poet and devises a test for Ambikapathy, which he fails, losing the princess's hand in marriage as a consequence. Allegedly, in the syncretistic tradition of South Asian cinema, the film contains a balcony scene that recalls Cukor's 1936 production. If *Ambikapathy* is of historical significance, then the 1953 spinoff, *Beneath the 12-Mile Reef*, is importance for its stunning use of underwater photography – something that Baz Luhrmann's *Romeo + Juliet* takes for theme. Essentially, the son (Tony) and daughter (Gwyneth) of rival sponge-fishermen develop an unlikely romance when one family invades the other's fishing 'turf'. In a deviation from Shakespeare's plot, it is Tony's father, Mike – not Mercutio – who is killed in an accident; Arnold, the Paris figure, proceeds to burn Mike's boat and steals his cargo. Hence, in order to recover his father's barely-afloat business, Tony, along with Gwyneth, takes a boat from Arnold's team and sets out to go sponge-fishing along the deadly 12-Mile Reef. When Thomas and Arnold apprehend the lovers, Arnold and Tony fight and, in the process, Thomas is persuaded to grant Tony permission to marry his daughter. This spinoff thus offers a happy ending, tempered by Mike's tragedy.

What is lacking in the above films, despite offering faithful transpositions of the major themes and plot of *Romeo and Juliet*, is a profound sense of the *tragic inevitability* that fuels Shakespeare's play. This, as we shall see, is what distinguishes a truly Shakespearean version of *Romeo and Juliet* from the hundreds of 'wannabes' that seek access to the play's affective capital. Rival social structures always inform this tragic trajectory – typically, those pertaining to class, race, and/or religion; interestingly, those spinoffs that tackle race and/or religion, rather than those revolving around class differences, tend to occupy the border between spinoff and adaptation. Tragic inevitability and the inscrutable workings of Karma are the subject of the epic *Romeo and Juliet* spinoff *Qayamat Se Qayamat Tak (From Judgement Day to Judgement Day)*. In this 1988 South Asian film, Shakespeare's plot is adhered to quite extensively: caught in an ancient rivalry, Raj falls in love (at first sight) with Rashmi, despite her betrothal to another. Raj's love deepens when he goes (undetected) to a party thrown by Rashmi's father Thakur, as Raj risks life and limb just to see her face. When the two families wind up vacationing in the same location, Raj and Rashmi officially fall deeply in love. Thakur, outraged, seeks to speed up his daughter's marriage to his chosen suitor, Roop, and it is immediately after the 'engagement' party that Raj and Rashmi elope, fleeing to a dilapidated temple in the country (significantly, the depiction of 'Mantua' as a ruinous borderland or liminal space has become a commonplace in *Romeo and Juliet* films). However, the doomed lovers are hunted down by Thakur's hired men and, in the midst of an effort to kill Raj, Rashmi is murdered in a move that cleverly conflates Mercutio and Juliet's character. When Raj sees that his best friend/lover is dead, he prevents his own murder by killing himself with a dagger, echoing Juliet's manner of suicide in Shakespeare's play. As Doug Lanier astutely observes, '(t)he tragic fatedness of the lovers is signaled early on when Rashmi takes photographs of Raj during a sunset, an omen of death; the final shot of the dead lovers, sunset in the background, recalls this motif'.[15]

This inescapable sense of ill-fatedness – of being star crossed – is the defining feature that separates a spinoff from an adaptation. Indeed, long before it was a play by William Shakespeare, Romeo and Juliet was a legend – a genre which, as Linda Charnes has argued, is nothing if not haunted – engendering the desire to 'escap(e) prior encoding'; legends, in other words, confront their protagonists with the paradox of their belated arrival at the very scene of the stories they presume to animate and originate.[16] As I have argued elsewhere, Shakespeare's play actively struggles against the forces of the legendary, as evidenced in Romeo and Juliet's desire to be 'new baptized' at all costs (2.1.93).[17] We see the influence of the legend – and its peculiar history of literary, rather than oral transmission – appear in Romeo and Juliet's many references to the constraints posed by books, letters, and acts of writing; although Romeo and Juliet appear convinced that they can become the 'authors' of their own destiny, it is the auctoritas – the preexisting authority – of the legend that thwarts their efforts to divorce their bodies from the tragic referentiality of their names.[18]

[15] Lanier, p. 285.

[16] Linda Charnes, Notorious Identity: Materializing the Subject in Shakespeare (Cambridge and London: Harvard University Press, 1993), p. 99.

[17] Courtney Lehmann, 'Strictly Shakespeare? Dead Letters, Ghostly Fathers, and the Cultural Pathology of Authorship in Baz Luhrmann's William Shakespeare's Romeo + Juliet', Shakespeare Quarterly: Vol. 52.2 (Summer 2001): pp. 189–221.

[18] For an extensive reading of the play in these terms, see Courtney Lehmann, Shakespeare Remains: Theater to Film, Early Modern to Postmodern (Ithaca and London: Cornell University Press, 2002). especially Chapter One, 'Shakespeare Unauthorized: Tragedy "by the book" in Romeo and Juliet', pp. 25–53.

There is no better example of the encroachment of the legend on Romeo and Juliet's best-laid plans than Juliet's inscription of its *auctoritas* in her commonplace book which, naturally, contains 'sententious' quotations from other sources, including an alliterative comparison of Romeo with 'rosemary' (2.3.195) – nothing less than the herb sprinkled on the bodies of the dead. In other words, no matter what fate they desire or attempt to authorise, Romeo and Juliet are destined to die by the cultural weight – the historically entrenched *auctoritas* – of the legend, which bears down upon Shakespeare's play even, it seems, against the playwright's own wishes. Hence, no film of *Romeo and Juliet* can crossover from a spinoff to an adaptation without some representation of this tragic inevitability, which must be implied or produced through fore-shadowing techniques (such as the sunset in Mansoor Khan's film) or allusions to the lovers' distinctly 'star-crossed' fate (Romeo and Juliet embody clashing faiths, social classes, races, or ethnic groups). As we shall see, Baz Luhrmann's adaptation goes one step further, alluding to Romeo and Juliet's tragic predestination through the narrative front-loading of lines like Romeo's statement after he consumes the poison ('th(e) drugs are quick') as well as through scenes that actually flash forward to the death of the lovers.

There are several more spinoffs that are of interest for their conceptual genius, such as the Nepalese-themed saga *1942: A Love Story*, along with *Dakan* (Mohamed Camara 1997), the first African film to feature a homosexual relationship between the 'Romeo' and 'Juliet' characters. Additionally, *This is the Sea* resituates the *Romeo and Juliet* legend amidst sectarian violence in Northern Ireland, while *Solomon and Gaenor*, which is set in Wales in 1911, features a forbidden relationship between a Jewish salesman and a Welsh miner's daughter. Only the soundtrack, which contains recitations of rabbinical liturgy and Welsh lamentation, creates the harmony that is impossible for the doomed lovers. The final borderline adaptation that I will point to here is, in the tradition of the lesser-known films cited above, a politically daring version of *Romeo and Juliet*, titled *Torn Apart* (Jack Fisher and Barry Markowitz 1989). This film tells the story of childhood friends Ben Arnon and Laila Malek; Ben and Laila find themselves reunited in Israel when Ben is performing his obligatory service to the Israeli Army. The problem is that Laila is Palestinian, and, naturally, their respective families are violently against the match. Moreover, a fellow Palestinian, Moustapha (the Paris figure), actively pursues his hope of marrying Laila, while Laila's relative Fawzi (the Tybalt character) is engaged in anti-Israeli terrorism. Professor Mansour, similar to Friar Laurence, is Ben's only mentor and ally; though he will sacrifice his own life to assist the lovers in their forbidden relations, Professor Mansour also serves as a variation on the Chorus in *Romeo and Juliet*, as the character who explains the Israeli-Palestinian conflict. With so much stacked against them, Ben and Laila try to flee to New York City, but are apprehended by soldiers. Upon their return with the captives, the soldiers get involved in a funeral riot and, as Laila tries to save Ben from harm, she is killed by a single gunshot, collapsing into Ben's embrace. The key to considering this film as more of an adaptation than a spinoff is, once again, the very real tragic inevitability that continues to loom over the Gaza strip today. And, as Doug Lanier points out, nothing in the film escapes complicity in the ongoing antagonisms between Jews and Muslims – not even the building blocks of cinematic narration – for although `(r)epeated wide shots of the land remind the viewer (t)hat the war is over', the `soundtrack contains continual reminders of the conflict'.[19] It is a testament to the power

[19] Lanier, p. 287.

of the Romeo and Juliet legend that it has been brought to bear on history itself and, yet, cannot change the tragic course of modern times.

Issues for adaptation

- **The setting**: *Romeo and Juliet* has proven to be the most 'adaptable' play in terms of its setting – as we have seen in this chapter, the sky's the limit (cats?). But since setting doesn't guarantee a given film's success, how do a director and screenwriter choose a setting for which the legendary, predetermined nature of the lovers' tragedy becomes believable – or, better yet – inevitable?

- **The principals**: even more than setting, casting the proper leads is the single-most important decision that is made in adapting *Romeo and Juliet* for the screen. How do a casting director and filmmaker choose *believable* young actors who are mature enough to handle the demanding roles?

- **The balcony scene**: among the more than thirty adaptations and two-hundred and thirty identified spinoffs and/or citations of *Romeo and Juliet*, the most referenced tableau is invariably the balcony scene. Clichéd to a fault, the balcony scene presents a unique challenge for filmmakers, who must inflect it with enough originality and immediacy to convince the audience that what they are seeing is real as opposed to 'staged'. What does a director have to do to insure that the balcony scene is not merely cinematic but more importantly, cinematographic, or, a visually meaningful threshold event in the young lovers' lives?

- **Image versus word**: for adaptations or transpositions similar to *West Side Story*, which does not retain a single line of the play, how are the film's 'Shakespearean' qualities rendered? How do a director and cinematographer rise to the challenge of creating a 'rhetoric' of images that is capable of replacing Shakespeare's poetry? Is it necessary to privilege one language over the other?

- **The soundtrack**: long before Baz Luhrmann's 'MTV'-style *Romeo + Juliet* was released, music and dance played a significant role in shaping the story – particularly noticeably during the Capulet Ball – of the two ill-fated lovers. The success of *West Side Story* has overshadowed many of the contributions of subsequent soundtracks, composers, and choreographers which (with the exception of Franco Zeffirelli's and Baz Luhrmann's adaptations), have gone largely ignored. How do a director, composer, and choreographer create music and dance numbers that can stand on their own, as they do in all three of these films?

- **Foreshadowing**: how does a director create the all-important sense of tragic inevitability for the audience while sustaining the belief that somehow, Romeo and Juliet will cheat death?

Now showing: *West Side Story*

I dreamed so much of walking in the future here
That sometimes I seemed to have remembered it.
> – Louis Aragon

There's a place for us
Somewhere a place for us.
> – Tony and Maria, *West Side Story*

It is somewhat ironic that the first truly phenomenal adaptation of *Romeo and Juliet* contains not a single line from Shakespeare. Sweeping the 1961 Academy Awards with ten Oscars (the most ever for a musical), *West Side Story* won Best Picture, Best Director, Best Supporting Actor, and Best Supporting Actress, along with Oscars for Color Cinematography, Color Art Direction/Set Direction, Sound, Scoring, Film Editing and Color Costume Design. These honours also make *West Side Story* the most critically-acclaimed Shakespeare adaptation of all time. Of course, there is some argument as to whether or not a Shakespeare film that retains none of Shakespeare's language still 'counts' as an adaptation, in the

---

[1] Louis Aragon, 'La nuit de Moscou', in Le roman inachevé (Paris: Gallimard, 1956), p. 231.

way that Franco Zeffirelli's and Baz Luhrmann's versions indisputably do. Developing his own definition as to what constitutes a Shakespeare 'adaptation', Michael Friedman argues against situating *West Side Story* alongside these two films, disagreeing with my claim that '(w)hereas conventional adaptations closely rely on the text and period proper to a given Shakespeare play, transpositional films alter the historical or cultural setting of the play but may or may not update the language, as the difference between *West Side Story*. . . and Baz Luhrmann's *William Shakespeare's Romeo + Juliet*. . . illustrates'. In response, Friedman contends: 'Lehmann's "transpositional" classification lumps *West Side Story* and *Romeo + Juliet* together in the same category, but I would argue that . . . the choice between using Shakespeare's language and modern dialogue (i)s a crucial distinguishing characteristic'.[2] While Friedman's point is well taken – and, to be sure, there are distinct challenges that come with the decision to use Shakespeare's language – I want to demonstrate in this chapter how moving away from this all-important notion of the Shakespearean 'Logos' can illuminate ways in which film adaptations employ devices that approximate Shakespeare's language without being bound to its direct citation. Such is the case, I shall argue, with *West Side Story*.

As discussed in the previous chapter, even when a film modelled on *Romeo and Juliet* resists the retention of Shakespeare's language, this should not necessarily be grounds for discounting it as an adaptation – provided the film establishes an *equivalent*

---

[2] Michael Friedman, 'Introduction: "to think o' th' teen that I have turned you to": The Scholarly Consideration of Teen Shakespeare films'. *Shakespeare Bulletin* 26.2 (Summer 2008), p. 6, n. 2. Friedman refers to my classificatory scheme in 'What is a Film Adaptation? Or, Shakespeare Du Jour', *Shakespeares After Shakespeare: An Encyclopedia of the Bard in Mass Media and Popular Culture*, edited by Richard Burt. Vol. 1 (2 Vols.) (Westport, CT: Greenwood Press, 2007), pp. 74–80.

means of rendering the imminent and implacable force of tragic inevitability. In his reflections on adapting the Broadway musical into a musical film, Ernest Lehman observes that

> *West Side Story* was not an easy film script to write. I found it difficult reshaping an iconic stage musical into a movie. I noted that some of the production numbers on stage seem to be in the wrong place for a film. I wanted the film to flow with rising dramatic movement, with no intermission to break that tension. This meant no comic interludes after the rumble to break the escalating sense of inevitable tragedy.[3]

But the problem he encountered was, without Shakespeare's words – without Juliet's 'ill-divining soul' and Romeo's 'misgiv(ing)' mind (1.4.104; 3.5.54), not to mention the Chorus's opening announcement that 'a pair of star-crossed lovers take their life' (Pro. 6) – how was this 'sense of inevitable tragedy' to be conveyed? On more than one occasion, Lehman thought he had discovered his solution: to take the musical out of the musical. But every time he did so, he explains:

> I found myself haunted by a vision. I would walk into the quintessential Broadway restaurant, Sardi's, and there, seated, would be the creative forces behind the original stage show staring at me, with fans of the Broadway show milling about with that same accusatory look. Their eyes were saying what they

[3] Ernest Lehman offers an introductory letter, dated October 2002, as part of the front matter of the special 40th Anniversary Edition of *West Side Story* released as a two-DVD set with an accompanying booklet containing photos of the premiere, the screenplay, the original lobby brochure for the Broadway musical, and many other 'extras'.

were thinking. 'Listen, you interloper, have you mangled another Broadway show on the altar of Hollywood?'

So Lehman resolved to make his dialogue as honest and, yet, as 'invisible' as he could, in order to showcase the musical and dance numbers wherein – as we shall see – the 'escalating sense of inevitable tragedy' resides.

Indeed, although the practice of tweaking and tampering with Shakespeare's plays was occurring as early as the late seventeenth century, it was during the eighteenth and nineteenth centuries, as Peter Conrad explains, that there was a 'need to demonstrate that Shakespeare was a Romantic artist, which meant rewriting him into conformity with new aesthetic ideals – or, in some cases, unwriting him altogether'.[4] The primary example of 'unwriting' that Conrad provides is the nineteenth-century operatic trend in which Shakespeare's 'words are dissolved by music in a series of adaptations of *Romeo and Juliet*'.[5] Citing Bellini's 1830 opera *I Capuleti e I Montecchi* and Berlioz's 1839 *Roméo et Juliette*, Conrad makes an extremely compelling case for why Shakespeare can *still* be Shakespearean 'when his words are taken away'; after all, he continues, there is 'an arcane logic to the process, made clear by Walter Pater's decree in *The Renaissance* that all arts should aspire to the condition of music'.[6] What happened during the Romantic era is that poetry came to stand in for music – and drama – because '(p)oetry musically canceled the sense of words and emphasised their raving, rapturous sound'.[7] Likening what we

---

[4] Peter Conrad, *To be Continued: Four Stories and Their Survival* (Oxford: Clarendon Press, 1995), p. 47.

[5] Ibid.

[6] Ibid.

[7] Conrad, p. 48.

might think of as the ecstatic 'beyond' forged by Shakespeare's poetry to 'the sibilant rush of (Shelley's) west wind' or 'the unintelligible art' of his skylark, Conrad explains that 'Shakespeare, in the Romantic view, had a special need for . . . lyrical salvation: his poetry had to be rescued from its adulteration by drama'; the Romantics, in turn, looked back to Classical times to justify their rescue mission, for 'Poets were singers first, when Apollo gave Orpheus his golden voice . . . .'[8]

Kenneth Rothwell observes that '(d)irect calls for music in the text certify to the presence of live musicians onstage in the Elizabethan playhouse'.[9] For instance, listening to Juliet repeat the rhyming vowels of Romeo's name during the balcony scene, Romeo replies: 'It is my soul that calls upon my name:/How silver-sweet sound lovers' tongues in night,/Like softest music to attending ears' (2.1.210–12). Shortly thereafter, just prior to their wedding in Friar Laurence's cell, Romeo actually attempts to convince Juliet to sing an impromptu duet with him:

> Ah, Juliet, if the measure of thy joy
> Be heaped like mine, and that thy skill be more
> To blazon it, then sweeten with thy breath
> This neighbor air, and let rich music tongue
> Unfold the imagined happiness that both
> Receive in either by this dear encounter.
>
> (2.5.24–29)

[8] Ibid.

[9] See Kenneth's essay 'Zeffirelli's *Romeo and Juliet*: Words into Picture and Music', *Literature/Film Quarterly* (Fall 1977), p. 326.

Similarly, in the *aubade* scene, Romeo 'sets up an elaborate quibble on "division", which to the Elizabethan musician meant "the execution of a rapid melodic passage" but which could be taken more generally in the sense of "departure": "Some say the lark makes sweet *division*/This doth not so, for she divideth us"'.[10] But if there is a precedent for music in *Romeo and Juliet*, then what of dance? Conrad reminds us that at the ball, Romeo is reluctant to dance, as if he were 'refus(ing) in anticipation (of) be(ing) cast in the ballets Prokofiev and Leonard Bernstein eventually composed for him'.[11] Indeed, Romeo laments to his fellow-revelers: 'You have dancing-shoes/With nimble soles; I have a soul of lead/So stakes me to the ground I cannot stir' (1.4.12–14). But Romeo will soon make an exception for Juliet, depending on how their meeting is depicted on stage or screen. What is critical about Romeo's somber confession for our reading of *West Side Story* is precisely the tension between body and soul of which he speaks. As we shall see, all of the dancers in *West Side Story* have 'nimble soles' and 'souls of lead', as the defeat of their youthful exuberance is daily recorded in their taut, anxious bodies – bodies that carry the legendary tragedy with them everywhere they go. Similarly, despite the inspired choreography of Jerome Robbins, the dance numbers in this musical film are characterised by a constant tension between leaping, which signifies escapism, and landing, which reflects the gravitational pull of reality – indeed, the legendary – as the characters inevitably sink back down into a life of poverty, racism, familial neglect, and urban decline.

---

[10] Rothwell, "Zeffirelli's *Romeo and Juliet*", p. 326
[11] Conrad, p. 57.

In establishing *West Side Story* as a legitimate adaptation of *Romeo and Juliet*, it is imperative to explore the ways in which the force of the legend – its predetermination of events and outcomes that the protagonists presume are theirs to create – impacts this musical film. If, as I have suggested, Shakespeare's Romeo and Juliet are plagued by the sense that they have arrived – as Benvolio fears – 'too late' (1.4.103) at the scene of their own lives, then *West Side Story* extends this experience of fatalistic predetermination to the *entire social structure* of Manhattan's West Side, as the characters' failure to elude tragedy is reinterpreted, in the words of the film, as 'a social disease'. In so doing, *West Side Story* radicalises Shakespeare's play for the purpose of social commentary, anticipating what Michael Hardt and Antonio Negri define as the central problem of late capitalism: namely, a world in which 'war is becoming a permanent social relation . . . War, that is to say, is becoming the primary organising principle of society'.[12] Peter Conrad observes that

> *West Side Story* scarily internationalizes the conflict. Even Bellini could only extend the feud through the Italian peninsula; but the squabbles in New York, engaging another undercurrent of paranoia in the American 1950s, are a preparation in miniature for a world wide combat. The film opens with an ominously silent overture, during which the camera aerially tracks its way up Manhattan from South Ferry to the slums above Columbus Circle. On the way it makes an abrupt detour to the East Side, so that the United Nations headquarters can be included in the

---

[12] Michael Hardt and Antonio Negri, *Multitude: War and Democracy in the Age of Empire* (New York: Penguin, 2004), p. 12.

survey. Manhattan is a global island, and the gangs inevitably deploy the language of the Cold War.[13]

On an obvious level, *West Side Story* features a 'war' – a word that is referenced constantly in the film – between first-generation, impoverished, white juvenile delinquents (the Jets) and the newly-arrived Puerto Ricans (the Sharks), who fight each other for territory, indeed, a place to call their own. The stakes of this war are very real for both parties, since the Jets, who hail from dysfunctional homes, have no place to return to at night, and the Sharks have left their homeland behind, only to find that America's arms aren't open to 'their kind'. But more importantly, as Conrad suggests, this is the beginning of a forever-war in microcosm; Anita, for instance, describes the climactic rumble as 'an excuse to start World War III', and her words are prophetic, as the Cold War, in all its incarnations, has served the US as a distraction from its own factious identity – a land, in the second half of the twentieth century, defined more as the 'home of the brave' rather than the 'free' – for who is free when home is a place constituted by real and social violence against a presumed 'other'? Although Tony and Maria try to break this brutal cycle of bigotry by converting relentless warfare into reciprocal welfare, their musical numbers serve as a constant reminder that the same 'crossed stars' that shined on Romeo and Juliet preside over them as well.

Before delving into an analysis of the ways in which *West Side Story* translates the tragic inevitability of Shakespeare's language into music and dance routines, it is useful to establish the plot parallels between the play and film. Similar to the beginning of Shakespeare's play in which the Capulets and the Montagues

[13] Conrad, p. 98.

goad each other into an all-out brawl, *West Side Story* opens with the Jets and the Sharks mutually antagonising each other, until at last the Prince Escalus character, Officer Krupke, arrives to break up what has escalated into an unplanned rumble (typically, the gangs hold 'war councils' before official rumbles). The players on both sides are all 'Mercutios' and 'Tybalts' in their own way, all hotheads who are literally dying to fight, as their lives are otherwise meaningless without the hatred that defines them. Importantly, parental figures are conspicuously absent from the entire film, which explains why the Jets and the Sharks are willing to sacrifice anything to maintain their 'turf' as the only place they can truly call home. In this respect, the teen angst that superficially plagues Romeo in the form of unrequited love (from Rosaline) becomes, in *West Side Story*, a very real social pathology that has spread to every 'juvie' on the mean streets of 'Hell's Kitchen', an area of Manhattan which, in the fifties and sixties, earned its name as a bastion of poverty and gang warfare. (Ironically, due to its proximity to Broadway, it has since become a more upscale actors' 'ghetto'.) Although Maria's father repeatedly calls her inside during the balcony scene (reminiscent of the Nurse's promptings in Shakespeare's play), not a single parental figure is ever shown on screen, which is no subtle indication that these 'children' are raising themselves. The implications of this change of focus are considerable, for whereas Shakespeare's Romeo and Juliet fall victim to their parents' 'ancient grudge', *West Side Story*'s Tony and Maria are up against the whole of society – a society divided by ethnic tensions, Cold War xenophobia and paranoia, the broken promises of US capitalism, and the extreme poverty that perpetuates all of the above.

As in *Romeo and Juliet*, Tony's best friend, Riff (a combination of both Mercutio and Benvolio), talks him into going to a dance where, Riff claims, Tony might find what he's been looking for. (Tony, we learn, has been having auspicious dreams about something – or someone – who is 'right outside the door . . . just around the corner', as he enthusiastically informs the bewildered Riff, whose only concern is getting Tony to rejoin the Jets.) And yet, just like Romeo, who fears that some 'consequence yet hanging in the stars/Shall bitterly begin its fearful date with this night's revels' (1.4.105–107), Tony, too, adds something of a premonition to the rhyme that he and Riff have bonded over since they were little kids:

RIFF: Womb ta tomb!
TONY: Birth ta earth! *An' I'll live to regret this!*[14]

A break in the primitive (and foreboding) rhyme that Riff and Tony share, Tony's devil-may-care attitude toward his destiny nevertheless betrays the force of the legendary, which is placed here – as Romeo's premonition is – mere moments before Tony will meet his Juliet. Expectedly, at the dance in the local gym (a far cry from the sumptuous Capulet Ball), Tony and Maria's eyes meet, followed by their hands, and lips, after which, nothing – not even Maria's dis-approving big brother, Bernardo – can sunder them. As in future treatments of this pivotal moment, brilliant cinematography – a partial dissolve that effectively erases everyone else around the two characters – creates the illusion that Tony and Maria are alone in the room, utterly lost in each other. Zeffirelli will employ a similar tactic, locating the lovers on the periphery of the older generation's circular dances in order to set them apart from the cyclical force of the legend that defines the historic antagonisms between the Montagues and the Capulets. But it is not long before the ill-fated nature of Tony and Maria's meeting is acknowledged, or, rather,

---

[14] Emphasis mine.

announced in the film. The revelation that Maria is the little sister of Bernardo, the leader of the Sharks, and that Tony is, in Nardo's words, 'one of them (whites)', is revealed with the same intensity as when Romeo cries, 'Is she a Capulet?/O dear account! My life is my foe's debt' (1.4.230–31) and, shortly thereafter, when Juliet exclaims: 'My only love sprung from my only hate/Too early seen unknown and known too late. Prodigious birth of love it is to me/That I must love a loathéd enemy' (251–54). Romeo and Juliet's lapse into the formality of rhymed couplets, arguably the most constraining of poetic forms, points to the imposition of the 'Social', that is, the intrusion of the prevailing ideology that urges Verona's factions into a state of (upper) class warfare which, ultimately, defeats the lovers' attempts to improvise their destiny. Similarly, in *West Side Story*, such prohibitive and irreconcilable social antagonisms emerge at the dance:

BERNARDO:	Get your hands off, *American*!
TONY:	Take it easy, Bernardo.
BERNARDO:	Stay away from my sister!
TONY:	Sister?
BERNARDO:	Couldn't you see he's one of them?
MARIA:	I saw only him.

As Maria is rushed out of the dance by her escort Chino (the Paris figure), Tony is being urged by Riff to head over to Doc's Candy Store for the pending 'war council'. But Tony is 'still lost in a dream',[15] according to the stage directions, as the scene shifts imperceptibly to the night streets that Tony wanders, lost in his rhapsody for 'Maria'. Naturally, the ensuing scene should be the balcony scene, but director Robert Wise and screenwriter Ernest Lehman begin to

[15] Lehman, p. 33.

insinuate the rise of the legendary in the choral numbers that bracket Tony and Maria's duets. Indeed, from this point forward, we see Romeo and Juliet's battle against the Chorus's tragic prediction transposed into a battle between a literal Chorus – specifically, ensemble numbers that reinforce the *impossibility* of averting tragedy – and Maria and Tony's 'impromptu' duets, which strive to create an alternative world, one that will be realised only in death.

Hence, the classic song 'I like to be in America' intercedes between Tony and Maria's balcony meeting, giving the audience a sense of the forces that the two are up against.

GIRLS: (chorus) I like to be in America,
Okay by me in America,
Everything free in America.

BERNARDO: *For a small fee in America.*

ANITA: Buying on credit is so nice.

BERNARDO: *One look at us and they charge twice.*

CONSUELO: I'll have my own washing machine.

CHINO: *What will you have, though, to keep clean?*

ANITA : Skyscrapers bloom in America.

ANOTHER GIRL: Cadillacs zoom in America.

ANOTHER GIRL: Industry boom in America.

BOYS: (chorus) *Twelve in a room in America.*

ANITA : Lots of new housing with more space.

BERNARDO: *Lots of doors slamming in our face.*

ANITA : I'll get a terrace apart<u>ment</u>.

BERNARDO : (with exaggerated Mexican accent)[16]
Better get rid of your ac<u>cent</u>.

ANITA AND THREE GIRLS: Life can be bright in America.

---

[16] This is a telling stage direction from Lehman's *Screenplay*, suggesting the filmmakers' conflation of Puerto Ricans with all Latinos. pp. 41–42.

BERNARDO:	*If you can fight in America.*
ALL GIRLS:	Life is all right in America.
ALL BOYS:	*If you're all white in America.*

Stunningly subversive lyrics even for a relatively contemporary musical, Bernardo's rejoinders, along with the boys' chorus, repeatedly underscore their fatalistic certainty that things will *never change*, even as the girls cast their naïve eyes unblinkingly towards a brighter future – one that includes, significantly, an homage to fifties' 'time-saving appliances' – the social accoutrements of the perfect female domestic (servant). Indeed, this song has been the subject of outrage on the part of Latino and Latina audiences alike. Characterising what has become the standard response to this Rita Moreno-led number, which evolves as a variation on the Shakespearean theme of sticomythia, Blanca Vasquez asks the rhetorical question: 'And what did the "real" Puerto Rican, Anita, do, in the film? She not only was another Latina "spitfire", she also sang a song denigrating Puerto Rico and by implication, being Puerto Rican . . . I remember seeing it and being ashamed'.[17] Alberto Sandoval recalls with total aversion 'those who upon my arrival (in the US) would start tapping flamenco steps and squealing: "I like to be in America?"'[18] In addition to serving as an homage to commodity culture as well as a critique of the selectivity of the American Dream, this number has helped to solidify an already existing stereotype of Latinos 'as inherently musical and performative subjects, ready to wear their sexualised identity at the

[17] Blanca Vázquez, 'Puerto Ricans and the Media: A Personal Statement', *Centro* (Winter 1990–91), p. 5.
[18] Alberto Sandoval, quoted in Frances Negrón-Muntaner, 'Feeling Pretty: *West Side Story* and Puerto Rican Identity Discourses', *Social Text* 63, 18.2 (Summer 2000), p. 84.

drop of a hat'.[19] Moreover, Frances Negrón-Muntaner adds that, in this particular routine, which coincided with 'significant racial and social unrest', Latinos 'are doing exactly what they are expected to do . . . singing and dancing the night away'.[20]

Like the starry-eyed Juliet who struggles against her father's insistence that she marry against her will to shore up a socio-political alliance, the girls' chorus – and Anita in particular – clearly have no real say in matters of national security, as they are being constantly overruled by the cynical bravado of their male counterparts. In fact, the Sharks' gang leader, Bernardo (a cross between Tybalt and Old Capulet) will play this same paternalistic, blocking-figure role with his sister Maria, absolutely forbidding her to contest the racial barriers that lend meaning to the boys' lives as gang members, who are sworn to protect their 'turf' which, in *West Side Story*, is not just geo-spatial territory but also gendered territory that extends to the bodies of women. Yet, as Negrón-Muntaner observes, even in spite of the film's stereotyping of the girls as naïve advocates for assimilation and the boys as nationalistic 'criminals', Puerto Ricans suddenly 'acquired several previously denied possibilities, including social and visible representability' in *West Side Story*.[21] Indeed, '*West Side Story* represented Puerto Ricans as part of a community and allowed them to be central in the narrative, although depending on the community of spectators, the Sharks are seen as antagonists, victims, or even heroes'.[22] And unquestionably, it is the 'America' number in particular that opens up the exploration of intra-ethnic tensions between assimilation

[19] Negrón-Muntaner, p. 85.
[20] Ibid.
[21] Ibid., p. 86.
[22] Ibid.

and nationalism. 'If anything', notes Negrón-Muntaner, '"America" portrays an ambivalent picture of life in the United States, with all its oppression and promise. The level of irony, social critique, and protagonism of the women contrasts with most of *West Side Story* in its subtlety and insight'.[23] Importantly, this number – updated by Sondheim from the stage version to include more scathing lyrics and converted from an all-girls number to a co-ed, chorus-style number – not only explores conflicting intra-racial attitudes toward life in 'America' but also suggests how such competing perspectives can arise from relative gender entitlement. In fact, even though 'it is the leading "authentic" Puerto Rican actress who is singing the praises to America, and the "brownface" Bernardo who critiques the United States'.[24] Rita Moreno's Anita convincingly demonstrates what Puerto Rican women have to gain in American society, which, while patriarchal, is not nearly as protectionist as Latino culture. There is no better statement of the extent to which attitudes toward 'America' are gender specific in this film than in the following exchange in which Anita defends Maria's desire to remain at the dance:

ANITA: Girls here are free to have fun,
She (Maria) is in America now.

BERNARDO: Puerto Rico is in America now!

End of story.

Well, not exactly, for *West Side Story* proceeds with its tragic momentum headlong into a recapitulation of the balcony scene – only this time, a fire escape serves the same purpose. Just as Juliet warns Romeo of the danger he faces in courting her on Capulet grounds, Maria begs Tony to leave:

MARIA: It is dangerous. If Bernardo knew –

TONY: We'll *let* him know. I am not 'one of them', Maria.

MARIA :   But you are not one of *us*, and I am not one of you.

Despite Maria's concerns, it is clear from this scene, in which they sing the famous love song 'Tonight', that they are destined to be together – a point that the camera's special effects makes plain. Indeed, while they sing, the sky, the buildings, and the night itself 'see(m) to take on a magical quality'.[25] However, lest we get lost in the moment, Steven Sondheim's lyrics remind us – ever so subtly – of the Shakespearean source that has predetermined the lethal outcome of this romance, when the two sing: 'For here you are/ And what was just a world is a star/Tonight!' It is no coincidence that, at the very mention of the word 'star', the scene 'fades back to reality', accompanied by the sobering off-screen voice of Maria's father calling her inside.[26] Still, as in *Romeo and Juliet*, Maria will call Tony back several times, till they have exchanged vows of love, and have arranged to meet the next day – of all places – at the bridal shop where Maria works.

One can hardly begin to discuss the doomed relationship between Tony and Maria without raising the thorny issue of casting, which was far from colourblind in the transition from stage to screen. As Negrón-Muntaner notes: 'Although Jerome Robbins had requested Rita Moreno to audition for the Maria character for the Broadway show, once the play was transformed into a Hollywood production, the likelihood that a Puerto Rican or Latina actress

[25] Lehman, p. 47.

[26] Ibid.

would be granted the lead role considerably diminished'.[27] Had Robbins gone on to cast Moreno in the lead role,

> the union of Tony and Maria could have created anxiety in 1961 . . . as any sexual contact between them could have resulted in interracial love and offspring. One way to alleviate this anxiety and allow white audiences to enjoy the interracial seduction without its consequences was to cast an actress whom everyone knew to be white.[28]

Natalie Wood was eventually cast as Maria, and made to speak her lines with an exaggerated accent; similarly, George Chakiris, who played Riff (the leader of the Jets) in the London theatrical run, was evidently not-quite-white *enough* to play the part for Hollywood; instead, he became Bernardo, the cruel leader of the Sharks. This character change is particularly interesting, for Chakiris, the son of Greek immigrants, is naturally darker than the actor who plays Tony in the film. Yet, Jerome Robbins and Robert Wise made the controversial decision to have him wear 'brownface', for the role, unnaturally darkening Chakiris's skin with heavy make-up, while casting 'unnaturally blonde' boys to play the Jets.[29] Ironically, thereafter, Chakiris was often typecast as the quintessential 'Latin lover'. All this begs the question as to why – with two excellent singers and dancers eligible for the role of Maria and Tony (Rita Moreno, a 'real' Puerto Rican, and George Chakiris, respectively) – would the filmmakers choose Natalie Wood and the singularly bland Robert Beymour? In one respect, the casting decisions for *West Side Story* tell us much about the cultural pressure that the

[27] Negrón-Muntaner, p. 91.

[28] Ibid., pp. 91–92.

[29] Ibid., p. 91.

filmmakers were up against when they converted their Broadway play into a blockbuster Hollywood film; in a less flattering sense, however, their willingness to compromise the authenticity of the production – both in terms of casting and singing – to appease the anxieties of audiences who were violently opposed to even the illusion of miscegenation, provides us with a measure as to just how far the filmmakers would go to convert a controversial play into a popular movie. Significantly, unlike Wood and Beymour, both Moreno and Chakiris achieved a kind of revenge against the bigotry that haunts even the film's paratext, as both were the only two actors to win Oscars for their performances.

What is particularly interesting about *West Side Story*'s treatment of the Romeo and Juliet legend is the way in which its tragic implications infect *everyone*, for all the young men (and the women who fall for them) are digging their way to an early grave. Indeed, Riff proclaims: 'Them cops believe what they read in the papers about us cruddy j.d.'s, so that's what we give 'em – somethin' to believe in!'. Similar to the ways in which the compulsion to act out premonitions ultimately (and unconsciously) compels Romeo and Juliet to assume their tragic destinies, so, too, in *West Side Story*, a 'legend' of sorts – the boys' bad reputations – determines the behaviour of the gang members, who are hell-bent on living *down* to others' low expectations. Importantly, however, these kids are not remorseless sociopaths; quite the contrary, as Anita observes to Maria: 'You saw how they dance: like they have to get rid of something, quick. That's how they fight'. One interpretation of what the boys carry in their ever-tensed bodies – as Romeo and Juliet do in their names – is the legend of their juvenile delinquent status, a phenomenon that they believe they can't beat, so they join, making Krupke's point that they will never amount to anything a self-fulfilling prophecy. Although the boys make fun of their status as they prepare for the 'PRs' (Puerto Ricans) to arrive at Doc's Candy Shop, their sung tribute to Officer Krupke (whom they impersonate) has chilling implications. In one exchange, Riff, playing himself, explains to A-Rab (who impersonates a psychiatrist) that

> My Daddy beats my Mommy,
> My Mommy clobbers me,
> My Grandpa is a Commie,
> My Grandma pushes tea.
> My sister wears a mustache,
> My brother wears a dress.
> Goodness Gracious, that's why I'm a mess!

To which A-Rab, still playing the shrink in a German accent, replies:

> Yes!
> Officer Krupke, you shouldn't be here.
> This boy don't need a couch, he needs
> a useful career.
> Society's played him a terrible trick,
> And sociologically he's sick.

As the chorus chimes in 'We are sick, we are sick, we are sick, sick, sick' we can't help but see that the cards dealt to them are not much different from those handed to Tony and Maria, it's just that the boys don't fight against their predetermined lives whereas Tony and Maria do. Shortly after this revealing number, when Doc gets ready to reprimand Action for his manners, beginning with the sage saying, 'Why, when I was your age –' Action explodes: 'When you wuz my age? When my old man wuz my age? When my brudder wuz my age! *You wuz never my age, none a ya!* Da sooner you creeps get hip ta dat, da sooner ya'll dig us!' Doc replies: 'I'll dig your early graves, that's what I'll dig'. In this painful exchange, we can read between the lines to see that, like A-Rab, these boys were, in effect, 'born dead', without the options that constitute what it means to live – indeed, to be – which explains the carelessness with which they treat their own bodies, as if they were already ghosts. And who can blame them, when they have nothing to lose? Indeed, what is particularly important about the use of Doc's Candy Shop as a meeting ground – along with the other primary sets like the playground and the park – is the fact that all three raise the spectre of stolen childhood, reminding us that underneath their world weary skins, all the players are really just a bunch of scared kids.

Tony and Maria try to intervene in this vicious cycle when Maria begs Tony to call off the rumble, which he temporarily succeeds in doing by challenging the Jets and the Sharks to engage in a 'fair fight' – two men, no weapons, just skin-to-skin. Bernardo agrees to the conditions because he believes that he gets to fight Tony, but the Jets appoint 'Ice' as their man, and Bernardo must begrudgingly comply with the rules. Before they can negotiate any further, the dense Lieutenant Schrank shows up to make some racist comments and throw the PRs out, who exit Doc's Candy Shop whistling 'My Country 'Tis of Thee'; the audience is left to fill in the second line, 'Sweet land of liberty', and the irony of this quintessentially American anthem is lost on no one. As in *Romeo and Juliet*, however, before the fateful fight goes awry, Tony and Maria 'marry' one another – in the bridal shop – where they prop up dress dummies to play their parents, the best man, and maid of honour. But Maria has a condition: Tony must stop the fight *altogether*, fair or unfair; and, of course, she knows not what she does, for Tony, who will attempt to make peace with Bernardo just as Romeo does with Tybalt, will eventually come between Bernardo and Riff, and Riff will be killed, leading to the cycle of retribution that will ultimately claim Tony's life. But in the meantime, Maria and Tony believe that they can change their fates just as enthusiastically as Romeo and Juliet do.

TONY: We're untouchable, Maria! We have magic!

MARIA: Listen and *hear* me. You must go and stop it.

TONY: It means that much?

MARIA: Yes.

TONY: All right, I will, then.

MARIA: Can you?

TONY: You don't want even a fist fight? There won't be *any* fight. There.

MARIA: I believe you! You *do* have magic!

But not even magic is enough to temper the potent force of the imminent tragedy, for during the faux wedding ceremony, screen-writer Ernest Lehman inserts distinctly foreboding language. When Tony grabs a male dummy for 'Riff', he utters their old friendship pledge, exclaiming: 'Here we go, Riff! Womb to tomb!' – an image that Baz Luhrmann will literalise in his use of the Capulet swimming pool as a place of birth and death – as well as an equation drawn by Friar Laurence in Shakespeare's play, who employs the same couplet: 'The earth that's nature's mother is her tomb;/What is her burying grave, that is her womb' (2.2.9–10). As if this line testifying to their interwoven fates wasn't disturbing enough (Riff's death will lead to Tony's murder of Bernardo and, finally, to Chino's murder of Tony), when Tony looks at the dress dummy playing his mother, he says to Maria: 'Look, Mom's crying already', as if even this inanimate soul knows what's to come. Almost immediately thereafter, Tony offers a reprise of 'Tonight', which, this time, includes the lines:

Tonight, tonight
Won't be just any night
Tonight there will be no morning
Star.
Tonight, tonight,
I'll see my love tonight.
And for us, stars will stop
where they are.

But the stars won't stop; rather, they will cross and double-cross the best laid plans of these young lovers – and there 'will be no morning star' for Tony, who will die before dawn. This is precisely the kind of escalating sense of tragic inevitability that makes *West Side Story* a legitimate adaptation of *Romeo and Juliet*, despite the decision to retain not a single word of Shakespeare's play.

Immediately following and eventually interspersed with this number, the Jets and the Sharks perform their own unique versions of 'Tonight' in ensembles which, as several critics have remarked, off-set the heterosexual trajectory of Tony and Maria's love with homoerotic dance routines – though such scenes are often coded as homophobic. For example, from the film's earliest moments, images of one group stalking the other from behind – in close proximity – suggests a predatory sexuality. In the fight scenes in particular, the erotic dimension of the gangs' movements become self-evident, as they roll around on top of each other, some straddling their victims close to the face, with the antagonists' crotches at point blank range. Provocatively, in a scene that Zeffirelli virtually copies to introduce the Capulets, the Sharks enter the picture with the camera focused on their groin region, where their fingers 'click' to the beat of the music. Even *within* each gang there is an unmistakably 'queer' air about the dance numbers, which are choreographed with pirouettes and other distinctly balletic moves, rather than drawing on more masculine, 'contemporary' dance genres. Moreover, whether the men are performing for each other or against the rival gang, there is no getting around the fact that in such routines, they are transformed into an all-male 'chorus line' – a homosocial activity that is coded homoerotically – based not only on the reality that the boys' admiring, emulating gazes are fixed on one another, but also because the choreography itself, which frequently demands leg-lifts and, even, splits by the ensemble, creates the constant effect of 'crotch-shots'. And, as in so many fifties films starring the likes of Rock Hudson (among others), the lyrics in *West Side Story* provide several opportunities for double entendres. Particularly after the theatrical version's run in London, where the word 'bugger' can mean 'sodomise', lyrics such as 'Here come the Jets,/Yeah! And we're gonna beat/Every last buggin' gang/On the whole buggin' street!' give us pause. Similarly, in the 'Tonight' number mentioned above, it is the Sharks who are given the homoerotic or, properly understood, homophobic language, with their allusion to their backsides, or 'rumps', in the couplet formed by 'rumpus' and 'jump us':

We said 'okay, no rumpus,
No tricks' –
But just in case they jump us,
We're ready to mix
Tonight!

Recalling that all the filmmakers – Sondheim, Wise, Robbins, and Lehman – were themselves gay, as well as the fact that the musical is a genre overwhelmingly patronised by gay audiences, it is hard not to chuckle with recognition at embedded lines like 'The Jets are comin' out . . . Tonight'. More importantly, though, as we shall see in Zeffirelli's adaptation, a queer perspective opens up the film to a variety of thought-provoking readings, with 'queerness' defined as 'a simultaneous attraction to a person and a resistance to a normalising personhood' – a point to which I will return.[30]

Mirroring the structure of the play, the film quickly reinstates (hetero) 'normalcy' by including a version of Juliet's 'Come night, come Romeo, come thou day in night' speech (3.2.17), as Maria anxiously awaits the consummation of her 'marriage' to Tony. She sings:

Today
The minutes seem like hours,
The hours go so slowly,
And still the sky is light...
Oh, moon, grow bright,
And make this endless day endless night!

Here again, Maria knows not what she says, since Tony will all too soon experience the endless night of death. While Maria is singing her song of anticipation, Tony, similar to the dynamic between Mercutio, Tybalt, and Romeo, will show up at the appointed place to stop the fight, bearing all kinds of physical and verbal insults from Bernardo until at last Riff is shamed into taking on Bernardo himself. Tony tries to break up the fight, grabbing Riff's shoulder and delaying him just long enough to make him vulnerable to Bernardo's killing blade. When Tony retaliates by killing Bernardo, he sinks to his knees

---

[30] Stacy Wolf, '"We'll Always Be Bosom Buddies": Female Duets and the Queering of Broadway Musical Theater', *GLQ: A Journal of Lesbian and Gay Studies* 12.3 (2006), p. 357.

and, rather than crying 'O, I am fortune's fool!' (3.1.136), as Romeo does, he simply shouts, agonisingly, 'Maria!' Maria's reaction to the news of Bernardo's death shocks Chino, the messenger, who can't believe that Maria keeps asking about Tony rather than her own brother; when the truth dawns on her, she falls to her prayers before a small shrine to the Virgin Mary – an image that both Zeffirelli and Luhrmann employ in their distinctly 'Catholic' adaptations. More brutal than the death of Tybalt, who is Juliet's cousin, the death of Maria's only brother stuns her into praying that her life be exchanged for his; but as she utters this wish, Tony appears at her window. Like Juliet's initial response to the news of Romeo's murder of Tybalt, Maria screams and hits Tony, crying 'killer killer killer killer killer –' but she quickly relents and collapses into his arms. When he offers to turn himself in to the police, she refuses to allow it and, together, they come up with a plan to meet at Doc's and escape to 'Somewhere'. The music for this most famous of love ballads begins, as Tony and Maria frantically try to reassure each other:

TONY: We'll be all right. I know it.
We're really together now.

MARIA: But it's not us! It's everything around us!

TONY: Then I'll take you away, where
nothing can get to us, not anyone
or anything . . .

Tony proceeds into the line we've all been waiting for: 'There's a place for us', but not even this transcendent musical number can alter the trajectory of their fate. As if testifying to the force of the legend, Maria's above reminder to Tony that 'it's not us – it's every-thing around us' is all too true; indeed, their love, like Romeo and Juliet's, is thwarted by a 'social disease'. Whereas Romeo and Juliet are up against deeply entrenched feudal codes of conduct, Tony and Maria face the bigotry of those who, like Anita, insist that Maria 'stick to (he)r own kind'. Hence, it is Anita who seals their fate when, in a variation on the role of Friar John, she refuses to convey a message to Tony that Maria has been delayed – a decision she makes only after enduring a near gang-rape by the Jets (who don't trust her as a messenger). Instead of conveying Maria's message, Anita tells them spitefully that Chino has killed Maria. Doc (a cross between Friar Laurence and Balthazar), overhears and tells Tony, who, like Romeo, responds by seeking out his own suicide – in this case, by running out into the streets and begging Chino to 'get me too'.

The scene at Doc's is disturbing on many levels; whereas the near-rape and certain humiliation of Anita is the subject of most critical commentary, Anita's betrayal of Maria is also a threshold moment, following hard upon what Stacy Wolf refers to as their 'queer pedagogical duet' in the preceding scene. 'The female duet', Wolf explains, 'occupies a space in between the norm and the deviation; it is more intimate and direct than the all-women's chorus number and more active and transformative than the male-female love song'.[31] As an example, Wolf analyses the song 'A Boy Like That'/'I Have a Love', which Anita and Maria perform immediately before the fateful trip to Doc's. During 'A Boy Like That' Anita angrily attempts to persuade Maria to dump Tony for '(o)ne of (he)r own kind'; but Maria passionately insists that what is 'true for you, (is) not for me'. Here, as Wolf contends, the tension between alliance and opposition is extremely challenging to navigate; however, both women 'express their commitment in the same musical vocabulary'.[32] As each tries to persuade the other of the

[31] Ibid., p. 359.
[32] Ibid., p. 368.

veracity of her feelings, Anita and Maria learn lessons from each other; and, gradually, '(t)heir intimate conversation locates them as a musical couple, each striving to be understood by the other'.[33] This burgeoning sense of understanding leads to the exquisite duet 'I Have a Love', which 'develops and deepens the pedagogy of emotion set out in the first section'.[33] Moreover, the way in which this song is performed by Maria and Anita – in Maria's bedroom, directed not at an audience, but towards one another – emphasises the fact that 'this song makes sense only as one that creates a relationship, a mode of communication'; in fact, 'by the end, they are likely sitting or standing, facing each other, looking longingly into each other's eyes, holding hands, and singing the same note'.[34] Wolf identifies this extraordinary song as a 'queer pedagogical duet' because as 'one woman teaches the other a lesson, the latter's character shifts. By the end, they sing together' (rather than contrapuntally as in the first half of the duet), which insures that 'they agree, the lesson has been learned, the couple has been solidly formed'.[35] That this song is the last one in the film invests it with further significance, and, interpreted 'queerly', it makes the scene at Doc's all the more tragic; for not only does Anita's 'message' lead directly to Tony's death and, therefore, the destruction of the film's most compelling heterosexual relationship, but, also, it forces the homosocial bond between Anita and Maria to dissolve. In effect, all forms of desire – heterosexual, homosexual, queer – are negated at the end of *West Side Story*.

Thus, in a variation on Luigi Da Porto's ending, where Romeo sees that Juliet is alive just before he dies from the poison, Tony, still

[33] Ibid.
[34] Ibid.
[35] Ibid., p. 369.
[36] Ibid., p. 370.

calling out wildly for Chino to kill him, glimpses Maria running across the playground toward him. Just as the two crash into each other's arms, Chino fires a gun at Tony's back, and he collapses instantly. Yet even to the very end, Tony is convinced that he can change a fate that is indelibly inscribed in the stars that hover over him, as he gasps, blaming himself: 'I didn't believe hard enough.' 'Loving is enough', replies Maria. 'Not here', Tony whispers: 'They won't let us be'. Appropriately, the lovers' final exchange leads into a brief, faint reprise of 'Somewhere':

MARIA:		Then we'll get away.
TONY:		Yes, we can. We will.
MARIA:	(sings)	Hold my hand and we're halfway there.
		Hold my hand and I'll take you there,
		Someday,
		Somehow . . .

Tony tries to sing the second line with Maria, but dies before he can complete it. Subsequently, Maria like Juliet before her, threatens to join her lover in death when she takes Chino's gun and cries: 'How many bullets are left, Chino?' But suddenly, in a complete rage, she points the gun at all of them and assumes the role of the Prince in Shakespeare's play, delivering the film's 'moral':

YOU ALL KILLED HIM!
And my brother and Riff! Not with
bullets and knives! WITH HATE!
WELL I CAN KILL TOO! BECAUSE NOW
I HAVE HATE![37]

[37] Ibid., p. 125.

She continues, still sounding very much like Juliet: 'How many can
I kill, Chino? How many – and still have one bullet left for me?' But
when Officer Shrank shows up to collect the body, Maria relents
and runs to protect Tony. She gestures to two Jets and Chino to
come forward and bear the body off the playground; when Tony's
leg falls, Pepe, another Shark, steps in to become the fourth pall
bearer. '*Te adoro*, Anton', Maria whispers, and, unlike the ending of
Shakespeare's play, the reconciliation of the feuding factions is
quite uncertain, as the final stage directions attest:

> At last, she (Maria) gets up and, despite the tears on her face,
> lifts her head proudly, and triumphantly turns to follow Tony's
> body, being borne off by Jets and Sharks who appear, for the
> moment to have found an understanding, in tragedy. The adults
> – Doc, Schrank, Krupke – stand watching, bowed, alone, useless.
> And nearby, looking across at each other uneasily, and then
> moving off in opposite directions, are the few Jets and Sharks
> who have not joined the procession, who are not yet ready,
> perhaps never will be ready, to give up war as a way of life.[38]

Commenting on earlier, operatic treatments of the legend, Peter
Conrad asks what, if any, wars 'can be resolved by music?' After
further reflection, he replies: 'Song prolongs life and sweetens death
in Bellini, and Gounod's Roméo dies with a reminiscence of the
nightingale and lark which accompanied his night with Juliet. These
are small but valuable victories for the morale of the characters';
but how, he concludes, 'will music ever persuade WASPs and
Latinos to love or at least live with each other, let alone prevent

[38] Ibid., p. 125.

Americans and Russians from blowing up the world?'.[39] Conrad admits to being 'baffled' by the conclusion of *West Side Story*.[40] In a behind-the-scenes retrospective, Ernest Lehman explains that, originally, 'Maria was to have an aria with a gun. And I wrote a dummy lyric. And Lenny could never set it to music . . . He said "I can't find the music." And that dummy lyric is the speech they give till this day.'[41] Bernstein did indeed struggle with Maria's final 'song' many times over: 'I tried once to make it cynical and swift. Another time like a recitative. Another time like a Puccini aria. In every case, after five or six bars, I gave up. It was phony'.[42] It may have been phony, but it was honest; Bernstein didn't – perhaps couldn't – give Maria music because, in the Romantic tradition, music is transcendent, capable of conveying the ineffable, of 'describ(ing) a mystery that is beyond the reach of words'.[43] Yet, as the first decade of twenty-first century suggests, war will always be 'a way of life' for some, indeed, for too many, and words – unlike weapons – remain beyond the reach of those who need them most. 'But words', Conrad concludes, 'are all that Bernstein has to give Maria at the end of *West Side Story*, and they challenge us with social and political realities which are unmoved by the lullabies of music'.[44] Ultimately, then, the silence at the end of *West Side Story* might be read as an act of conscientious objection, indeed, a refusal to allow music to pacify us in the face of tragedy. For we,

[39] Conrad, p. 93.

[40] Ibid., p. 92.

[41] Quoted in the 'Behind-the-Scenes' retrospective, titled West Side Memories, which is bundled with the DVD celebrating the 40th Anniversary of the original release of West Side Story.

[42] Quoted in Conrad, p. 93.

[43] Ibid.

[44] Ibid.

too, remain 'baffled' by the reality that *West Side Story* is a show that plays not in a distant 'somewhere', but, rather, *everywhere*, all the time, around the world – and we have yet to figure out a way to avert the tragic ending.

Shakespeare with a view: Zeffirelli's *Romeo and Juliet*

Although Zeffirelli recalls meeting 'Lenny' Bernstein while enjoying New York's social scene during the late 1950s, he acknowledges no debt to *West Side Story* in his 1968 *Romeo and Juliet* – the first traditional, 'doublet-and-hose'-style Shakespeare film ever to cross-over into youth culture. Based on his acclaimed 1960 theatrical production at the Old Vic, Zeffirelli's 1968 film adaptation proved to be an international success, as the young, paradoxically angst-ridden, peace-loving, 'flower-child' generation came out to the cinemas in force. Perfectly attuned to the impact of popular music on this group of rebels with a cause, the film made its way into audiences' hearts through its musical score in particular, composed by the legendary Nino Rota. One of the numbers performed at the Capulet Ball, for example, features a male troubadour singing 'What is a Youth?', a haunting ode to the transience of time that inspired the producers of the long-running US soap opera, *The Young and the Restless*, to commission from Rota a markedly similar instrumental for the show's theme song. The lyrics of the former piece are as follows:

What is a youth?
Impetuous fire.
What is a maid?
Ice and desire.

The world wags on
A rose will bloom,
it then will fade.
So does a youth,
so does the fairest maid.

Comes a time when one sweet smile
Has its season for a while
Then Love's in love with me.
Some may think only to marry.
Others will tease and tarry.
Mine is the very best parry,
Cupid he rules us all.

Caper the caper; sing me the song,
death will come soon to hush us along.
Sweeter than honey and bitter as gall,
love is the past-time that never will pall.
Sweeter than honey and bitter as gall,
Cupid he rules us all.

A rose will bloom,
it then will fade.
So does a youth.
So does the fairest maid.

Appropriately, Nino Rota's famous lyrics harken back to similarly morbid Renaissance poems such as Robert Herrick's 17th-century exhortation 'To the Virgins, to Make Much of Time':

Gather ye rosebuds while ye may,
Old Time is still a-flying:
And this same flower that smiles to-day
To-morrow will be dying.
The glorious lamp of heaven, the sun,
The higher he's a-getting,
The sooner will his race be run,
And nearer he's to setting.
That age is best which is the first,
When youth and blood are warmer;
But being spent, the worse, and worst
Times still succeed the former.
Then be not coy, but use your time,
And while ye may, go marry:
For having lost but once your prime,
You may for ever tarry.[1]

Both songs could be said to thematise Zeffirelli's adaptation, which has nothing if not a 'carpe diem' mood. And it is little wonder, for 1968 was a miraculously impetuous year, marked not only by the infamous May riots in France, which included massive worker strikes and bloody student protests as well as the shocking assassination of presidential-hopeful Bobby Kennedy, the rising tide of anti-Vietnam War sentiment, deteriorating relations between the Soviets and the West, and Mao's Cultural Revolution in China. A ripple effect in the world of film ensued, as *Cahiers du Cinema* contributors Jean-Luc Comolli and Jean Narboni published their manifesto 'Cinema/

---

[1] Robert Herrick, 'To the Virgins, to Make Much of Time', in *The Norton Anthology of English Literature*, 8th edition, Vol. 1 (2 Vols.), edited by Stephen Greenblatt (New York and London: W.W. Norton, 2006), pp. 1659–60.

Ideology/Criticism', calling for an end to the 'closed-circuit' whereby '"what the public wants"' means "'what the dominant ideology wants"'[2]. Jean-Luc Godard, for example, rose to the challenge by pushing the boundaries of the already avant-garde *Nouvelle Vague* (New Wave) with *La Chinoise* (1967), which took abstraction and hand-held camerawork to an unparalleled extreme – to the chagrin of some and the applause of others. Released in Britain in March and the US in September, Zeffirelli's 1968 adaptation of *Romeo and Juliet* was far from insulated from these turbulent times. Significantly, the film was to begin with a kind of primitive graffiti – the carving of the title in Verona's ancient walls – an image that alludes to the 'inspirational' phrases of the Sixties. For example, among the more memorable acts of graffiti inscribed during the May riots, two sentiments in particular capture the opposing forces of 1968. One, teeming with idealism, reads: 'Be realistic, demand the impossible'; another, consumed with outrage, says, simply, 'Be cruel', while another expounds upon this theme: 'A single nonrevolutionary weekend is infinitely more bloody than a month of total revolution'. The world of music was permanently affected by this crisis of idealism versus aggression. The Pretenders' song 'When Will I See You' cites the 'demand the impossible' slogan quoted above and refers to those people who, like Romeo and Juliet, 'fill streets at night' and count themselves among the 'starry eyed', whereas the other end of the spectrum is epitomised by groups like The Rolling Stones, who responded to the political climate with the insurrectionist number 'Street Fighting Man'.

---

[2] Jean-Luc Comolli and Jean Narboni, 'Cinema/Ideology/Criticism' (1969) in *Film Theory and Criticism*, edited by Gerald Mast, Marshall Cohen, and Leo Braudy, 4th edition (New York and Oxford: Oxford University Press, 1992), p. 685.

This same internal conflict between dreaming and fighting, optimism and nihilism, defines Zeffirelli's 1968 adaptation, in which the lovers' naïve romanticism exists in constant tension with the cultural violence all around them. As Peter S. Donaldson astutely remarks: 'the film participates in the general loosening of restrictions on the representation of sexuality on film of the period, and it seemed to endorse of number of the values of the international youth movement: pacifism, distrust of elders, and sexual liberation'.[3] Rounding out this portrait of the disaffected teen-lovers, Russell Jackson observes that '(w)hat is "contemporary" in Zeffirelli's version resides in the couple's frank expression of sexual desire and in their (long) haircuts, and in a fundamental ordinariness'.[4] Jackson goes one step further, noting the film's ongoing relevance, for although the 'director had announced his project as "a cinéma-verité documentary . . . on Renaissance Verona"', in 'social behavior, festivity, fighting and religious observance, Zeffirelli's Renaissance Italy seems closer . . . to the experience of the audience. This version of Verona is somewhere we might live – or at least visit – with just a few adjustments of costume'.[5]

Romeo and Juliet opens with a God's eye view of a hazy Verona, with Laurence Olivier performing the Prologue's bleak monologue in voiceover. Remarkably, Zeffirelli recalls fondly that Olivier, his boyhood idol, just so happened to be in the area filming *The Shoes of the Fisherman* and, when he learned of the neighbouring production, '(n)aturally he felt an almost proprietary

[3] Peter S. Donaldson, *Shakespearean Films/Shakespearean Directors* (Boston: Unwin Hyman, 1990), p. 145.

[4] Russell Jackson, *Shakespeare Films in the Making: Vision, Production and Reception* (Cambridge and New York: Cambridge University Press, 2007), p. 208.

[5] Ibid., p. 197.

interest in any film of a Shakespeare play'.[6] When Zeffirelli offered him the role of the Prologue, Olivier, a bit crest-fallen, replied: 'Of course . . . But isn't there anything else?' 'I think he would have played Romeo if he'd thought there was half a chance', Zeffirelli recalls with a laugh, but,

> (i)n the end I got him to dub Lord Montague, who'd been played by an Italian with a thick accent. By now unstoppable, Larry insisted on dubbing all sorts of small parts and crowd noises in a hilarious variety of assumed voices. The audience never knew just how much of Laurence Olivier they were getting on the soundtrack of that film.[7]

For Zeffirelli – not an unsuperstitious man – this was an auspicious beginning for his underfunded production, about which backers remained highly skeptical. In fact, he notes that even '(b)efore we started shooting, there was a particularly good omen: Christine Edzard . . . and Richard Goodwin, the associate producer of British Home Entertainment, . . met for the first time during our "commune", fell in love and later married. It seemed the perfect start to *Romeo and Juliet*'.[8] The couple went on to create Shakespeare films of their own.

Indeed, long before Kenneth Branagh would insist on creating a 'family' feeling among the castmembers of his Shakespeare films, Zeffirelli rented a series of country homes on a small estate not far from Rome, and brought his own family, along with the major

[6] Franco Zeffirelli, *Zeffirelli: An Autobiography* (New York: Weidenfeld and Nicolson, 1986), p. 229.

[7] Ibid.

[8] Ibid., p. 227.

actors, together for the entire summer. It is little wonder, then, that, at this time that Zeffirelli told *Vogue* magazine his *Romeo and Juliet* 'will really be a documentary for the period as well . . . . I know my Romeo and Juliet, but, oh, how I also know my Italy'.[9] Indeed, as Ace Pilkington observes, '(f)or Zeffirelli, the Italian towns which became his Verona . . . are part of the plot, an "additional character" indeed, with the beauty of Renaissance Italy but also with a sinister energy which drives the tragedy inexorably on'.[10] But it is easy to lose the 'sinister' aspects of the mise-en-scene in Zeffirelli's magical shooting locations in Tuscania, Pienza, and Gubbio – let alone the mini-estate where he and the others resided. 'There we all were', he remembers, 'living as if in a cheerful, busy commune; Olivia and Leonard rehearsing on the lawn; Nino Rota writing the music in the salon; Robert Stephens and Natasha Parry learning their lines or swimming in the pool – it was a dream world'.[11]

But Zeffirelli's dream world was haunted, just as Romeo and Juliet are, by the fear that 'Destiny' would keep his story from going forward, due not only to the film's incredibly low budget – $800,000 – but also to events in Zeffirelli's own life. Significantly, just before scouting exterior locations in an around the Rome-based studio Cinecittá, the director was attempting to put on a production of *Aida* in – of all places – Egypt. Despite enjoying himself, the many attractions, and the Egyptian people immensely, Zeffirelli recalls having 'the most terrible premonition', and, subsequently, he and the entire cast of *Aida* 'caught the first – and the last – plane back

[9] Quoted in Ace Pilkington, 'Zeffirelli's Shakespeare', in *Shakespeare and the Moving Image: the plays on film and television*, edited by Anthony Davies and Stanley Wells (Cambridge: Cambridge University Press, 1994), p. 165.

[10] Ace Pilkington, p. 172.

[11] Zeffirelli, *An Autobiography* p. 227.

to Italy. The day after we returned . . . the Six Day War began . . .'[12] Not surprisingly, then, the forces of idealism and aggression that characterised the climate in which Zeffirelli found himself trying to film a love story took on an almost allegorical quality: it would be the dreamers versus destiny, and who would prevail, no one really knew. And how could the young stars of the film, Leonard Whiting and Olivia Hussey – then the youngest pair ever assembled to play *Romeo and Juliet* on screen – *not* defy their star-crossed fate in the summer of 1968, a time when *anything* seemed possible?[13]

As early as the opening credits, however, foreshadowing of the bloody business to come is evident. As Olivier concludes the Prologue, the camera zooms in on the sun, at which point the screen reads, 'William Shakespeare's', as if to imply that the Bard is the light of the world or, alternatively, *Italy*'s native 'son'; but all too quickly, the scene and credits change when a cut to battlements – a structure that can barely contain its implicit violence – announces '*Romeo and Juliet*'. In keeping with his superstitious nature, Zeffirelli explains that in his adaptation '(t)he central idea is that of a puppeteer, Destiny, who handles all the characters. They are all puppets on a stage and no one is fully responsible. The whole tragedy is permeated with the idea of fate. There is nothing to do. Juliet is the only valuable opposition to it'.[14] What, then, is the source of this tragic predetermination in the film? As we shall see, Zeffirelli boldly suggests – through his selective use of a large, gold crucifix

---

[12] Ibid., p. 226.

[13] Actually the first known attempt to cast actors close in age to Shakespeare's Romeo and Juliet was undertaken by William Poel in his 1905 stage production, which featured a fourteen year-old Juliet (Dorothy Minto) and a seventeen year-old Romeo (Esme Percy).

[14] This excerpt from Zeffirelli's interview with *The Guardian* (5 March 1968) is cited in Jackson p. 195–96.

– that God himself has preordained Romeo and Juliet's death. But before we can begin to see this case unfold, we must return to the beginning of the film, where Zeffirelli, professing to use a cinéma verité style, employs an impressive range of hand-held camerawork to capture the frenetic, hyper-violent qualities of the opening fray between the Montagues and the Capulets.

Indeed, more so than any other adaptation before it, the opening brawl looks more like the battle scenes from Kenneth Branagh's *Henry V*, as characters are not merely beaten but murdered: run-through, decapitated, or violently disfigured (one combatant gets a sword in his right eye). Not even the women and children are spared as they attempt to flee from the melee. Then, suddenly, the camera whirls 360 degrees and tilts up to authorise the Prince as the figure who, based on the literally heightened value ascribed to him by the camera angle, declares death henceforth for anyone who creates mutiny among his subjects. Mirroring the camerawork that has preceded his entry, the Prince – poised aristocratically astride his white horse – turns round and round in an effort to address the crowd that encircles him. Yet throughout this scene, it is Michael York's swashbuckling Tybalt who most captures our attention; not only does he cut a fine figure in his doublet and hose, but also, Zeffirelli has given him a cap which, with its brim folded up, makes him appear as though he has devil horns (Luhrmann will extend this suggestive sartorial flourish by having Tybalt wear a devil's costume at the Capulet Ball). Zeffirelli recalls York's disappointment when he informed him of the role he would play: ''"Not Romeo . . . Mercutio?" asked York, despondent. "No, Tybalt". Zeffirelli replied firmly, but reassuringly added, "(e)ven with only twenty-four lines, it will be a major role when you see what we will do"'.[15] Moreover, as Zeffirelli

[15] Zeffirelli, *An Autobiography*, pp. 215–16.

notes, another auspicious event occurred when he noticed that 'Michael (York) was having a good time. A photographer called from *The Sunday Telegraph* to do a story on us and – another good omen for *Romeo and Juliet* – the two of them were soon inseparable. They eventually married and have always made a wonderful couple . . .'[16]

Michael York's twenty-four lines turn out to be a lot in this production, in which Zeffirelli cuts more than half of the play. As we have come to expect from directors who adapt Shakespeare, visual language becomes as important – If not more so – than the text. Hence, in his first scene, Romeo carries a flower, which tells us all we need to know; denied all of his bad Petrarchan poetry, Romeo, upon seeing the wounded, cries only: 'What fray was here?/Yet tell me not, for I have heard it all:/Here's much to do with hate, but more with love'. Disgusted, the peacenik dashes the flower to the ground and walks away from the confused Benvolio. As in earlier versions, the scene proceeds to Paris's attempt to woo Juliet through Old Capulet, as the aristocratic Count stakes his claim to her: 'Younger than she are happy mothers made', to which Capulet replies, eyeing his disenchanted wife across the way, 'And too soon marred are those so early made'. Lady Capulet adds an exclamation point to this statement by slamming a window shut, preventing both her husband and Paris from catching any glimpse of Juliet. In various other examples of 'stage business' such as this, Zeffirelli makes it plain that the marriage between Juliet's parents is a bad match, to say the least. Significantly, one such match – known for its turbulence – played an unexpected role in Zeffirelli's ability to move forward with a film that no one (except the cast) seemed to believe in: the then-notoriously

[16] Ibid., p. 228.

fiery couple who had starred in Zeffirelli's 1966 *Taming of the Shrew*, Richard Burton and Elizabeth Taylor, to whom the director showed early footage of his *Romeo and Juliet*. Though both were enamored with what they saw, what they heard was another matter, as Burton pointed to a problem with the verse. Perhaps it was this remark that prompted one of the more amusing outbursts in the early stages of shooting, when Zeffirelli allegedly told the classically-trained Romeo, played by Leonard Whiting, to 'stop thinking about your Granddaddy Shakespeare and speak the lines naturally!' Privy to Whiting's personal copy of the script, Russell Jackson observes that '(a) version of this advice is probably reflected in a note Whiting jotted down on the back of his script: "Don't quiver voice sounds phony"'.[17]

Playing opposite Whiting, Olivia Hussey's Juliet is first introduced to us wearing a sumptuous red dress that barely contains her bosom. Guilding her pale skin is a large golden cross, an ornament that first becomes a focal point in *West Side Story*. In his rich psychoanalytic reading of Zeffirelli's film, Peter S. Donaldson notes that from the very beginning, Juliet is positioned in the middle of a series of disturbing triangulating relationships. As noted above, we are first introduced to her as an object of barter between Paris and her father, and, shortly thereafter, Juliet becomes the subject of the Nurse's bawdy banter when Lady Capulet awkwardly attempts to broach the subject of marriage with her daughter. Yet, upon our first sight of Juliet, her independent spirit is showcased by dint of the fact that, as Donaldson observes, she is 'seen apart from her father's gaze' and, consequently, 'comes to life' on her own.[18] Indeed, Zeffirelli's

[17] Zeffirelli, 'Filming Shakespeare', in *Staging Shakespeare: Seminars on Production Problems*, edited by Glenn Looney (London and New York: Garland, 1990), pp. 239–71, p. 249.

[18] Donaldon, p. 162.

hope-against-hope that Juliet will somehow remain 'the only valuable opposition (to Destiny)' informs his tendency to underscore her aggressive optimism and open sexuality, as her 'there's a place for us' moments temporarily prevail over fate and force of circumstance alike. Indeed, Donaldson affirms this perspective when he asserts that although Juliet is 'enmeshed in the triangular structures of (the) feud and the generational displacements of patriarchal marriage brokerage, she seems to have the possibility of her own life, her own space'.[19]

Despite being two hours and twenty minutes in length, the pacing of Zeffirelli's adaptation is swift, for the scene proceeds immediately to a vision of Mercutio and his band of merry men carrying torches in the piazza. The combination of Zeffirelli's direction and John McEnery's deeply-nuanced portrayal of Mercutio – the mercurial foil to Michael York's fiery Tybalt – has forever changed the way that this role is interpreted. Indeed, McEnery's 'Queen Mab' speech smacks of a barely-contained lunacy that no film actors have been able to master since. More importantly, this scene has become the basis of subsequent renderings that suggest Mercutio's homoerotic attachment to Romeo, as Zeffirelli presents Mercutio as a man 'desperate . . . to retain Romeo's (attention) by keeping him loyal to the values of the male pack'; in fact, Donaldson claims that '*Romeo and Juliet* was also, for its time, perhaps the most daring of all Shakespeare adaptations in its bringing to the surface homoerotic aspects of Shakespeare's art'.[20] This, as he contends, is the likely source of Mercutio's often violent misogynistic speeches and gestures, which reach a breaking point when his Queen Mab speech is derailed by the subject of the heterosexual imperative:

[19] Ibid.
[20] Ibid., p. 145, p. 158.

This is the hag, when maids lie on their backs,
That presses them and learns them first to bear,
Making them women of good carriage.
This is she – This is she – This is she . . .

Donaldson argues that Mercutio's 'final, sad "*this* is she" suggests a partial awareness that his inventiveness and improvisation mask an identification with the (devalued) women his discourse and antics invoke. He himself is Queen Mab: she arises from his own pain and confusion'.[21]

Whether or not Romeo recognises Mercutio's repressed identification with Mab, it is clear that he acknowledges his friend's 'pain and confusion'. Upon seeing that Mercutio is raving and desperately alone at the end of his famous speech – which echoes hauntingly throughout the empty courtyard into which Mercutio has fled – Romeo clasps Mercutio's face to his in an effort to console him. Filmed in a tight profile, this two-shot shows Romeo and Mercutio's foreheads resting softly against one another. Staring eye-to-eye with their lips parted, their impassioned and deeply private exchange is as romantic – in its own, subtle way – as the scenes between Romeo and Juliet themselves. 'Peace, peace, Mercutio, peace/Thou talk'st of nothing', whispers Romeo; measuredly, Mercutio replies, swallowing his incipient tears:

> True, I talk of dreams
> Which are the children of an idle brain,
> Begot of nothing but vain fantasy,
> Which is as thin of substance as the air,
> And more inconstant than the wind who woos
> Even now the frozen busom of the north . . . .

[21] Ibid, p. 158.

In Zeffirelli's production, these words resonate with a heightened intimacy; one even wonders if Mercutio is encoding his unrequited love for Romeo in his talk of 'fantasy' and 'inconstancy', as he tries to break through the 'frozen bosom' of his best friend. Indeed, as Mercutio is reluctantly coaxed away by the 'pack' of lusty young men, a long take of him walking backwards – his angst-ridden gaze fixed on Romeo – resembles that of a jilted lover.

Significantly, the movement in this scene thus leaves Romeo alone in the empty courtyard, at which point he utters his fear that he will arrive 'too early' at the Ball, concerned that

> Some consequence yet hanging in the stars
> Shall bitterly begin his fearful date
> With this night's revels, and expire the term
> Of a despisèd life closed in my breast
> By some vile forfeit of untimely death.

Based on the unconventional blocking of this scene, Romeo's musings draw heightened attention to the overwhelming force of 'Destiny' in the film, as the gang literally – albeit unwittingly – abandons him to his Fate. That Mercutio has instilled this morbid mood in Romeo, and the fact that their destinies are inextricably intertwined, is also suggested by the foreboding death mask that Mercutio wears throughout the scene. But, at least at this juncture, Romeo is able to master his fear with a gaze up at the heavens, as he concludes, clearly referring to God: 'But (H)e that hath the steerage of my course/Direct my suit'.

As we shall see in the following chapter, though Zeffirelli does not go to the lengths that Luhrmann does to escape the very 'Destiny' that he so forthrightly acknowledges, Zeffirelli nevertheless eliminates *all* of the remaining speeches that allude to the 'tragic inevitability' embedded in Shakespeare's play. It is almost as if the director believes that by simply cutting Shakespeare's foreboding language, his film will find 'a place' for the lovers beyond the grasp of the legend. For example, in the play, Juliet – after meeting Romeo but yet unaware of his identity – exclaims: 'If he be married,/My grave is like to be my wedding bed' (1.2.247–48). Zeffirelli removes this line, as well as Juliet's many violent visions of Romeo; during the balcony scene, Juliet responds to Romeo's wish, 'I would I were thy bird', rather ominously: 'Sweet, so would I,/Yet I should kill thee with much cherishing' (2.1.229–28). There is no such mention of Juliet's peculiar reply in Zeffirelli's adaptation; moreover, he deprives Juliet of her famous 'Gallop apace, you fiery-footed steeds' (3.2.1) speech and, in so doing, forgoes Juliet's half-erotic, half-morbid speculation 'Give me my Romeo; and when he shall die,/Take him and cut him out in little stars,/And he will make the face of heaven so fine,/That all the world will be in love with night . . .' (3.2.21–24).[22] So, too, following Romeo's slaying of Tybalt, there is no mention of Juliet persuading her mother that 'Indeed, I never shall be satisfied/With Romeo till I behold him – dead – ' (3.5.93–94), a vision that all too soon proves true. The continuation of these lines (also eliminated from the film) is more disturbing still, for Juliet inadvertently predicts the means by which Romeo will die: 'Madam, if you could find out but a man/To bear a poison, I would temper it,/That Romeo should, upon receipt thereof,/Soon sleep in quiet' (3.5.96–99).

Yet another inauspicious omen, which likewise plays right into the hands of the tragic itinerary of the legend, occurs when we learn of Juliet's equally disturbing written words about Romeo. This peculiar scene, which likewise does not appear in the film, occurs when the Nurse asks Romeo:

[22] As indicated earlier, Juliet's musings about night produce a provocative textual crux; while Levenson chooses the reading "when *I* shall die," the line can also read "when *he* shall die."

'Doth not Romeo and rosemary begin
 Both with a letter?'
'Ay, Nurse, what of that? Both with an "R"'.
'Ah, mocker, that's the dog's name. "R" is for the – no, I know it begins with some other letter; and she hath the prettiest sententious of it, of you and rosemary, that it would do you good to hear it'. (2.3.195–201)

In writing such 'sententious' phrases – also known as *auctoritas* – In her commonplace book Juliet knows not what she does, for rosemary, as Renaissance audiences were well aware, was typically sprinkled on the bodies of the *dead*. But the most conspicuous deletion from Zeffirelli's film Is the premonition that Juliet has – a vision that runs structurally parallel to Romeo's ominous musings just prior to entering the Capulet Ball – when she exclaims as Romeo leaves for Mantua: 'O God, I have an ill-diving soul!/Methinks I see thee now, thou art so low,/As one dead in the bottom of a tomb' (3.5.54–56). Despite Zeffirelli's efforts to derail this implacable process of literary accretion through conspicuous omissions, no degree of altering or excising the text will produce the sought-after 'happy ending'. Rather, both Romeo and Juliet are, in Mercutio's words, 'already dead' (2.3.12), victims of a tragic trajectory whose arc cannot be altered.

Whereas Baz Lurhmann invests in imagery through which he attempts to stave off the momentum of the legend, Zeffirelli, more in the tradition of *West Side Story*, employs music to this end, as Nino Rota's unforgettable love theme functions both as a source of imagined transcendence and tragic imminence, at once stalling and, at other times, hastening the lovers' fate. Appropriately, we first hear this haunting melody at the Capulet Ball, a scene that receives more than fifteen minutes of screen time, much of which is devoted to the 'Morisca' dance as well as vocal and instrumental versions of the famous ballad 'What is a Youth?' On the one hand, the lyrics are inescapably morbid, for as the song that will play whenever Romeo and Juliet are together, it is hard not to interpret phrases such as 'death will come soon to hush us along' as premonitory. On the other hand, these lyrics are voiced only once in the film, whereas the many instrumental versions, with their rising, transcendent crescendos, seem to work against the lyrics – that is, by carving out 'a place for' Romeo and Juliet where they are insulated from their inevitable fate. The meeting of Romeo and Juliet during an instrumental variation on Rota's theme is particularly poignant in this regard. Extending his arm from behind a pillar, Romeo reaches for Juliet's hand; a tight shot of Juliet's face reveals her closing her eyes in what appears to be an expression of ecstasy and, undoubtedly, erotic anticipation. When Juliet whirls around to see the beautiful face of the stranger who has quietly stalked her in his cat mask, she is as enamoured with what she sees as Romeo is. Accordingly, what starts with chastely clasped hands during the iteration of their famous sonnet, quickly leads to passionate kisses between Romeo and Juliet, as Rota's song swells in the background, literally underscoring the magnitude of their love. However, the love theme crescendos again when the pair recognise that they hail from rival households, this time suggesting the intrusion of 'Destiny' into their lives. At this delicate moment, a slight change to the play adds to this sense of drama when Juliet sends her nurse to *Tybalt* to find out who her lady's mysterious love-interest is; hence, when Tybalt, who has already been shunned for his attempt to throw Romeo out of the party, utters the word 'Romeo', it is with a sinister quality that further whets his revenge, while simultaneously reminding us that, along with Mercutio, Tybalt and Romeo's fates will triangulate and culminate in death.

Given Zeffirelli's apparent resistance to retaining Shakespeare's heavy-handed moments of foreshadowing, it is particularly odd that he chooses to transition into the balcony scene with a line that is rarely cited in stage or screen productions. While Benvolio and Mercutio call aloud for Romeo, who is busy making his way through the impressive natural barriers of the Capulet orchard, Mercutio, heard only in voiceover as the camera lights on Romeo, complains disheartedly: 'The ape is dead'. Romeo's curt 'answer', which we are far more accustomed to hearing on stage and screen, implies that Mercutio has never been in love: 'He jests at scars that never felt a wound'. This peculiar juxtaposition of lines serves Zeffirelli quite efficiently, for the 'exchange' emphasises the fact that Mercutio is a stranger to heterosexual love while also functioning on a literal and metaphorical level to disclose a significant development in Romeo's character. Metaphorically speaking, up until this point Romeo has been 'aping' or merely mimicking the stereotypical behavior, postures, and language of a lover; now, however, he has crossed the threshold to experiencing love as a life-altering, distinctly humanising phenomenon and, hence, his tendency to 'ape' the part of a lover is dead indeed. By the same token, in more literal terms, Romeo does, in fact, resemble an ape as he cavorts, jumps, and swings through the dense vines of the Capulet orchard, a scene that evokes Tarzan comparisons to this day.

The twisted vines of the Capulet grounds also provide the perfect backdrop to the lovers' constantly entwined bodies throughout the balcony scene, wherein the two youths kiss and engage in 'heavy petting' as Nino Rota's theme song waxes romantic yet again. As many scholars have remarked, this scene is noteworthy for its unadulterated passion, as Romeo and Juliet utter lines only when they come up for air from each other's mouths – a tableau perfectly fitting for an audience poised on the brink of the 'free love' era of the Seventies. Crucially, however, Zeffirelli does not simply represent Juliet as the object of our desiring gaze. Rather, as Donaldson asserts, 'Zeffirelli moves away from the conventions of mainstream cinema and toward a more reciprocal and unpredictable treatment of sexuality'.[23] By the same token, however, less sophisticated audiences are more likely to focus on Elizabeth Hussey's bust, which, on certain occasions, partially reveals her nipples beneath her corseted underdress – particularly when she leans over the balcony, breathing heavily from her rapture. Indeed, at this juncture is it worth noting Zeffirelli's first impressions of Olivia Hussey: 'She had some talent, but she was unfortunately overweight, clumsy looking and bit her nails constantly – hardly the delicate Juliet I dreamt of'. On a pure whim, however, Zeffirelli later called back several of the actresses whom he had rejected earlier, and it was then that he

> stumbled upon the amazing transformation of Olivia Hussey. She was a new woman: she had lost weight dramatically. Her magnificent bone structure was becoming apparent, with those wide expressive eyes and her whole angular self. She was now the real Juliet, a gawky colt of a girl waiting for life to begin.[24]

Hussey certainly had transformed, though how much weight she lost is impossible to discern through the enormous gowns that Zeffirelli outfits her in; especially when she appears next to Leonard Whiting's lean, tights-wearing Romeo, Hussey seems somewhat strangely matched with him. But if, as Donaldson notes, Zeffirelli 'translate(s) Juliet's self-assertion into physical activity' not only 'by emphasising *her* desiring look' but, also, by asserting 'her energetic physical

[23] Donaldson, p. 167.
[24] Zeffirelli, *An Autobiography*, pp. 225–26.

command of herself *and* of the scenes in which she appears', then a more robust Juliet makes perfect sense, particularly if Zeffirelli is, in fact, attempting to approximate – visually – 'parity between genders . . . .'[25] In more general terms, however, as many critics have speculated, the scarcity of women – compared with the sheer number of young attractive men in form-fitting clothing that populate Zeffirelli's Verona – may have more to do with the director's (at the time) closeted homosexuality than with any deliberate aesthetic decision. Indeed, Zeffirelli's first impression of Whiting is revealing: 'his looks were perfect for the role; he was the most exquisitely beautiful male adolescent I've ever met'.[26] The first shot of Romeo suggests the extent to which the camera is enamoured with him, as he emerges in soft focus, flower in hand. Indeed, Ace Pilkington asserts that '(o)f all Zeffirelli's films, Romeo and Juliet comes closest to the essence of the Shakespeare play on which it is based, perhaps in part because the beauty of Zeffirelli's actors and camerawork echoes (even as it replaces) the formal ornamentation of Shakespeare's verse'.[27]

On the glorious Tuscan morning that follows the balcony scene the audience is treated to a view of the countryside, as Friar Laurence goes about picking herbs and flowers. The Friar is looking among the wildflowers for one in particular, which he finds and holds up for the audience to glimpse – its unique periwinkle tint is unmistakably reminiscent of the flower that Romeo holds at the very beginning of the film.[28] Given the repeated use of a lone flower at

[25] Donaldson, p. 167.

[26] Zeffirelli, *An Autobiography*, p. 228.

[27] Pilkington, p. 173.

[28] In *Shakespearean Films/Shakespearean Directors* Peter S. Donaldson identifies the flower that Romeo holds as a mint flower; though he doesn't mention the color, it is clearly the mint varietal characterised by purple 'spikes', known as *Agastache rugosa*.

threshold moments in the film, we might conclude that in place of the foreboding speeches that Zeffirelli cuts from the screenplay, he inserts visual cues which, consciously or unconsciously, intimate the increasing force of the legend. Though somewhat different from the purple flower that Romeo holds at the beginning of the film, a single purple flower will be shown twice more, unmistakably yoking Romeo and Juliet's destinies to the intervention of the Friar. Both here – in the middle of the film – and nearing the end, the Friar will emerge holding the varietal that is the source of the sleeping potion – the floral device that will ultimately have a fatal effect on both lovers. This imagery is very subtly employed, providing the audience with a glimpse of the flowers just long enough to connect them through their common color scheme.

Far less subtle, however, is the cross imagery that begins to appear, appropriately, with the introduction of Friar Laurence. In addition to the cross that Juliet wears about her neck, an enormous golden crucifix adorns the cathedral in which Friar Laurence's cell is located. When Romeo arrives there, ecstatic from the preceding night's revels, the Friar proceeds to chide Romeo at length for his quickly-abandoned love for 'Rosaline'; this scene, however, makes little sense to the audience, since there is no mention of her name prior to this moment – although Russell Jackson points out that in the shooting script, Rosaline is identified as an elegant lady-in-blue at the Capulet Ball.[29] Not coincidentally, when the Friar ceases lecturing Romeo, he seeks inspiration by turning his gaze to the image of the crucifix; through shot-reverse-shot camera work, Zeffirelli makes it clear that the Friar's decision to marry the lovers has come from God himself. Of course, the most obvious reason for this decision is the fact that Friar Laurence desperately wants to

[29] Jackson, p. 202.

preempt Romeo and Juliet from engaging in the sin of premarital sex, for even within the hallowed interior of the cathedral, the two can barely keep their hands and lips off each other, and the Friar must labour constantly to part them. Zeffirelli's ensuing use of the cross, however, is far more brazen. Adding some stage business to the arrangements that the Nurse and Romeo are making for the secret ceremony, the camera focuses on the crucifix once again as Romeo attempts to pay the Nurse for her service. When she repeatedly refuses to accept the offering, Romeo goes to put the coin in the indulgence box, but the Nurse prevents him, and keeps it for herself. Thus, one can't help but wonder if, had Romeo proleptically purchased an indulgence, the story might be entirely different. Quickly, though, the ominous nature of the 'greater power' that will, ultimately, thwart their intents, is implied when Romeo, virtually lost in rapture, stares at the crucifix with wonder, blowing two kisses to it before dashing out of the cathedral. Subsequently, in a scene borrowed from Renato Castellani's adaptation, Juliet is shown doing needlework as she anxiously awaits the Nurse's news, and, after cajoling the nurse into telling her that Romeo awaits his bride-to-be, Juliet flies to Friar Laurence's cell to be married. As the liturgical music, sung acapella by women, rises and falls, Romeo takes one last confident look at the crucifix, before kneeling alongside Juliet only seconds before their fate is sealed.[30] The film proceeds to an 'INTERMISSION'.

[30] Supporting this claim, Patricia Tatspaugh observes that 'only Zeffirelli capitalises on the church which forms one side of the square. He associates the church, with its Romanesque arches, fading frescoes and mosaic pavement, exclusively with Romeo and Juliet', p. 142. See *The Cambridge Companion to Shakespeare on Film*, First Edition, edited by Russell Jackson (Cambridge: Cambridge University Press, 2000), p. 142.

In theatrical performances of the play, the intermission typically occurs following the death of Mercutio – when Romeo cries 'O, I am fortune's fool!' (3.1.136). Interestingly, mere moments before the fight, Zeffirelli plays up Mercutio's effeminacy. For example, before jesting obscenely with the Nurse, Mercutio is shown diligently pretending to sew his handkerchief; subsequently, before Tybalt can goad Mercutio into a fight, Mercutio decides to cool off in the drinking fountain, where he starts wringing out his laundry. Hence, when he begs Tybalt to couple his insulting 'word(s)' with 'a blow' (3.1.39), the homoerotic insinuation further inflames Tybalt, who splashes Mercutio indignantly and turns his attention to Romeo. What follows is an excruciating scene in which Mercutio, standing up for what he perceives to be an unpardonable affront to Romeo's character, playfully engages Tybalt in an epic swordfight – one that is filled with laughter, jests, and even a handshake between the opponents. Of course, Romeo is destined to come between them, exposing Mercutio's wiry, almost fragile frame, to Tybalt's unintended fatal blow. Indeed, Zeffirelli makes it clear that when the fun and games turn deadly, Michael York's Tybalt is utterly horrified at the sight of Mercutio's blood on his sword. What is so painful about Mercutio's final appearance on screen is the way in which John McEnery – in front of his crowd of adoring fans, plays the scene – for everyone, including Romeo, believes that Mercutio's groaning and stumbling is an elaborate joke, an impression that is heightened by Zeffirelli's tendency to shoot Mercutio's scenes with a hand-held camera, investing him with an energy that is his alone. Hence, in a tight, reverse two-shot of their earlier clench, Mercutio takes Romeo's head in his hands and whispers, plaintively, 'Why the devil came you between us?/I was hurt under your arm'. Once again, their heads tilt forward, one supporting the other, and Romeo begins to understand the gravity of the situation. When Mercutio at last gives up the ghost, still dogged by the laughter of his raucous friends, Romeo reaches for Mercutio's handkerchief and reveals the gaping wound that has claimed his life. The (albeit bloody) token is something that a woman would typically give a man as a sign of her favour towards him, and Romeo takes it up with a zeal that we have not seen even in his romantic interactions with Juliet. Clearly, from Zeffirelli's perspective, Romeo must prove his manhood – his dexterity with his sword – *before* he is permitted to consummate his relationship with Juliet.

In fact, the actual fight between Romeo and Tybalt is distinctly homoerotic, as the men eventually strip down to their billowing shirts and reveal increasingly more fit male flesh. At one point, without swords, the men roll around in the dust together, alternately assuming the 'power position'. And, when Tybalt dies, he collapses on top of Romeo, whose awkward arms await him. Four times Romeo repeats 'I am Fortune's fool!' as he runs from the scene. After the Prince metes out his surprising sentence of Romeo's banishment, the camera's gaze – perhaps in one last effort to bring Mercutio's ambivalent sexuality back to life – takes a definitive turn towards the homoerotic in the ensuing scenes. For example, the film immediately cuts to Romeo lying prone on the cold stone floor of Friar Laurence's cell; weeping hysterically, his sinewy body and backside 'faces' the camera, much as it will in the *aubade* scene. With Mercutio dead, it is now the unlikely suspects – the Nurse and the Friar – who must importune Romeo to regain his masculinity. Provocatively, the lines that Zeffirelli retains throughout this scene anxiously convey the fear that Romeo will be incapable of consummating his marriage to Juliet. Playing on the Renaissance meaning of 'stand' as slang for maintaining an erection, the Nurse commands Romeo: 'Stand up, stand up, stand an you be a man;/For Juliet's sake, for her sake, rise and stand' (3.3.88–89).

Similarly, Friar Laurence asks Romeo: 'Art thou a man? . . . Thy tears are womanish . . . Unseemly woman in a seeming man . . .' (3.3.108–109, 111). What we see here, Donaldson observes, is Renaissance patriarchy at its finest, 'an ideology requiring young men to assert their masculinity by violence, devalue(ing) women, and distance(ing) themselves' from the opposite sex at at all costs.[31] Hence, after much proverbial ringing of hands and further chastisement from both the Friar and the Nurse, Romeo is at last ready, both literally and figuratively, to 'rise and stand'; determined to regain his slighted sense of masculinity, Romeo steals away to his new wife's bedchamber. However, there is no lovemaking scene – a chaste cut to the two lovers lounging in bed the morning after.

Here we see an erotic shot of Romeo which parallels his position in the previous scene, as he lies on his stomach with his now-naked bottom tilted toward the camera. By contrast, Juliet remains modestly covered by the bed sheet. If this shot, as Russell Jackson points out, startled some critics at the time, who 'have not failed to point out the homosexual gaze represented by the camera's having dwelt on Romeo's neat backside',[32] then the subsequent shot of Romeo standing naked before the window, bathed in the light of dawn, is even more provocative, for he moves like an Adam in Paradise, unselfconsciously stretching in his beautiful skin. Referring to the camera's lingering views of Romeo, Jackson asserts that critics have oversimplified this scene by viewing the camerawork as an extension of the director's gaze. Rather, he continues, 'to accept the queer dimension of the film is to recognise a valuable asset'.[33] Jackson's perspective is informed by

---

[31] Donaldson, p. 153.
[32] Jackson, p. 209.
[33] Ibid.

Donaldson's intriguing contention that Zeffirelli capitalises on 'heterosexual film conventions governing the deployment of the male gaze, as well as on his own contrary or complementary presentation of *men* as objects of an admiring gaze', to create 'a spectatorial position neither simply male nor female nor simply identificatory or detached'. Instead, the camera produces distinctly 'bisexual identifications' and, even, 'a sense of loss in the presentation of heterosexual intimacy'.[34] The fact that Luhrmann will duplicate this gaze in his version of the *aubade* scene testifies to this more aesthetically and ideologically informed perspective, as well as the historical reality that compulsory heterosexuality often demands the curtailment of same-sex bonds – a point which, for Donaldson, Zeffirelli's production takes for theme. Indeed, in Romeo's case, we recognise this moment of rupture in Mercutio's death, which marks the official demise of the 'pack' of young men with whom Romeo has long haunted Verona's streets, whereas with Juliet, this sense of loss is anticipatory, as she will shortly be disowned by her parents and betrayed by her nurse.

In addition to loss, however, this scene is equally inflected with the spirit of transcendence, marking the director's final attempt to forestall the inevitable tragedy that otherwise occurs so precipitously in this play. When Romeo attempts to get dressed, offering yet another glimpse of his prone body, Juliet gazes dreamily at him – cueing the spectator to share her perspective – as she persuades him that it is the nightingale and not the lark that sings so beautifully 'on yon pom'granate tree'. Ecstatic, Romeo alights back onto the bed, exclaiming: 'Let me be ta'en'; as he does so, the love theme plays again and, for just a moment, we believe that these lovers might actually cheat death and defeat

[34] Donaldson, p. 170, emphasis his.

the legend after all. Rota's score begins to rise in volume, and, as already indicated, there is no accompanying reference to Juliet's 'ill-divining soul'. Instead, Juliet, more hopeful than apprehensive, asks Romeo: 'O thinkst thou we shall ever meet again?' Romeo replies, with utter confidence, 'I doubt it not; and all these woes shall serve/For sweet discourses in our times to come'. As the love theme reaches its crescendo, the lovers silently repeat their signature intertwined hand grasp. This crucial visual and thematic device is the source of the lovers' very first touch at the Capulet Ball; subsequently, it is repeated following the balcony scene, as Romeo reluctantly descends from Juliet's outstretched hand; finally, in this moment, a tight shot reveals the lovers' hands clasping and unclasping so gradually that we see an unmistakable allusion to Michelangelo's's famous depiction of God and Adam, who is brought to life by one touch of the divine. Thus, as the music plays, far more triumphant rather than foreboding, we forget the ironic truth that this is the very last time they will be together – alive – again.

The film proceeds at a face pace from this point forward and, yet, Zeffirelli slows the tragic momentum with an unusual amount of interpolated stage business in Juliet's ensuing confrontation with her father and, shortly thereafter, with Friar Laurence. Critics have all but overlooked the unique blocking of these two scenes, which serves to remind us that Romeo and Juliet are, and have always been, children who lack the support and guidance of their families. When Juliet rejects her father's decision to marry her off to Paris in forty-eight hours, Old Capulet violently flings her against the bedroom wall and the Nurse boldly intervenes, protecting Juliet with her own substantial body while bravely admonishing Capulet by shouting: 'You are to blame'. At this juncture, Juliet is visually reduced to a little girl, indeed, a child, as she is shown kneeling behind and clinging desperately to the Nurse's dress as both Capulet and Lady Capulet disown their only child. When Juliet cries, 'O sweet mother, cast me not away', Lady Capulet replies curtly, devoid of warmth: 'I have done with thee'. The Nurse is thus Juliet's last line of defence and, though she is clearly represented as acting with Juliet's best interests at heart, the Nurse proceeds to advise Juliet to marry Paris. Shocked, Juliet recoils from the Nurse's touch, and for the first and only time in the film, the love theme plays as Juliet sunders her relationship with her dearest friend. Although the surprising implementation of Rota's song at this juncture might be interpreted as misguidedly inconsistent or, alternatively, melodramatic, this decision marks a crucial turning point in the film, for the song will hereafter be repeated solely as a harbinger of tragedy, no longer exalting in its sweeping melodic refrain to whisk the lovers out of harm's way. The music also underscores Juliet's status as the orphan she always already was – a pawn in the Renaissance trafficking in women, who will be sold to the highest bidder.

This reading becomes more evident when, in the following scene, Juliet throws herself frantically at the Friar, clinging to his robes just as she had clung to the Nurse's skirts mere moments ago. Although the blocking of the characters in both scenes is the same, the significance of Juliet's desperate lunge at the Friar is heightened by the view of the dangling wooden cross and prayer beads that adorn the lower portion of his robes. Here, as suggested from the outset of this discussion, the use of the cross comes to signify the infringement of the legendary, writ large in Zeffirelli's adaptation as the 'greater power' that thwarts, ultimately, *everyone's* 'intents'. For even as Friar Laurence looks hopefully to the purple flower from which he derives the sleeping potion (the third and final use of the floral motif in the film), the cross that is carved out in his cellar door looms over the scene, backlit to emphasise its creation from purely negative space – a far cry from the transcendent, solid gold crucifix that inspired the Friar's earlier schemes to shield the lovers from harm. Complementing the reconstitution of the cross symbol as more sinister, the love theme plays again – this time in a minor key – as though it were operating in conspiracy with the will of God.

In the interests of maintaining dramatic momentum, Zeffirelli eliminates the Nurse and Juliet's parents' hyperbolic utterances over her 'dead' body, as the scene shifts abruptly to her solemn burial in the Capulet vault – a scene which, in contrast to the many sumptuous versions before and after it, looks more like the scant ritual afforded Ophelia than a funeral for 'the fair daughter of rich Capulet' (2.2.58). Replacing Shakespeare's peculiar insertion of Peter's comedic scene with the musicians, Zeffirelli adds his own touch of comic relief when Friar Laurence, preparing to administer Juliet's last rites, casts his eyes down at her and smiles furtively – Puckishly confident that his plan is working. But Romeo's man, Balthazar, who is hiding in the trees nearby, beholds Juliet and is immediately shown thundering past Friar John on his horse. In a scene resembling a cross between cinéma verité and *commedia del'arte*, Friar John lumbers awkwardly across the dusty countryside with his mule, arriving in Mantua long after Balthazar has broken the news to Romeo. Consistent with his earlier deletions of tragic portents, Zeffirelli eliminates Romeo's naïve recounting to Peter of his 'auspicious' dream in which 'methought I was this night already dead – . . . And that my lady Juliet came to me,/And breathed such life with kisses in my lips/That I revived and was an emperor' (5.1.5, 7–9). Instead, when Balthazar tells Romeo that Juliet is dead, Romeo bursts into what sounds like a non-sequitur: 'Then I defy you stars!' Recalling that Romeo's only other reference to stars in this film occurs in his speech just before he enters the Capulet Ball, this second reference makes little sense. Similarly, in cutting Romeo's trip to the apothecary, the director leaves the audience wondering how Romeo has obtained the poison that serves as the font of his suicide. Nevertheless, after posting straight to the Capulet tomb, Romeo, unimpeded by Balthazar or Paris, batters down the door and goes frantically in search of Juliet. Following several establishing shots of rotting corpses, the camera lights on Juliet's bright countenance. When Romeo lifts the shroud that covers Juliet's face, Rota's song is plucked by a solitary guitar; its effect at this juncture is rendered all the more powerful by the loneliness it implies, as Romeo gazes at the bright remnant of his departed love. Only stones would not be moved in this scene, which is rendered beautifully by Whiting's Romeo, who pours amazedly over Juliet's body, ever-hoping that Juliet is still alive because he is convinced that 'death's pale flag is not advanced there' – and tragically – he is correct in his surmise.

In fact, it is almost as if Romeo knows that something is amiss, because while his heart apprehends the tragedy, his mind forces him to question what his eyes see, as he asks: 'Ah, dear Juliet,/Why art thou yet so fair?' At this point Romeo spies the pale body of Tybalt; seemingly inconsistent with Zeffirelli's decision to leave Romeo's fatal encounter with Paris on the cutting room floor, the director includes Romeo's reconciliation with Tybalt, perhaps as one final effort to persuade Michael York that his character would indeed be one of the stars of the film. But this intervening scene serves as an emotional transition for Romeo, who returns to gaze at Juliet's body, now sobbing like the child that he has always already been. As he fully comprehends the death of his love and the gravity of the desperate act he is poised to commit, Romeo utters his final speech while hugging Juliet's body from head to foot.

When he at last resolves to drink the poison, Romeo tilts his head back to swallow the fatal drink and the love theme – paralleling the exact strain when Juliet tosses back the sleeping potion – swells for the last time within the narrative-proper. Romeo stumbles as his body revolts from the intrusion of death, pausing to draw a faint kiss from Juliet's hand – the site of their first touch and the connection that Zeffirelli has rendered thematic from first to last – and falls to the floor.

Moments later, the Friar enters to find how horribly his plan has gone awry, and he attempts to shield Juliet from the sight of Romeo's body. Fittingly, we are made aware of Juliet's waking by a tight shot of her hand, which unfurls and, having regained its strength, makes a fist, as if already in solidarity with Romeo's resolve to die rather than live without love. 'Where is my Romeo?' are her first words, uttered with soft anticipation, which the Friar responds to by trying to escort Juliet out of the monument. When the Watch sounds, however, the Friar waxes pale; Juliet discovers Romeo's body and Friar Laurence, panicked, exclaims: 'A greater power than we can contradict hath thwarted our intents'. The Watch sounds again, and he cries, determined against his better judgment to leave her to her grief, 'I dare no longer stay!' The otherwise calm and collected man suddenly raves like a madman, repeating 'I dare no longer stay' three more times as he flees the Capulet vault. Significantly, we do not see his character again, a decision that subtly raises suspicions about the Friar's integrity in ways that date back to the more skeptical visions of the early Italian treatments of the legend. As Juliet now dwells alone with Romeo, the love theme resumes, softly – without crescendos. Paralleling Romeo's painful confusion over Juliet's inextinguishable beauty, here, too, the height of the tragedy corresponds to Juliet's recognition that her lover's 'lips are warm'. Bursting into tears, she realises that little more than a minute has determined their fate. The extraordinary pathos with which this scene is rendered makes the audience feel as though they, too, are experiencing Romeo's death without foreknowledge, as if they are experiencing the tragedy – along with Juliet – for the first time. Subsequently, upon hearing the authorities entering the tomb, she simply cries, 'No!' and, with dogged determination, Juliet concludes: 'Then I'll be brief./O happy dagger/This is thy sheath!/ There rust, and let me die', stabbing herself and expiring on Romeo's chest. As she does so, Rota's theme ceases to be heard, ending as abruptly as Juliet's life.

If it is the nearly triumphant score, coupled with Zeffirelli's removal of many of the play's premonitory lines, which almost persuade us that Romeo and Juliet, too, will defy their fate, then it is the strategic deployment of this song during the credit sequence that convinces us that a 'greater power' has indeed prevailed once and for all. After the Prince utters his notorious last line, 'All are punished!' Zeffirelli aligns the feuding factions opposite one another (including, in another departure from the play, the parents of *both* Romeo and Juliet). As they process towards us and out of the cinematic frame, various gestures are made – the shaking of hands, embracing, sympathetic nods – as the offending parties exit the solemn scene, clearly having learnt their tragic lesson. In voiceover, Laurence Olivier utters a curtailed version of the concluding lines, assigned in Shakespeare's play to the Prince:

A glooming peace this morning with it brings;
The sun for sorrow will not show his head.

. . . .
For never was a story of more woe
Than this of Juliet and her Romeo.

As the credits roll, the processional scene slowly darkens. When the camera shifts to a shot of the battlements – the same, foreboding image on which the title 'Romeo and Juliet' was inscribed at the beginning of the film – Rota's love theme begins again. More than complementing the opening shot, this book-end image implies the victory of the legend in the very architecture it pictures. For battlements are a place of surveillance and violence, and as Rota's score begins to swell now for the last time, the musical theme betrays its true allegiance. Indeed, we are left with the disturbing feeling that it has never really been allied with the transcendence of the legendary forces against which Romeo and Juliet unwittingly conspire, but, rather, with their untimely, 'timeless end' (5.3.162), having merely teased us into believing – with its magnificent, overreaching strains – that it could usher the lovers into a world beyond the cycle of violence that the battlements encode. Appropriately, the final crescendo occurs in tandem with the fade to black, signaling the eternal night of death.

William Shakespeare's Romeo + Juliet: a cinematic detour through the play's textual origins

···

Man can create only in continuity, by making the potential actual, he is excluded, by his nature, from originality and innovation.

But this difference is an adaptation.

— Pierre Macherey, 'Creation and Production'[1]

'I've always wanted to do *Romeo and Juliet*', writes Baz Luhrmann. 'Shakespeare', he claims, was 'a rambunctious, sexy, violent, entertaining storyteller. We're trying to make this movie rambunctious, sexy, violent, and entertaining the way Shakespeare might have if he had been a filmmaker'.[2] Intent on realising what I would refer to as Shakespeare's legacy of 'cinematic thinking', Luhrmann has his work cut out for him, for in adapting a play that is simultaneously a

---

[1] Pierre Macherey, 'Creation and Production', in *Authorship from Plato to the Postmodern*, edited by Sean Burke (Edinburgh: Edinburgh University Press, 1995), p. 230.

[2] See 'A Note from Baz Luhrmann', in *William Shakespeare's Romeo + Juliet. The Contemporary Film, The Classic Play* (New York: Bantam Doubleday Dell, 1996), pp. i–ii (i).

legend, he must contend with ghosts.[3] In titling his film *William Shakespeare's* Romeo + Juliet, however, Luhrmann *appears* to have no aspirations to originality, a gesture that is perfectly in keeping with the status of authorship – or auteurship – within postmodern culture. According to Fredric Jameson, one of the 'essential messages' of the postmodern aesthetic involves, paradoxically, 'the necessary failure of art and the aesthetic, the failure of the new, (and) the imprisonment in the past'.[4] Yet even the past itself is 'condemned' – in Jameson's words – to engage with history only 'through our own pop images and stereotypes about that past, which itself remains forever out of reach'.[5] Missing this 'essential message', critics have been quick to dismiss Luhrmann's film as 'postmodern tomfoolery', mourning its alleged substitution of 'postmodern razzmatazz' for Shakespearean textuality and early modern history without realising the extent to which the film itself mourns these losses as symptomatic of the madness of its own mode of production.[6]

Rather than taking note of the provocative crisis of representation staged in *William Shakespeare's Romeo + Juliet*, critics take Luhrmann's adaptation to task for not being 'Shakespearean' enough, reading the film's title too literally. '*William Shakespeare's Romeo & Juliet* is deceptively titled', writes one reviewer, because

[3] See *Shakespeare Remains*, 'The Machine in the Ghost: *Hamlet*'s Cinematographic Kingdom', pp, 89–129.

[4] See Fredric Jameson, 'Postmodernism and Consumer Society', in *Movies and Mass Culture*, edited by John Belton (New Brunswick: Rutgers University Press, 1996), p. 190.

[5] Jameson, 'Postmodernism and Consumer Society', p. 194.

[6] See Jim Welsh, 'Postmodern Shakespeare: Strictly Romeo', *Literature-Film Quarterly* 25.2 (1996), p. 152, and Brian D. Johnson, 'Souping up the Bard', *Macleans* Nov. 11, 1996, p. 74.

'it is really Baz Luhrmann's *Romeo & Juliet*'.[7] *Rolling Stone* critic Peter Travers observes, 'It's a good thing that Shakespeare gets his name in the title, or you might mistake the opening scenes for Quentin Tarantino's *Romeo and Juliet*'.[8] Yet another review echoes this sentiment quite precisely: 'Good thing Shakespeare's name is included in the title. Otherwise, you might mistake this audacious version of his tale of star-crossed teen lovers for an extended music video'.[9] What is so striking and, in fact, symptomatic about these critical remarks is that they protest too much – that is, too much *in common* with each other. For in going to the same linguistic well to describe the film's titular strategy, these critics not only testify to the uncanny power of the legendary, which subsumes their purportedly original 'takes' on the film within a narrative form of repetition compulsion, but more importantly, their comments act out the problems of authenticity and authority embedded in the very cultural logic they set out to critique. To be sure, *William Shakespeare's Romeo + Juliet* is unabashedly replete with 'postmodern razzmatazz', however, the critical reception of Luhrmann's film tends to rest too easy with this complex cultural category, drowning any discussion of the film's provocative negotiation of its own historical dilemma in a self-indulgent, hipper-than-thou inventory of its aesthetic failures. A more productive project would involve calibrating the degree to which Luhrmann's film resists easy insertion into the postmodern 'legend' that originality is impossible – a legend which, as we shall see, sends us hurtling headlong back into the struggle of adaptation embedded in William Shakespeare's own *Romeo and Juliet*.

[7] Welsh, p. 152.

[8] Peter Travers, 'Just Two Kids in Love', *Rolling Stone* Nov. 14, 1996, p. 123.

[9] Welton Jones, 'Triumph of tragic love ensures long life of "Romeo"', *The San Diego Tribune* 12 April 1998: p. E1. Luhrmann did, in fact, release a music video and an MTV special to promote the film.

Before exploring how Luhrmann's film facilitates this provocative historical intersection of postmodern and early modern, it is first necessary to establish how *William Shakespeare's Romeo + Juliet* qualifies as specifically postmodern, since this is a label that the film's detractors have taken for granted. From its opening moments, Luhrmann's film announces its apparent overdetermination by the modus operandi of pastiche, the quintessential signifier of the postmodern aesthetic. For what indeed is the alternative in 'a world in which stylistic innovation is no longer possible'?[10] In such an environment, the new is replaced with the 'neo' and 'personal style' is replaced with 'the random cannibalization of all the styles of the past', leading to 'the well-nigh universal practice today of what may be called pastiche', or, what Jameson provocatively refers to as 'blank parody'.[11] The formal consequence of the postmodern preoccupation with pastiche is the 'emergence of a new kind of flatness or depthlessness, a new kind of superficiality in the most literal sense'.[12] Not surprisingly, the most striking formal feature of Luhrmann's appropriately dubbed 'neo-*Romeo*' film[13] is its barrage of incongruent surfaces that reproduce the complex textuality of Shakespeare's play at the level of mise-en-scène, generating the pastiche visual nightmare known as 'Verona Beach' – itself a curious hybrid of Shakespeare's Veronese setting, LA's Venice Beach, and the film's on-location shots of Mexico City,

[10] Jameson, 'Postmodernism and Consumer Society', p. 190.

[11] Jameson, 'Postmodernism, or The Cultural Logic of Late Capitalism', in *Postmodernism: A Reader*, edited by Thomas Docherty (New York: Columbia UP, 1993), p. 74. I am working with several different versions of Jameson's work on postmodern culture because each of them offers a slightly different perspective on his theory of aesthetic production.

[12] Jameson, 'Postmodernism, or The Cultural Logic of Late Capitalism', p. 68.

[13] Johnson, p. 74.

along with the coastal city of Vera Cruz. The opening scene of Luhrmann's film builds on this sense of rupture by calling into question not only the film's location but also the spectator's orientation in space and time. Declaring open season on the viewer's visual loyalties, the cinematic frame yields to a television screen as a news anchorwoman delivers Shakespeare's prologue in bleak monotones. This unique interpretation of a dramatic Chorus is quickly eclipsed by another shift of medium as a violent montage of newsreel footage, newspaper headlines, and prime-time drama shots of the awestruck faces of Capulets and Montagues collectively document the ongoing war in Verona Beach. The prevailing feel of this bizarre opening sequence is pure pastiche: evening-soap fiction meets evening-magazine 'real life', but the lines separating titillation from truth, melodrama from docu-drama, are fuzzy at best. True to postmodern form, Luhrmann introduces us to *William Shakespeare's Romeo + Juliet* in a manner wholly attuned to a 'consumers' appetite for a world transformed into sheer images of itself and for pseudo-events and "spectacles"'.[14]

By the time we arrive at the first scene of Shakespeare's play involving the confrontation between the Capulets and the Montagues, the spectator's sense of being unstuck in space and time suffers further displacement in the midst of the bizarre ethnic mix created by Luhrmann's cast. Sizing up the cultural differences between the Capulets and the Montagues, one critic observes that the 'Montagues are a motley crew with a kind of *Apocalypse Now* dress code, army surplus Hawaiian shirt and semi-punk hair. The Capulets are smooth, sleek, groomed and feline, Latin cowboys in

---

[14] Jameson, 'Postmodernism, or The Cultural Logic of Late Capitalism', p. 74.

close-fitting black, accessorised with silver trimmings and images of the Virgin Mary'.[15] Essentially, the south-of-the-border-*cum*-spaghetti-western Capulets are characterised by an excess of ethnicity, while the pasty-faced Montague boys sport a lack of thereof, becoming, in effect, 'beastie boyz' as they rap, grind, and signify in classic wanna-be style. The stereotypes operative in both the Capulet and Montague gangs offer pointed testimony to the postmodern loss of 'personal style' and the compensatory predominance of pastiche. But this loss extends beyond the diegetic reality to encompass the film itself, which creates a visual vernacular for audiences weaned on popular film through a relentless cinematic intertextuality. Indeed, the opening scene alone 'is filled with glancing references to and overt borrowings from the cinema of violence: the Western, the gangster movie, the kung-fu pic, the urban drama, the crime thriller, (and) the action comedy'.[16] Such borrowings keep the spectator's gaze hostage to the shifting, shimmering surfaces of Luhrmann's film, demonstrating the extent to which, as Jameson argues of the 'remake' film, intertextuality has become 'a deliberate, built-in feature of the aesthetic effect' designed to tap into 'our awareness of the pre-existence of other versions'.[17]

Playing on the audience's awareness of Franco Zeffirelli's lusty, busty, flower-child version of *Romeo and Juliet* starring Olivia Hussey and Leonard Whiting, Luhrmann stages several intertextual echoes of and overtly parodic gestures toward Zeffirelli's film. While Lady Capulet is introduced primping and preening in Zeffirelli's film, in

---

[15] Hawker, Philippa. 'DiCaprio, DiCaprio, Wherefore Art Thou, DiCaprio?' *Meanjin*, March 1997, p. 6.

[16] Ibid.

[17] Jameson, 'Postmodernism, or The Cultural Logic of Late Capitalism', p. 76.

Luhrmann's 'remake', she becomes a monstrous crossbreed of Southern debutante and Hollywood diva. And whereas Zeffirelli shows Lady Capulet and Tybalt merely dancing together at the ball, Luhrmann heightens this erotic suggestion in the direction of incest, as they become 'kissing cousins' on the dance floor. Similarly, while Zeffirelli only hints at Mercutio's homoerotic attachment to Romeo, Luhrmann's Mercutio is a black-skinned, white-sequined, drag queen who seems desperately disturbed by Romeo's heterosexual awakening. Less problematic and more clever is Luhrmann's revision of one of Zeffirelli's most famous set pieces – the Morisca – at the Capulet Ball, which involves a dizzying interweaving of hands, gazes, and bodies; in Luhrmann's film this motif is revisited in the form of Romeo's ecstasy trip which mimics the frenzied whirl and hum of love-at-first-sight. Finally, just as Zeffirelli showcases the song 'What is a Youth?' as the memorable (and now clichéd) centrepiece of his film, Luhrmann converts this theme into Mercutio's drag rendition of 'Young Hearts'. Thus we glimpse the postmodern confrontation between Shakespeare, Zeffirelli, and Luhrmann's sex, drugs, and rock-and-roll rendition of star-crossed love through the magnifying glass of a rabid intertextuality, which now becomes 'a constitutive and essential part of the film's structure . . . as the operator of a new connotation of "pastness" and pseudo-historical depth, in which the history of aesthetic styles displaces "real" history'.[18]

In what sense, then, does this film live up to its title as *William Shakespeare's Romeo + Juliet*? And, for that matter, to what extent does Shakespeare's own play deserve this attribution? Before we can answer this question, we must acknowledge that early modern authorship takes its cues from the medieval ideology of *auctoritas*,

[18] Jameson, 'Postmodernism, or The Cultural Logic of Late Capitalism', p. 76.

which reduces the figure of the author to a pastiche ensemble of other voices. Indeed, what we see at work here is a literalisation of Jameson's definition of pastiche or 'blank parody' as 'speech in a dead language', an unhealthy linguistic environment that is 'amputated of the satiric impulse, devoid of laughter and of any conviction that alongside the abnormal tongue you have momentarily borrowed, some healthy linguistic normality still exists'.[19] Indeed, the early modern author is bound to speak in a 'dead language' as a figure whose work is constituted by the words of *auctors* – essentially, dead authorities – whose wisdom is preserved through cultural regimens of repetition. Although the phrase 'ghostly father' invokes the description of Friar Laurence in Shakespeare's *Romeo and Juliet*, it is a particularly apt description of the *auctor* which, as Mary Carruthers reminds us, designates a reiterative, text-centered mode of production that bases its promulgation of *sententiae* on the authority already contained in other texts. Representing this tradition of authority, Friar Laurence is a figure who is always spouting aphorisms and sententious phrases; and despite the fact that he briefly acts upon his own authority in helping Romeo and Juliet, he ultimately concedes to the 'greater power' or *auctoritas* of law and religion which, he tells Juliet, 'hath thwarted our intents' (5.3.153–4). Thus, we might conclude that whereas early modern authorship emerges in the spirit of adaptation to the still culturally-dominant demand for *purposeful* cannibalisation of past styles and preexisting authority, postmodern authorship is fueled by the more *random* cannibalisation, or pastiche, of precedents drawn from the past. In other words, the challenges of early modern and postmodern authorship converge, provocatively, along the axis of 'blank parody'.

[19] Jameson, 'Postmodernism, or The Cultural Logic of Late Capitalism', p. 74.

From this historical perspective, then, there appears to be no such thing as William Shakespeare's *Romeo and Juliet*, let alone a film claiming that authority. But in *practice*, specifically, dramatic practice, there are opportunities to articulate new or emergent 'structures of feeling' towards authorship and authority,[20] as W.B. Worthen argues. In contrast to the ideological strictures that govern the production of nondramatic texts, dramatic texts do not engage in the mere blank parody of preexisting authority; rather, in their 'surrogate' existence as performances, they engender an authority of their own. Dramatic performance, as Worthen explains, should not be conceptualised as a straightforward 'performance *of* the text but as an act of iteration, an utterance, a surrogate standing in that positions, uses, signifies the text within the citational practices of performance' and which, as a result, achieves a semi-autonomous existence *apart from* the text.[21] What Worthen identifies as 'surrogation' is the capacity of performance to utilise the multiple citational practices of the stage in order to transform the potentially 'dead language' of the text. Surrogation can even transform fundamental notions of priority and origins, for it is an 'act of memory and an act of creation (that) involves not the replaying of an authorising text, a grounding origin, but the potential to construct that origin as a rhetorically powerful *effect of performance*'[22] Worthen's emphasis on the transformative as opposed to the merely translative power of surrogation stresses the liberating provisionality of performance without simply reverting to the incapacitating dialectic of the text-versus-performance

[20] The term 'structures of feeling' is borrowed from Raymond Williams, *Marxism and Literature* (Oxford: Oxford University Press, 1977).

[21] Worthen, W.B. 'Drama, Performance, Performativity'. *PMLA* (October 1998), p. 1101.

[22] Ibid.

paradigm. But is to possible for 'authors' to engage in counter-hegemonic performances themselves – even if originality, as Macherey reminds us, is, ultimately, 'impossible'? Indeed, I will show how this contestatory presence may be traced back to Shakespeare's play only by way of its surrogates, which are activated by the provocative citational practices of performances like Baz Luhrmann's *William Shakespeare's Romeo + Juliet* as a film that wages resistance to the legend – both postmodern and early modern – that reduces the project of adaptation to a blank parody of the past.

Legends embody a narrative form that has received significantly less attention from critics than other genres such as myths, fables, and folktales. In the absence of more extensive and specific treatment of legends in narrative theory, I find Roland Barthes' concept of déjà-lu – the already read – to be particularly useful in the case of the Romeo and Juliet legend, which, as we have seen in Chapter One, is distinguished by a long line of almost exclusively literary, rather than oral, transmission.[23] Without specifically referring to legends, Peter Brooks explains the narrative pathology of déjà-lu in terms of what he calls the 'anticipation of retrospection':

> If the past is to be read as present, it is a curious present that we know to be past in relation to a future we know to be already in place, already in wait for us to reach it. Perhaps we would do best to speak of the *anticipation of retrospection* as our chief tool in making sense of narrative, the master trope of its strange logic. We have no doubt forgone eternal narrative ends . . . yet

[23] Barthes explores the concept of *déjà lu* throughout *S/Z*, translated by Richard Miller (New York: Hill and Wang, 1974).

still we read in a spirit of confidence, and also a state of
dependence, that what remains to be read will restructure
the provisional meanings of the already read.[24]

Offering a variation on this theme, the characters of Romeo and
Juliet seem to operate under the assumption that what remains to
be *written* will restructure and, ultimately, enable them to avert, the
tragic fate that they have *already read* in their crossed stars. If we
continue to read forward from the early modern to the
postmodern, then, we find that Baz Lurhmann's *William Shakespeare's Romeo + Juliet*, with its fetishistic appropriation of the plus
(+) sign, indicates – regardless of the contemporary, historical, and
legendary forces he is up against – that he, too, wishes to 'add'
something of his own invention to this story. Engaged in a constant
struggle with the forces of the 'already read' and already known,
William Shakespeare's Romeo + Juliet is nothing less than an
allegory of 'adaptation'.

Precisely because the legend of Romeo and Juliet is distinguished by a literary as opposed to oral history, it is a particularly
useful source for exploring the legends that accrue to authorship –
literary or filmic – in the age of blank parody. Appropriately,
Luhrmann seeks to overcome the citational clutches of preexisting
textual authority with the creation of a distinctly cinematographic
language. In creating a contemporary screen adaptation,
however, Luhrmann is not only faced with the sedimented *literary*
history of the legend but also with the legendary status of
Shakespeare's own play in contemporary popular culture – a status
that is perpetuated by the standard inclusion of *Romeo and Juliet*

---

[24] See Peter Brooks' *Reading for the Plot: Design and Intention in Narrative*
(Cambridge: Harvard University Press, 1984), p. 23.

in high school curricula, the success of adaptations such as *West Side Story*, and the rising star of Leonardo DiCaprio, whose popular reception as the ultimate 'Romeo' uncannily culminates in his star-crossed 'sequel' to *William Shakespeare's Romeo + Juliet*: *Titantic*. Thus, as Shakespeare's play-ending couplet inscribing 'Romeo' and 'woe' triangulates all too easily to include 'DiCaprio', we are reminded that the legend, despite its reworking in the predominantly visual medium of cinema, can return as a 'dead letter' – a *fait accompli* – to inscribe even the most powerful performances within its consuming textuality. And though Luhrmann seizes every opportunity to convert the potentially 'dead language' of Shakespeare's *Romeo and Juliet* into a distinctly cinematic visual language, such repressions of the text, as Geoffrey Nowell-Smith argues, return as 'hysterical' moments in the mise-en-scène.[25] Richard Vela sees a similar impulse at work in his reading, noting that 'Luhrmann's allusive technique tends to subvert rather than reinforce the meanings displayed on screen'.[26] Remarkably, it is the abundant baptismal and, simultaneously, womb-like water imagery, unanimously considered by critics to be the most innovative aspect of Luhrmann's film, which exposes the steady encroachment of the

[25] For a discussion of an unacknowledged precedent of Luhrmann's aggressive attempt to pit image against word, see Douglas Lanier's brilliant exploration of Peter Greenaway's *Prospero's Books*, titled 'Drowning the Book: *Prospero's Books* and the Textual Shakespeare' in *Shakespeare, Theory, and Performance*, edited by James C. Bulman (New York and London: Routledge, 1996), pp. 187–209. The concept of the hysterical return of the repressed is invoked throughout Nowell-Smith's extensive work on mise-en-scène criticism.

[26] Richard Vela, 'Post-Apocalyptic Spaces in Baz Luhrmann's *William Shakespeare's Romeo + Juliet*', *Apocalyptic Shakespeare: Essays on Visions of Chaos and Revelation in Recent Film Adaptations*, edited by Melissa Croteau and Carolyn Jess-Cooke (Jefferson, NC: McFarland, 2009), p. 91.

legend and, specifically, of Arthur Brooke's own poetic imagery on Luhrmann's cinematic tour de force. Rife with images of fish, water, and baited hooks, Brooke's *Tragicall Historye* contains a lure that not even Luhrmann can resist – so strong is the pull of this 'ghostly father' reluctantly entombed in Shakespeare's play.

> Every artist is a cannibal, every poet is a thief.
> All kill their inspiration and sing about their grief.
> – U2, 'The Fly', from *Achtung Baby!*

In discussing *William Shakespeare's Romeo + Juliet*, Luhrmann has rather oddly asserted that Shakespeare 'did not write *Romeo and Juliet*, he stole it', a remark that undermines the fidelity to Shakespeare advertised in the film's title.[27] In virtually the same breath, however, Luhrmann implies that his filmic realisation of the Romeo and Juliet legend *is* based exclusively on Shakespeare's version of it, for as his subsequent comments imply, he admits only a vague familiarity with the fact that Shakespeare's play was based on 'a long poem' that was in turn derived from 'an Italian novella'.[28] The connection between Luhrmann's film and Brooke's poem therefore seems to be a coincidence but, as we shall see, it is a coincidence so provocative as to be classifiable only as 'uncanny'. Another curiosity related to the film's title and its apparent privileging of Shakespeare is Luhrmann's cutting of more than one-third of Shakespeare's play from his screenplay; more significantly, when pressed to discuss the film's distinctly 'Shakespearean' qualities, Luhrmann somewhat disdainfully indicates that the standard quota of 'witty epigrams' and 'speaking in perfect sonnets' will be hard to

---

[27] 'An Interview with Baz Luhrmann', *Cinema Papers* (Feb. 1997), p. 13.
[28] Ibid.

find in *William Shakespeare's Romeo + Juliet.*[29] But it is precisely in these mild condemnations of the world's most famous love story that we see Luhrmann's own ambitions to 'originality'.

As we enter Luhrmann's distinctly postmodern mise-en-scène, it is tempting to read what remains of Shakespeare's *Romeo and Juliet* in the bleak spotlight of blank parody. Signs representing the 'Globe Theatre Pool Hall', 'The Merchant of Verona Beach', and 'Out Damned Spot Cleaners', as well as advertisements for consumable goods such as 'Pound of Flesh' fast food, 'Rosencrantzky's' restaurant, and 'Prospero's whiskey' refigure the high-cultural status of Shakespearean verse as an homage to postmodern consumer culture. But what is most striking about Luhrmann's conversion of these Shakespearean hallmarks into sites of consumption is his literalisation of the aesthetic cannibalism that links postmodern film adaptation to the early modern blank-parody function of imitating *auctoritas* – a function that would-be 'authors' such as Ben Jonson uncannily defined in terms of the metaphor of *digestion*:

> The third requisite in our *Poet*, or *Maker*, is *Imitation*, to bee able to convert the substance, or Riches of another *Poet*, to his owne use. To make choise of one excellent man above the rest, and so to follow him, till he grow very *Hee*: or, so like him, as the Copie may be mistaken for the Principall. Not, as a Creature, that swallowes, what it takes in, crude, raw, or indigested; but, that feedes with an Appetite, and hath a Stomacke to concoct, divide, and turne all into nourishment.[30]

---

[29] Ibid.

[30] Ben Jonson, *Timber: Or, Discoveries Made upon Men and Matter* (1616), *The Collected Works of Ben Jonson*, Vol. 8 (11 Vols.), C.H. Herford, P. Simpson, and E. Simpson, eds. (Oxford: Clarendon Press, 1925–52), lines 2466–75.

Similarly, Luhrmann 'feedes with an Appetite' on Shakespeare's words, seeking to 'concoct and divide' them into a kind of cinematic mincemeat. And where his camera fails to commodify and consume Shakespearean verse, Luhrmann adopts an ironising, literalistic approach to the language. For example, at the Capulet Ball, Luhrmann playfully converts Juliet into Romeo's 'bright angel' (2.2.26) as she emerges decked out in an angel costume. Luhrmann has even more fun with Shakespeare's memorable account of Paris as a 'precious book of love' that only 'lacks a cover' (1.3.87, 88); in the film, Paris is given a literal cover when 'Dave Paris' is introduced to us as a cover boy, featured as *Timely Magazine*'s 'Bachelor of the Year'. Naturally, Paris shows up to the Ball sporting the 'all-American' look of an astronaught. In the spirit of Jonsonian imitation, then, these tongue-in-cheek visual variations on a Shakespearean theme suggest Luhrmann's more serious, carnivorous desire to authorise a version of the legend that occupies a distinctly cinematic register – not the tragic registry of 'sour misfortune's book' (5.3.82).

This desire is not without precedent, however, for Shakespeare's play attempts to authorise a new version of the legend in his own terms by staging an escape from the tragic referentiality of Romeo and Juliet's language. As we have seen, Shakespeare's lovers are in search of a properly poststructuralist universe in which signifier and signified exist in arbitrary relation to each other – where Romeo, as Juliet describes him, is neither 'hand, nor foot, nor arm, nor face, nor any other part' belonging to the deadly inscription of his legendary name (2.1.83–84). Thus what distinguishes Shakespeare's play from its source in Brooke's poem is the fact that

> while Brooke had told his story in a mercilessly prolix succession
> of poulter's measure couplets, Shakespeare now gave voice to

the most various linguistic range of any play that had yet appeared on the English stage. Colloquial prose, rhymed and unrhymed blankverse, Petrarchanism both sincere and parodic, stichomythia, epith alamion, aubade, bawdy, song, pun, lament, soliloquy, epistle, flyting, gnomic 'sentence', the conceits that clownage keeps in pay, and even an elegant embedded sonnet are among the many rhetorical styles that vie for center stage in the course of the two hours' traffic.[31]

Whereas Shakespeare filters Brooke's lethal (re)capitulation of the legend through an extraordinary range of poetic styles, Luhrmann continues this game of cat-and-mouse by exploiting a radically fluctuating cinematic rhetoric. 'Let's talk about that cinematic language', proclaims Luhrmann, 'You get a lot of people saying, "Oh my god, you change style every five minutes. How MTV"'. To this charge, Luhrmann offers a somewhat unexpected reply: 'Well, have you ever seen a Hindi movie? Please. That idea of low comedy one minute, a song, then *Rebel Without a Cause*, is aligned with Shakespeare's need to keep changing style, to keep clarity, to keep surprising the audience, to keep ahead of them'.[32] As far as Luhrmann is concerned, then, what qualifies as 'strictly Shakespeare' is strictly pastiche. However, Luhrmann's stylistic investment in pastiche is distinctly *not* aligned with the 'dead language' of blank parody. For what is most striking about his commentary is its invocation of the life-infusing, transmigratory mystique of Hindu culture and cinema, which Luhrmann manipulates as a means of linking the metamorphoses of Shakespearean

---

[31] E. Pearlman, 'Staging *Romeo and Juliet*: Evidence from Brooke's *Romeus*', *Theatre Survey* 34 (May 1993), p. 23.

[32] Luhrmann, 'Interview', p. 14.

verse to his own ever-changing cinematic language. But why is Luhrmann so concerned with the principle of dynamic change in the first place? Is it possible that the somewhat peculiar 'needs' he ascribes to Shakespeare – the need, for example, 'to keep changing style' and 'to keep ahead of the audience' – expose his own sensitivity to the pull of the legendary? Simply put, there is an unmistakable urgency in *William Shakespeare's Romeo + Juliet* that does not exist in Luhrmann's other work; and this urgency, I would argue, stems from the fear that he may, in fact, fall one step *behind* the audience or, more importantly, the legend, having exhausted his quota of new steps in *Strictly Ballroom*, as well as his follow-up film, *Moulin Rouge!* (2001).

Baz Luhrmann's *William Shakespeare's Romeo + Juliet* is perhaps best described as a combination of his other 'Red Curtain Trilogy' plays: *Strictly Ballroom* and *Moulin Rouge!* Luhrmann's first commercially released film, *Strictly Ballroom* (1992) serves as a provocative prequel to his tango with the Romeo and Juliet legend. Particularly illuminating are the parallels between this earlier film's principal character, Scott Hastings, and Shakespeare's Romeo. Like Romeo, whose every move is circumscribed by literary conventions, Scott Hastings is a dance legend-in-the-making who remains 'boxed-in' by the rules of the Australian Dance Federation. 'Maybe I'm just sick of dancing someone else's steps all the time', exclaims Scott, eager to authorise new moves expressly forbidden by the Federation and the cultural dictates of 'strictly ballroom' dancing. Defying the will of his parents, Scott partners up with a girl from the wrong side of the tracks and together they break the cycle of convention and corruption that has plagued the Pan-Pacific Dance Championships for generations – by dancing, quite literally, out of bounds. Subsequently, the generation-long feud between rival households is ended when universal enthusiasm for

Scott's fabled 'new steps' proclaims victory against the old guard. Replete with Luhrmann's signature death-defying camera angles, *Strictly Ballroom* is *Romeo and Juliet* with a happy ending. Noting the striking likeness between *Strictly Ballroom*'s dance-duo and DiCaprio and Danes's Romeo and Juliet, one reviewer observes that '(t)hey would be just a slight variation on the romantic couple in *Strictly Ballroom*, if only the film-makers weren't stuck with Shakespeare's downbeat ending'.[33] Indeed, in one of *Strictly Ballroom*'s particularly 'downbeat' moments, we are reminded of a theme that applies more strictly to *Romeo and Juliet*: 'You can dance any steps you like', says a Federation Judge to Scott, '(but) that doesn't mean you'll win'. In other words, defying the *auctoritas* of tradition comes with a price. If *Strictly Ballroom*'s vision of defiance *without* consequence succeeds temporarily in keeping the letter of Federation law suspended, then the letter's debt returns in *William Shakespeare's Romeo + Juliet* with a vengeance.

Although it might seem peculiar to leap forward to *Romeo + Juliet*'s 'sequel', *Moulin Rouge!* – the third and final film in the series that Luhrmann has named the 'Red Curtain Trilogy' – with the help of historical hindsight, we find that Luhrmann's anticipation of this final film could not help but have influenced the decisions made during his creation of *Romeo + Juliet*. Combining generic elements from both *Strictly Ballroom* and *Romeo + Juliet*, the musical film *Moulin Rouge!* includes elaborately choreographed dance numbers and a recitative-style 'sung' narrative. Moreover, in addition to form, the content of this final 'Red Curtain' film strikes a classic compromise formation; for in contrast to the total idealism of *Strictly Ballroom*, where both lovers survive, and the absolute nihilism of

---

[33] Peter Mathews, 'Rev. of *William Shakespeare's Romeo + Juliet*', *Sight and Sound* 7.4 (April 1997), p. 55.

Romeo + Juliet, wherein both perish, *Moulin Rouge!* temporarily achieves a happy ending as the lovers cheat death at the hands of an assassin, only to leave Sateen performing her literal 'Swan Song' as she dies on stage, leaving her 'Romeo'/Christian behind with the Hamlet-like imperative to 'write their story' for the benefit of posterity. Having typed his last word, Christian's conclusion is read in voice-over, as the bereaved author describes a story that is about 'people' and 'places' but, above all, is 'a story about love. A love that will live forever. The end'. Thus, *Moulin Rouge!* is nothing less than the dialectical synthesis of *Strictly Ballroom* and *Romeo + Juliet*, as a film that produces a 'third term', indeed, an alternative ending, to a story of star-crossed love that audaciously inscribes its own version of the 'Romeo and Juliet' plot onto the palimpsest of this very legend, almost – but not quite – arresting its tragic trajectory.

On one level, then, knowing that all three films are part of a trilogy suggests that the consolation afforded by the films that buffer *Romeo + Juliet* allow Luhrmann to confront *this* Ur-love story in all its fatalistic splendor; then again, the fact that Luhrmann tackles the primal scene of star-crossed love not once but three times suggests a certain level of repetition-compulsion at work in the director's own psyche, as a manifestation of the will to master trauma. Akin to Christian's predicament in *Moulin Rouge!*, Luhrmann's cinematic opus is haunted by the cultural trauma of being 'obsessed with love' but bound to live – and, ultimately, to write – the tragic ending he seeks so vehemently to avert. Unquestionably, *William Shakespeare's Romeo + Juliet* marks a return to a primal scene for Luhrmann, who seems at once drawn to legendary themes and intent on modeling alternatives to their debilitating logic.

Viewing the 'Red Curtain Trilogy' films in sequence, we might conclude that, having successfully thwarted the legend of star-crossed love in his *Strictly Ballroom*, Luhrmann ups the ante in

William Shakespeare's Romeo + Juliet, attempting to do something original with Shakespeare's 'original' as the ultimate test of his directorial aspirations. Consonant with Alexandre Astruc's watershed conception of the *auteur* as a film artist who uses the camera as a figurative 'stylus' or pen, Luhrmann invents a whole new language to encompass the twists and turns of his own need to keep one step ahead of the Romeo and Juliet legend, as the filmic action unfolds through the rhythms of whip pans, lightning cuts, super macro slam zooms, static super wide shots, tight on point-of-view shots, and other vertigo-inducing angles courtesy of crash crane camerawork.[34] This highly texturised, frenetic mise-en-scène is the trademark, or, in keeping with the name of Luhrmann's production company, the 'Bazmark' of his cinematic language. And according to long time set designer and fellow collaborator Catherine Martin, Luhrmann succeeds in leaving his mark on a film whose title insists only on the mark that 'William Shakespeare' has left on the Romeo and Juliet legend: 'Whether you love or hate the film, it's completely unique and very much a director's film – it has Baz's vision stamped all over it'.[35] Martin is not alone in her assessment of the film's auteurist innovations. For example, one critic observes that '(f)rom its first image . . . Baz Luhrmann's new version of *Romeo and Juliet* proclaims its origins and originality'.[36]

[34] These camera movements are representative of Luhrmann's stylistic repertoire and are recorded throughout the screenplay by Pearce and Luhrmann. Even before the pioneering work of journals like *Cahiers du Cinema*, the earliest articulations of what would become auteur theory came from figures like Alexandre Astruc, who was writing, along with Roger Leenhardt, for *L'Ecran Français* in the early 1940s.

[35] Catherine Martin, quoted Bryce Hallet's article, 'British Love *Romeo* and Leave *Titanic*', *Sydney Morning Herald* 21 April 1998, p. 7.

[36] Hawker, p. 6.

But isn't this a paradox? How can something proclaim both its 'origins' *and* its 'originality'? As Linda Charnes might argue, such comments about Luhrmann's film bespeak an unwitting complicity in the ideology of the legendary, for

> a legend is a cultural product which depends upon the naturalizing or 'forgetting' of its own history as a manufactured thing. Always read as a paradigm for some authoritative reality, the legendary elides the space that originally existed between its own constructedness and that 'reality' to which it refers, imposing both its values and its authority as *originary* rather than derivational.[37]

Indeed, considering their stylistic innovations alone, Shakespeare's play and Luhrmann's film participate in the fantasy of eliding the gap between source and adaptation – between, in Ben Jonson's terms, 'Copie' and 'Principall' – by aspiring to produce 'original' versions of this legend of star-crossed love. But if, as the proverb implies, it is a wise character who knows his author, then it is a wise auteur who knows the character of his source: Luhrmann's 'quarrel' is not with Shakespeare but with Shakespeare's 'master', that is, *his* source. Ironically, then, in attempting to baptise the Romeo and Juliet legend anew by recontextualising the tragic referentiality of Shakespeare's language within the new citational protocols of cinematic language, Luhrmann misses the mark, paying his outstanding debt to the legend by reproducing Arthur Brooke's imagery 'to the letter'.

---

[37] Linda Charnes, *Notorious Identity: Materializing the Subject in Shakespeare* (Cambridge: Harvard University Press, 1993), p. 2.

Sticks and stones may break my bones but words will surely kill me.
– Hortense Spillers, 'Mama's Baby, Papa's Maybe:
An American Grammar Book'[38]

Luhrmann's passing reference to the 'long poem' that serves as Shakespeare's principal source for *Romeo and Juliet* clearly indicates that his desire to understand or represent the complex history of this legend is quite secondary to his hopes of placing his own 'Bazmark' on it. The relationship between Luhrmann and Brooke that emerges in *William Shakespeare's Romeo + Juliet* must, therefore, be considered in light of what Freud classifies as 'uncanny'. According to Freud, the experience of the uncanny stems from precisely this kind of vague or seemingly 'neutral' knowledge which, having been 'estranged only by the process of repression', returns in the form of a very real menace, often as a 'morbid anxiety' that serves as a harbinger of death. More important for our understanding of the signifying operations of the legendary, Freud explains that, whatever the repressed content is, this psychic and semiotic terrain cannot be traversed '*without preserving certain traces of it which can be reactivated*'.[39] As we have seen, Luhrmann reimagines *Romeo and Juliet* through the invigorating lens of his cinematic language – repressing, in the process, the primacy of Shakespeare's language. In so doing, however, he activates a far more potent force: the uncanny return of the legend and its tragic inevitability, which materialises in the correspondences between the film's cinematic innovations and their source in the

[38] Hortense Spillers, 'Mama's Baby, Papa's Maybe: An American Grammar Book', *Diacritics* (Summer 1987), p. 65.

[39] Sigmund Freud, 'The Uncanny' (1919), *Studies in Parapsychology* (New York: Collier Books, 1963), pp. 46–47, emphasis mine.

death-devoted imagery of Brooke's poem. Thus, *William Shakes-peare's Romeo + Juliet* really *is* William Shakespeare's *Romeo and Juliet* in more ways than Luhrmann could have possibly anticipated, for he inherits Shakespeare's own battle with Brooke, and, in so doing, Luhrmann confronts both the early modern and postmodern legend that reduces authorship to the 'speech in a dead language'.

Even before we explore Brooke's impact on Luhrmann's visual language, our first indication that this ghostly father is traversing *William Shakespeare's Romeo + Juliet* is suggested by the fact that the film's spoken language is, in fact, dominated by the familiar rhythms of rhymed couplets. Though rhymed couplets may seem to be the most comprehensible form of Elizabethan dialogue and, therefore, most user- and audience-friendly, Luhrmann's cast-members – with the exception of Claire Danes's Juliet – articulate the couplets in a way that draws attention to their forced, artificial, and constraining nature. Not only does this most conventional of poetic forms suggest the encroaching itinerary of the legend's signifying chain in its contrived, premeditated logic of succession, but also, these rhymed couplets bypass Shakespeare's stylistic deviations and reproduce the monolithic cadence of Arthur Brooke's poem, which is composed *exclusively* in rhymed couplets. And, lest we forget, the alienating predictability of 'witty epigrams' and 'perfect sonnets' is precisely what Luhrmann claims to *avoid* in his film. Further evidence of the possibility that Luhrmann is dealing with an itinerary more potent than his own directorial vision emerges in the prevailing image of Romeo as a knight in shining armour. While the film's depiction of Juliet as Romeo's 'bright angel' derives from Luhrmann's clever conversion of Shakespearean metaphor into cinematic pun, the parallel image of Romeo as Juliet's 'knight' is only implicit in the 'night's cloak' that panders to the lovers' clandestine affair in Shakespeare's play (2.1.117).

However, in Brooke's poem, Romeo is repeatedly referred to and described as a 'knight'. This powerful but derivative image of Romeo-as-knight suggests Luhrmann's grail-like battle against the legend even as it inscribes the impossibility of originality on the shining surface of Romeo's body.

Other details of plot and character not contained in Shakespeare's play likewise seem to cue Luhrmann's film at crucial moments. For example, both Brooke and Luhrmann build scenes of foreshadowing into Romeo and Juliet's first encounter. Just before his first meeting with Juliet, Romeo, still in the throes of an ecstasy trip, suddenly exclaims '(t)he drugs are quick' – precisely the line he utters over his own dead body once he has swallowed poison in the Capulet tomb. This example of foreshadowing remarkably reproduces Brooke's early indication of the fatal bent of Romeus's love for Juliet, as Romeus gazes upon her and proceeds to 'swallo(w) down loves sweete empoysoned bait' – lured into a love for which there is no remedy, as Brooke concludes: 'so is the poyson spred throughout his bones and vaines' (l. 211). However, the fact that in Luhrmann's film, Romeo oddly announces his 'empoysoning' even *before* he meets Juliet suggests the momentum that the legend has gathered since Shakespeare's own contention with Brooke four hundred years earlier. Another provocative correspondence between film and poem occurs immediately after Romeo and Juliet meet; before they are able to exchange words, the lovers' discourse is preempted with an invitation to dance. Brooke explains that just as Romeo is about to address himself to Juliet, another 'comely' suitor 'did fetch her forth to daunce' (l. 246); so, too, in Luhrmann's film, the 'comely' figure of Paris kidnaps Juliet as his dance partner before she and Romeo can properly introduce themselves. Luhrmann and Brooke even agree on minor plot details involving the functions of secondary characters. At the lovers' nuptial, for instance, both Luhrmann and Brooke have the Nurse bear witness to the marriage ceremony, but in Shakespeare's play she is conspicuously absent from this scene. Similarly, whereas Paris is missing from the conclusion of Luhrmann's film and Brooke's poem, he *is* present at the end of Shakespeare's play, where he dies by Romeo's hand. Yet the ongoing irony of the film's title lies in the fact that Luhrmann's film, by virtue of its correspondences with Brooke, remains *William Shakespeare's Romeo + Juliet* through and through; In other words, by inadvertently eliminating the mediation of his Shakespearean source, Luhrmann takes on Brooke 'directly' – just as Shakespeare did.

In the spirit of *Strictly Ballroom*'s liberating embrace of the *passadoble* and *Moulin Rouge!*'s thwarted attempt to bypass its own tragic ending, *William Shakespeare's Romeo + Juliet* introduces a pair of new moves that delimit both the success and failure of Luhrmann's cinematic attempt to finish the business begun by his Shakespearean source. Sizing up these innovations, *People* critic Leah Rozen disparagingly notes that Luhrmann 'piles on religious iconography and bathes the whole (film) in pointless water imagery'.[40] But these two crucial innovations couldn't be more pointed, particularly when we consider the fact that the film's ubiquitous water imagery and cross iconography are inextricably linked through the rite of baptism – specifically, the new baptism demanded by Shakespeare's Romeo as a means of escaping the tragic referentiality of his name: 'Call me but love, and I'll be new baptised:/Henceforth I never will be Romeo' (2.1.93-94). In describing the significance of water in the film, Luhrmann explains that water serves as his motif of choice for 'escape'. Romeo and Juliet 'escape into water. They use water for silence, for peace and', he adds, 'their

[40] Leah Rozen, 'Picks & Pans', *People Magazine* Nov. 1, 1996, p. 21.

"there's a place for us" moments'.[41] Water, in other words, emerges as a distinctly cinematic substitute for the ebb and flow of language through which the lovers' relationship unfolds in Shakespeare's play. For example, Juliet is first introduced to us under water as she emerges, face-up, from submergence in the bath tub; later, Romeo undergoes a similar purifying ritual when an underwater camera frames his attempt to cleanse the ecstasy from his senses, plunging his head into a basin at the Capulet Ball. Romeo and Juliet experience love-at-first-sight through the tropical waters of an aquarium – a twist to be topped only by Luhrmann's staging of the balcony scene in a swimming pool. And, finally, on the eve of the newlyweds' consummation, Romeo arrives wet with rain and leaves the next morning by way of the Capulet pool. Of course, the omnipresence of the ocean at Verona Beach locks the entire mise-en-scène into the tidal swings of Luhrmann's manic version of Shakespeare's depressing play. As in *Strictly Ballroom*, then, 'the most telling, powerful moments between Romeo and Juliet are silent ones',[42] suggesting at least a symbolic return to a pre-linguistic economy of representation, wherein image is anterior and, indeed, preferable to language. As Diana Harris speculates, ever since Australian director Jane Campion's pathbreaking film, *The Piano* (1992), 'the associations of water with a pre-symbolic, pre-meaning, fluid and free state of ideal, non-fixed being have been absorbed . . . by the Western movie-going culture, especially Australasia'.[43] Nevertheless, if the silent flow of water is Luhrmann's preferred motif

[41] Luhrmann, 'Interview', p. 14.

[42] Hawker, p. 11.

[43] I wish to thank Diana Harris for generously providing me with a copy of her unpublished conference paper, 'Violent Delights, Violent Ends: Baz Luhrmann's Romeo + Juliet', which was also presented at the Centenary Conference of Shakespeare and screen scholars in Malaga, Spain, Sept. 21–24, 1999.

for realising Romeo and Juliet's desire to be 'new baptised' into a world without referentiality, then his recourse to the clichéd description of water as Romeo and Juliet's '"there's a place for us" moments' suggests the extent to which the legend is already one step ahead of Luhrmann's attempt to liquidate it; for as we know too well, the source of this cliché is none other than that staple of Western movie-going culture, *West Side Story*, which remains *the* most famous contemporary incarnation of the Romeo and Juliet legend.

Though water is evoked in early versions of the legend through nautical references, in Brooke's poem, water imagery is deployed uniquely, serving as the singular metaphor through which he relays the 'tragicall historye' of the young lovers. For example, descriptions of desire that connect 'quenching' with 'drenching', as well as images of the sea, ships, tempests, and fishing with baited hooks flow throughout the poem. In several instances it even seems as if Brooke's distinctive use of water imagery actually provides Luhrmann with stage directions. The most stunning example of this uncanny choreographic influence emerges in Romeo and Juliet's first meeting from opposing sides of an enormous fish tank, a scene that is the most technically brilliant, affectively engaging, and seemingly original sequence in the entire film. Luhrmann's camera produces a series of floating eye-line matches that follow Romeo and Juliet's gaze as they dart about in search of each other through the strobe-like glint of water, fish, and wonder that characterises this surreal love-at-first sight sequence. At times the lovers blend so perfectly with the scenery that it is difficult to distinguish their flirtatious eyes from the flitting motion of the fish that both pander to and prevent Romeo and Juliet's face-to-face meeting. It is remarkable, then, to find that this stunning scene is virtually duplicated in Brooke's poem, which describes a similar dance of gazes between the lovers. This passage begins with Romeus experiencing the whirlwind emotions of love-at-first-sight, and bears quoting at length:

> When Romeus saw himselfe in this tempest tost
> Where both was hope of pleasant port, and daunger to be lost,
> He doubtefull ska(r)sely knew what countenance to keepe;
> In Lethies floud his wonted flames were quenched and drenched deepe,
> Yea he forgets himselfe . . . .
> But onely seeketh by her sight to feede his houngry eyes.
> Through them he swalloweth downe loves sweete empoysonde baite,
> How surely are the wareless wrapt by those that lye in wayte?
> So is the poyson spred throughout his bones and vaines . . . .
> At last her floting eyes were ancored fast on him,
> Who for her sake dyd banishe health and fredome from eche limme . . . .
>
> His whetted arrow loosde, so touchd her to the quicke,
> That through the eye it strake the hart, and there the hedde did sticke.
> It booted not to strive, for why, she wanted strength:
> The weaker aye unto the strong of force must yeld at length.
> The pomps now of the feast her heart gyns to despyse
> And onely joyeth when her eyen meete with her lovers eyes.
> When theyr new smitten heartes had fed on loving gleames,
> Whilst passing too and fro theyr eyes ymingled were theyr beames,
> Eche of these lovers gan by others lookes to knowe
> That frendship in their brest had roote, and both would have it grow.   (l. 211–15; 218–21; 225–6; 233–422)

Unwittingly, and with extraordinary economy, Luhrmann's salt water aquarium converts Brooke's encumbered poetry into unspoken eloquence.

Precisely in its *deviations* from Shakespeare, then, Luhrmann's film reveals its 'primal baptism' as *William Shakespeare's Romeo + Juliet*, unconsciously reproducing the Bard's head-on confrontation with Brooke's *Tragicall Historye*.[43] Apropos of the film's peculiar repressions and displacements, Geoffrey Nowell-Smith has argued that, inherent to the project of adapting literature into film, is the uncanny process whereby repressions of plot and dialogue return as hysterical moments in the mise-en-scène. So, too, Luhrmann's repression of Shakespeare's language and details of plot return to haunt his mise-en-scène in the form of Brooke's increasingly *sinister* water imagery. In fact, in Brooke's poem, water does not function in the same way as it does in Luhrmann's film. Far from signifying escape, water connotes entrapment, becoming a crucial accessory in the legend's quest to bait, ensnare, and hook its unwitting victims.

---

[43] It is important to note that words – especially names – according to early modern linguistic theory, are easier unsaid than undone. For example, when Romeo exclaims 'call me but love/and I'll be new baptised', he is denying his 'primal baptism', or, the preordained plan that names were believed to contain for their recipients. The argument favored in the Renaissance maintained that there was a likeness and perhaps even a destiny inferable in the relationship between words and the things they characterised. This view, clearly based on the logic of *auctoritas*, conceived of words as conferring knowledge 'not immediately obvious', but rather, as 'a legacy of the wisdom of the past'. (See Jane Donawerth, *Shakespeare and the Sixteenth-Century Study of Language* [Urbana: University of Illinois Press, 1984] p. 31). This claim was particularly compelling when it came to names – including descriptive titles such as *William Shakespeare's Romeo + Juliet* – for as the educator Richard Mulcaster argued: 'God himself . . . doth plainlie declare . . . what a cunning thing it is to giue right names, and how necessary it is, to know their forces, which be allredie giuen' (quoted in Donawerth p. 29).

Accordingly, as the volume of water steadily increases in Luhrmann's film – from establishing shots of Romeo and Juliet through the domestic waters of bath tubs and sinks, to their courtship by way of an aquarium and, finally, to Luhrmann's brilliant inversion of the balcony-as-swimming pool – the more we realise that what these images conjure is not escape but *enclosure*. Indeed, the fear that Romeo and Juliet may be drowning in the waters of their new baptism is implied by their frequent lunges under water to avoid the ubiquitous eye of the Capulet surveillance cameras. During the balcony scene, for example, as the guard dog barks and the security camera pans the rippling surface of the pool, Romeo and Juliet submerge themselves; with their hair streaming under water, they stare at each other – as Luhrmann directs them – 'like two beautiful fish', suggesting a surreal but eerie sequel to their initial courtship through the aquarium.[44] But Romeo and Juliet, while certainly beautiful, will drown if they cannot come up for air, despite the fact that Luhrmann makes it look as though they can breathe underwater indefinitely through each other's mouths. This swimming pool scene thus marks the beginning of the 'hysterical' and, indeed, tragic conversion of Luhrmann's mise-en-scène, as the film follows the flow of *The Tragicall Historye*'s scenery and staging from pleasure to 'poyson'. Consequently, in *William Shakespeare's Romeo + Juliet*, the next image of fish underwater is inflected with gratuitous violence, as Mercutio is shown shooting fish with his gun while wading into the ocean – a proleptic vision, much like the earlier allusion to the 'drugs' from which Romeo will die – of the gunshot with which Juliet, the 'beautiful fish', will lay herself to rest at the film's conclusion.

[44] Baz Luhrmann and Craig Pearce, *Screenplay. William Shakespeare's Romeo + Juliet. The Contemporary Film, The Classic Play* (New York: Bantam Doubleday Dell, 1996), p. 66.

It has long been acknowledged that in Shakespeare's play the tragic turning point occurs following the deadly clash between Tybalt and Romeo, which is also the scene that critics have traditionally identified as the structural knot or figurative 'navel' of the Romeo and Juliet legend. In Brooke's poem the far-reaching effects of this pivotal encounter are registered in the chaos of the natural elements, as Brooke likens the fight to a meteorological disturbance:

> Even as two thunderboltes, throwne downe out of the skye,
> That through the ayre the massy earth and seas have power to flye,
> So met these two. (l. 1031–1033).

In Luhrmann's film, this same image of thunderbolts crackling over the seas is produced through cinematic special effects, specifically, through an optical insert of a storm breaking over the ocean as Romeo and Tybalt fight. Following this fatal conflict, Romeo gazes up into the sky and, as a mixture of blood and rain stream down his face, he sways deliriously from side to side, crying: 'O, I am fortune's fool!' In Brooke we find a parallel description of Romeus as a 'broosed barke in cruell seas betost' (l. 1363) – a personification not only of ficklo Fortune, but also of the male body in pain – a spectacle that Luhrmann's camera fetishises throughout this sequence. Both poem and film proceed to describe the storm giving way to a calm as Romeo arrives at Juliet's chamber soaked with rain and weary from battle. Brooke's version of this scene could easily provide the voice-over for Luhrmann's silent rendering of Romeo and Juliet's bittersweet reunion and sexual consummation:

In stormy wind and wave, in daunger to be lost,
Thy steerless ship (O Romeus) hath been long while betost.
The seas we new appeased, and thou by happy starre
Art comme in sight of quiet haven and, now the wrackfull barre,
Is hid with swelling tyde, boldly thou mayst resort
Unto thy wedded ladies bed, thy long desyred port. (l. 799–804)

But this calm after the storm is short-lived, for Romeo must speed to Mantua as decreed by his banishment. In keeping with the sea-faring metaphors that predominate in *The Tragicall Historye*, Brooke's friar proceeds to assure Romeo that while he is gone, Juliet will remain the 'ancor of (his) blisse', for

Unto a valiant hart there is no banishment,
All countrys are his native soyle beneath the firmament.
As to the fishe the sea. (l. 1443–1445).

From the perspective of the film, however, there appears to be something fishy about this assurance, for as Luhrmann's Romeo departs Juliet's bedchamber with a dramatic plunge into the pool, he sinks under the weight of her 'ill-divining soul', which proves to be anchored to the itinerary of the legend. Staring down at her 'beautiful fish' as the water folds ominously over him, Juliet's silent admiration is suddenly usurped by Shakespearean verse and her own disembodied voice, as she articulates this tragic itinerary through clenched teeth:

O God . . .
Methinks I see thee, now thou art so low,
As one dead in the bottom of a tomb.

At this moment all three versions of the Romeo and Juliet legend enter into alignment with each other, as Shakespeare's verse and Brooke's imagery conspire to convert Luhrmann's baptismal fantasy of rebirth into a watery tomb.

To describe this sequence as the structural knot of Luhrmann's film is also to imply its connection with hysteria, for what emerges in this scene is a revealing equation of 'tomb' and 'womb'.[45] In the context of Lacanian psychoanalysis, the navel and the knot are interchangeable signifiers for the knotted scar that closes off re-entry to the womb and with it, the possibility of returning to a pre-linguistic or 'imaginary' universe that precedes the subject's alienation into language and the responsibilities of the symbolic order. Long considered to be hysteria's mythical locus of origin, the womb is both a site and a symbol that inspires fantasies of self-creation and fears of mortality, encoding 'a message about how we are haunted by the elusive and protean sense of vulnerability, implenitude, and fallibility, even while the mise-en-scène of desire created by phantasy work seeks to hide this traumatic knowledge'.[46] Though

[45] While the womb/tomb equation may be found throughout Shakespeare's plays and, for that matter, throughout literature in general, the point to be stressed here is that this hysterical conversion is driven by Brooke's poem. For Luhrmann's attempt to prioritize his visual language over Shakespeare's language traces an imagistic arc directly back to Brooke's *Tragicall Historye*, exposing the legendary 'origin' of Luhrmann's presumed 'innovations'. For an example of the womb/tomb analogy in Romeo and Juliet – a couplet that Luhrmann omits – see Friar Laurence's reflections on 'the grey-eyed morn': 'The earth, that's nature's mother, is her tomb./ What is her burying grave, that is her womb' (2.3.9–10).

[46] See Elisabeth Bronfen's extensive analysis of hysteria in *The Knotted Subject: Hysteria and Its Discontents* (Princeton: Princeton University Press, 1998), pp. xv. Lacan's concept of the imaginary, symbolic, and Real stages of identification are fundamental to his theory of psychoanalysis and may be found throughout his work.

no longer classified as a clinical phenomenon, the hysterical performance typically revolves around the conversion of psychic trauma into bodily symptoms that serve to camouflage the real source of the problem and, consequently, prevent the cure that would put an end to its protective fantasies of self-fashioning. In its dizzying subversion of origins, hysteria, as Freud frequently lamented, baffles not only diagnosis but also the fabled psychoanalytic 'talking cure' and, in effect, language itself. It follows, then, that a film might simulate an hysterical performance by displacing a disturbance of its textual narrative onto its imagery or mise-en-scène. If so, our understanding of hysteria – with its self-conscious sense of performance, provisionality, and multiplicity – must be extended beyond the psychoanalytic to the realm of *cultural* pathologies. In the context of contemporary culture, Elisabeth Bronfen persuasively argues that the hysterical performance has been most provocatively redefined as a powerful and quintessentially postmodern trope 'for dissatisfied desire in general'.[47] We might consider, therefore, how the seemingly pathological subversion of linguistic origins performed by Luhrmann's film might function *homeo*pathically to counter the dead language of the legend, as well as to perform enabling alternatives to the theoretical diagnosis of and prognosis for authorship within postmodern culture. But the hysterical crux of *William Shakespeare's Romeo + Juliet* – the point at which its repressed legendary origin returns to haunt the film's fantasy of escape – occurs when Romeo mouths the word 'adieu' as he disappears beneath the dark surface of the Capulet pool, for this is an image that knots together Luhrmann's cinematic vision of new baptism with Brooke's tenacious inscriptions of death-by-drowning. At this moment Luhrmann's suggestive image of the pool-as-

[47] Bronfen, p, 384.

birthing-apparatus from which to create a new version of the legend undergoes a conversion from life to death, womb to tomb – an image which, as we have seen in *West Side Story*, recurs in Riff and Tony's refrain, 'Birth ta earth!'/'Womb ta tomb'.

While this scene occurs just after the midpoint of Shakespeare's play, in Luhrmann's film fewer than twenty minutes of running time remain – a clear indication that the legend is gaining momentum en route to its destination. Luhrmann has one more visual trick up his sleeve, however, for the film's omnipresent cross imagery replenishes the promise of rebirth where the baptismal waters run dry. But in this postmodern world filled with kitschified Mary and Jesus figurines, the crosses that appear on every surface from flesh to formica are all but emptied of their redemptive power. It is no wonder, therefore, that most critics have labelled Luhrmann's cross-laden mise-en-scène pointless, or worse, blasphemous. The real blasphemy lies in the fact that Luhrmann's exploitation of cross iconography is, perhaps, less concerned with exposing a religion bereft of devotion than it is with unveiling a whole new cult of the 'Bazmark' – the name of Luhrmann's production company. Recalling the comments made by set-designer Catherine Martin, this 'mark' emerges in her contention that *William Shakespeare's Romeo + Juliet* 'has Baz's vision stamped all over it'. Martin's comments invoke the classic and virtually obsolete conception of the *auteur*, whose stylistic signature is unmistakably inscribed in the film and is capable of overcoming all barriers to its articulation. What has replaced this romanticised figure, as Timothy Corrigan argues in *A Cinema without Walls*, is the Warhol-like spectacle of the 'commercially conditioned auteur', whose 'aesthetic', per se, resides in an easily duplicated marketing plan. Yet Corrigan also adds that if there are any authors 'alive' in postmodern culture, then they are to be found in film. Unlike their modernist counterparts, however, these commercially conditioned auteurs have no presumptions about becoming a controlling presence in film production; rather they focus their creative energies on proleptically generating 'commercial strategies for organizing audience *reception*'.[48] In this bottom-line environment, then, authorial originality is a by-product of supply and demand. But in Luhrmann's film this postmodern privileging of reception over production, commercial paratext over film-text, might prove to be the only means of escaping the itinerary of the legend. In other words, where Baz can't leave his mark on the legend, he leaves it safely outside its clutches, blazoning the cross trademark coined in the film's title on promotional trailers released before the film, an MTV special aired during the film, and the videocassette and DVD covers manufactured after the film's commercial run. Thus, with the help of the 'Bazmark', Luhrmann emerges as a 'brand-name vision that precedes and succeeds the film',[49] becoming a kind of legend in his own right.

This '+' or cross also marks one final point of resistance to the dead letter buried in Shakespeare's version of the legend, resonating as Luhrmann's most conspicuous attempt to replace word with image. In his effort to reach 'the street sweeper' as well as 'the Queen of England', Luhrmann recognises that his marketing of the film must dispense with the high cultural mystique of Shakespearean drama.[50] A particularly efficient means of announcing, if not accomplishing, this objective is to convert the 'and' in Shakespeare's title to a simple 'plus' sign, a commonplace of elementary maths as well as a symbol of religious devotion. But as Pierre Macherey explains of such

---

[48] See Timothy Corrigan's brilliant chapter entitled 'The Commerce of Auteurism' in his book *A Cinema Without Walls: Movies and Culture after Vietnam* (New Brunswick: Rutgers University Press, 1991), pp. 101–136, p. 103 (emphasis mine).

[49] Corrigan, p. 102.

[50] Luhrmann, 'Note', p. i.

attempts to desublimate works that give rise to 'the religion of art', before 'disposing of these works . . . men have to *produce* them'.[51] Paradoxically, he concludes, 'creation is the release of what is already there' and, therefore, the '"creative process" is, precisely not a process, a labour, it is a religious formula to be found on funeral monuments'.[52] There could be no more poignant literalisation of this fatalistic philosophy than the conclusion of Luhrmann's film, wherein no amount of creativity can convert Romeo and Juliet's funeral monument into a reversal of what's 'already in' the destination prescribed by the legend. In the superlative Capulet funeral monument, that is, the Catholic cathedral wherein Juliet's still-slumbering body has been placed, the redemptive force of Luhrmann's two 'innovations' – the baptismal water imagery and the cross iconography – flow together in the spectacular image of the neon-blue sea of crosses, inadvertently generating yet another uncanny invocation of Brooke's image of Romeus and Juliet living together 'in (a) place of endlesse light and bliss' (l. 2787). The force of this final image is so seductive that, if we just squint our eyes, we can imagine Romeo and Juliet floating, swimming in the bliss of their first rendezvous in the Capulet swimming pool. Luhrmann even delays the inevitable tragedy by having Juliet awake just before Romeo consumes the poison, dashing the vial from his lips after it is – barely – too late.[53]

[51] Macheray, p. 231

[52] Ibid., p. 232.

[53] It is important to note that even this seemingly innovative approach to the lovers' death has its origins not just in the Italianate tradition but also in early *performances* of the legend, such as the eighteenth-century theatrical productions of David Garrick as well as nineteenth- and twentieth-century opera stagings. Luhrmann, whose career extends to opera, would certainly be familiar with several variations on the play's conclusion.

And when Juliet kills herself with Romeo's gun, the camera cranes higher and higher to obscure any hint of blood. Significantly, Luhrmann's original plan for this scene was to have a 'wash of deep red blood floo(d) across them both', but it seems as though he couldn't bear the finality of that image.[54] Rather, the camera transports us from the sea of candles back to the swimming pool and a freeze-frame of Romeo and Juliet's underwater kiss. As the purifying baptismal waters rush over the lovers one last time, Luhrmann's remarks betray defeat: 'That final image when they kiss under water', he says with chagrin, 'it's just silence'.[55]

But this, too, is wishful thinking, for amid the faint aftershock of Juliet's fatal gunshot, we hear the whispers of 'ghostly fathers' other than Shakespeare and Brooke chiding Luhrmann for his presumption in seeking to escape the inevitable, as he did so deftly in *Strictly Ballroom*. If, as Slavoj Žižek explains, 'The letter which "arrives at its destination" is also a letter of request for outstanding debts',[56] then while *Strictly Ballroom*'s Scott and Frannie are able to overcome the ghostly agendas of dead-beat parents seeking to double-cross their best laid plans, Luhrmann's Romeo and Juliet must pay the debt left in their wake as the 'original' star-crossed lovers. Accordingly, Lacan contends that the letter arrives at its destination when 'the sender

54 Pearce and Luhrmann, p. 160.

55 Luhrmann, 'Interview', p. 14.

56 Slavoj Žižek, *Enjoy Your Symptom! Jacques Lacan in Hollywood and Out* (New York: Routledge, 1992), p. 16. While *Strictly Ballroom* is not a 'strict' treatment of the Romeo and Juliet legend, in that the animosity lies more with the parents' generation than with the youths, the film implies – had Luhrmann not altered the tragic trajectory – that the 'ancient grudge' would be perpetuated in the dance tastes and partner preferences of the younger generation. In other words, the parents' strife would have been reconstituted in the intersubjective network of their children.

... receives ... his own message in reverse form',[57] and, consequently, this is precisely what happens when we realise that the Bazmark – the insignia of Luhrmann's authorial agency – actually materialises the agency of the *legend* in the form of star-*crossed* love. Not even Luhrmann's final attempt to thwart this tragic itinerary in the film's ending, wherein Romeo and Juliet are only a blink away from escaping double suicide, can halt the momentum of the (dead) letter that seeks to settle outstanding accounts. For although this conclusion is nowhere to be found in Shakespeare's play or Arthur Brooke's poem, this ending is, ironically, a to-the-letter rendering of Matteo Bandello's conclusion – Arthur Brooke's principal source – and that of Bandello's source, Luigi Da Porto.[58] And so the slippery slope of the legend leads away from Brooke only to further entrench Luhrmann's film in the deadly echoes of ghostly fathers of other legendary accounts, all of them clamouring for breath. As Linda Charnes concludes, then, the legend, while 'steadily leading us toward the "promised end", ... promises absolutely nothing'.[59]

Yet Luhrmann has delivered the end he promised: to make a movie 'the way Shakespeare might have if he had been a filmmaker'. Luhrmann's glib leap from the early modern to the postmodern brings this analysis back to the peculiar questions with which we began. Is the Shakespearean text always already

---

[57] See Jacques Lacan's famous 'Seminar on "The Purloined Letter"', translated by Jeffrey Mehlman, in *The Purloined Poe: Lacan, Derrida, and Psychoanalytic Reading*, edited by John P. Muller and William J. Richardson (Baltimore: Johns Hopkins UP, 1988), pp. 28–54, pp. 52–53.

[58] What we have here, as Žižek might conclude, 'is an exemplary case of how "a letter arrives at its destination" when, in a totally contingent way, it finds its proper place' (*Enjoy Your Symptom!* 19). See *Enjoy Your Symptom! Jacques Lacan in Hollywood and Out* (London and New York: Routledge, 1992).

[59] Charnes, *Notorious Identity*, p. 75.

postmodern? Is Luhrmann's filmmaking practice indebted to something indelibly early modern? Initiating this dialogue between the early modern and the postmodern through the mediation of the legendary does not merely satisfy the urge, as Stephen Greenblatt memorably put it, 'to speak with the dead';[60] rather, as in *Hamlet*, this double projection poses a challenge *from* the dead who *talk back*. In *William Shakespeare's Romeo + Juliet*, this image of the dead who talk back emerges in the burned-out movie house of Sycamore Grove, the spectre, as Luhrmann describes it, of 'a once splendid cinema' in ruins.[61] In the futuristic landscape of Verona Beach, Sycamore Grove gestures bleakly towards the destination of cinema in the age of home theater, YouTube, and the digital revolution, as film itself becomes the victim of its own 'commercial conditioning' gone awry. It is almost as if, in staging the death of his own medium, Luhrmann takes his place as one more ghostly father calling out from the ruins for surrogate lives. But ruins imply an incomplete destruction – being at once degenerate and regenerate – and, as such, Sycamore Grove might be described as a monument to the difference between creation and adaptation. For if creation, in Machery's description, is 'the release of what's already there', then adaptation is what occurs in its aftermath. Contrary to the theoretical legends that explain it away as a compulsion to repeat the past, adaptation, in Leo Braudy's words, is 'unfinished *cultural* business',[62] a point which, as we shall see, is taken up with a vengeance in the film's tenacious afterlives.

[60] Greenblatt, *Shakespearean Negotiations* (Berkeley: University of California Press, 1988), p. i.

[61] Pearce and Luhrmann, p. 17.

[62] This idea is explored in Leo Braudy's 'Afterword: Rethinking Remakes' in *Play it Again, Sam. Retakes on Remakes*, edited by Andrew Horton and Stuart Y. McDougal (Berkeley: University of California Press, 1998), pp. 327–34.

PART 3:

Critical responses and the afterlife of the play's adaptations

West Side success

It is hard to believe that *West Side Story* was originally to be called 'East Side Story', featuring a forbidden love affair between a Catholic and a Jew during Easter/Passover. Jerome Robbins approached Bernstein with this proposal in January 1949; after some time, Arthur Laurents, who would eventually write the book on which both the play and film were based, complained that the project 'was *Abie's Irish Rose* to music and (he) wouldn't have any part of it'.[1] *Abie's Irish Rose*, which revolves around a relationship between a Jew (Abie) and a Catholic (Rose), focuses on issues of assimilation and the triumph of the 'melting pot' theory of America, and was the most successful Broadway show of the Twenties. Robbins argued that he had come up with something quite different, for the play he proposed would not only be a musical, but a tragedy – 'a contemporary version of *Romeo and Juliet* . . . .'[2] Laurents, Robbins, and Bernstein continued their discussions because they found themselves equally drawn to the theme of a socially impossible love story; however, by the mid-fifties, they agreed that the situation for Jews and, for that matter, the Irish, had improved substantially, and

---

[1] Laurents, quoted in Joan Peyser, *Bernstein: A Biography* (New York: Beech Tree, 1987) pp. 265–66.

[2] *Ibid.*

the pairing was not as compelling as it had been before the War. Bernstein wrote at the time that they were jazzed 'by the *Romeo* notion; only now we have abandoned the Jewish-Catholic premise as not very fresh, and have come up with what I think is going to be it: two teenage gangs, one the warring Puerto Ricans, the other 'self-styled' Americans'.[3] The new idea was truly a revelation, as it came to Bernstein as he sat at a pool in Beverly Hills, relaxing in the midst of writing the score for *On the Waterfront*. He recalls sitting there with Laurents and commiserating

> about what a shame it was that the original West Side Story didn't work out. Then, lying next to us on somebody's abandoned chair was a newspaper headline, 'GANG FIGHTS'. We stared at each other and realized that this – in New York – was it. The Puerto Rican thing had just begun to explode, and we called Jerry (Jerome Robbins), and that's the way *West Side Story* – as opposed to East Side Story – was born.[4]

Although enthusiasm was running high, when the group approached lyricist Stephen Sondheim, he was, at first, a surprisingly tough sell, bluntly telling Berstein that 'I can't do this show. . . I've never been that poor and I've never even met a Puerto Rican'.[5] Sondheim was eventually persuaded and, along with screenwriter Ernest Lehman, the five-member dream team collaboration was born.

[3] Leonard Bernstein, *Findings* (New York: Doubleday, 1993), p. 148.

[4] Bernstein, quoted in Al Kasha and Joel Hirschorn, *Notes on Broadway: Conversations with the Great Songwriters* (Chicago: Contemporary, 1985), p. 15.

[5] Stephen Sondheim, quoted in Alberto Sandoval, 'West Side Story: A Puerto Rican Reading of "America"', *Jump Cut* 39 (1994), p. 65.

Contrary to our expectations, given the success of the film, the Broadway musical that opened in New York in 1957 had a poor showing at the Tony Awards, losing in nearly every category for which it was nominated to *The Music Man*. The latter production evidently fit more comfortably into audiences' expectations for the musical genre which, not unlike Shakespeare's comedies, is driven by heterosexual pairings that often end – happily – in marriage. According to Stacy Wolf, the reviews of the Broadway version of *West Side Story* were generally 'positive but predictably anxious':

> critics commented on Robbins's astonishing use of dance to tell the story; on Bernstein's complex and unified, 'high art' score built on the short theme of a tritone plus a half-step up (the first three notes of 'Maria'); on Sondheim's capturing of an urban youth vernacular; and on the musical's contemporary, acerbic content and despairing ending. (366–67)

Latino reviewers, however, didn't waste any time criticising what they considered to be a racist treatment of Puerto Ricans, heaping blame on Sondheim in particular for his lyrics, which led him to revise the highly controversial 'America' number for the film version. But oh what a difference four years makes. By 1961, *West Side Story* swept the Oscars; and in a kind of historical irony, this film adaptation – originally focused on Jewish-Catholic relations – substantially beat its only major competitor: *Judgment at Nuremberg*.

After its world premiere at New York's Rivoli Theatre on 18 October, 1961, critics were nothing if not carried away by the film. Ecstatic, *New York Times* critic Bosley Crowther led with the headline 'Musical Advance', explaining that the film broke new ground for screened musicals. In his subheading 'Unconventional', Crowther contends that *West Side Story* 'departs from the convention that music and dance are used in motion pictures to convey only fun stuff or, at most, charming, tender sentiments. It bucks the esthetic barrier imposed by the photograph, the conditioning of the mind to expect the literal in strongly pictured quasi-reality'.[6] In other words, the film not only earned respect for the genre of musical film, but, also, it seamlessly combined cinematic realism with the theatrical suspension of disbelief, moving between these modes with an ease never before witnessed. However, a small minority of audience members didn't buy in to the film's narrative juxtapositions, as a 'few snickers . . . during the transitions from naturalism into fancifulness' were detectable; but, Crowther adds, 'this is to be expected with any effort to go beyond the bounds of the familiar. Moviemakers have always had to fight the inertia of the conventional-minded, especially with musical films'.[7] In other words, Crowther applauded the 1961 film adaptation as *the* definitive version of a story which, he argued, 'cried to be released in the freer and less restricted medium of the mobile photograph . . . .'[8] Be it the 'mobile photograph' or the 'moving picture', film – so the consensus among critics went – liberated *West Side Story* from the constraints of theatre, showcasing the talent of choreographer Jerome Robbins in particular, whose dance routines poignantly 'conveyed the wild emotion that burns in these youngsters' tough, lithe frames'.[9] Indeed, these young, tensed bodies carry the burden of the Romeo and Juliet legend with them everywhere they go, brilliantly betraying a world-weariness (as we have seen with characters like 'A-Rab' – 'you wuz

[6] Bosley Crowther, 'Musical Advance: The "West Side Story" Expands on Screen', *The New York Times* 22 October 1961, p. X1.

[7] Ibid.

[8] Bosley Crowther, 'Film at the Rivoli is Called Masterpiece', *The New York Times* 19 Oct. 1961: p. 39.

[9] Ibid.

never my age') that youths should neither know nor suffer. Interestingly, given the universal acclaim for Robbins, little was made of the fact that he was forced to abandon the production after approximately two-and-a-half months, leaving film's principal director Robert Wise to complete the all-important gymnasium and rumble routines. The only weakness in the production, according to most reviewers, was Richard Beymer's portrayal of Tony, the Polish boy who wants a way out of his dead-end life, which he finds, both figuratively and literally, in Maria.

In comparing both of Crowther's rave reviews, we find one particularly provocative theme, namely, the selective 'hearing' that this famous *New York Times* journalist – then in his mid-fifties – brings to bear on his analysis of the film. Clearly *not* a member of the younger generation, Crowther's sympathies lie elsewhere; paraphrasing Doc's moralising line as follows, 'You kids make this world lousy! When will you stop?' Crowther proceeds to herald this explanation as 'a cry that should be heard by thoughtful people – sympathetic people – all over the land'.[10] What he misses is the more poignant rejoinder to Doc's accusation, uttered by the incendiary man-child 'Action': '*We* didn't make it, Doc'. Ironically, inscribed in the reviews themselves is the yet-unbridged generation gap which, in both *Romeo and Juliet* and *West Side Story*, kills.

West Side Story was also a key player in what would soon materialise as the break-up of the Hollywood Studio System, which had dominated the industry with its constricting contractual arrangements, star system, and elaborate, strings-attached financing for more than half a century. Taking a long view of the 1962 Oscars, Murray Schumach explains that 'the awards this year were a dramatic illustration of how far the independent producer-directors

[10] Ibid.

have become the dominant creative forces of the American movie industry'.[11] Both *West Side Story* and *Judgment at Nuremberg* were produced without major studio backing, and released, as Schumach observes, 'through United Artists, which does not have a studio, and which finances only those movies made by independents'; in fact, as Schumach notes with irrepressible satisfaction, '(n)ot a single award went to a picture made by one of the major movie studios'.[12] Moreover, all of the five nominees for Best Picture were 'indies', continuing the precedent set by the 1960 Oscars, when Billy Wilder's *The Apartment* – also an independent film release by United Artists – won Best Picture. Speaking to the merits of musical film in particular, long considered 'box-office poison in Hollywood', Seymour Peck observed that *West Side Story* had almost single-handedly reversed this trend. 'One reason', according to Peck, for the lack of screen musicals' popularity 'is that foreign audiences, so important to the movie industry since American audiences drifted away to TV, have not responded to American musicals – possibly because their plots are insubstantial, or because all those songs in English, even when translated in subtitles, grow tiresome to moviegoers in Tokyo or Barcelona'.[13] But *West Side Story* changed all that, and in 1961, some twenty film musicals followed in its wake. In anticipation of the success of *West Side Story* (even before the film debuted), Warner Brothers broke a record in September of 1961 by paying $5,500,000 for the rights to screen *My Fair Lady*.[14] Jule Styne, a major

[11] Murray Schumach, '"West Side Story" Wins Oscar as Best Film', *The New York Times* 10 April 1962, p. 47.

[12] Ibid.

[13] Seymour Peck, 'Again the Movies Sing and Dance', 2 Jul. 1961: p. SM16.

[14] Eugene Archer, 'Filmed Musicals are on Increase', *The New York Times* 30 Sept. 1961, p. 16.

player in stage and screen musicals of the day, explained – rather prophetically – that what was needed to keep the trend alive was an entrepreneurial model (not unlike Timothy Corrigan's 'commercially-conditioned auteur') that wages 'a smart, long-range publicity campaign', including 'advance touring companies of stage shows in Europe, coupled with heavy promotion of American songs and records on television and radio disc jockey shows abroad'.[15]

This formula worked brilliantly for *West Side Story*, for internationally, both the play and the film were a sweeping success and, it bears mention, much less controversial. Even the Queen of England herself 'braved a London snowstorm' to watch the picture. Evidently the first time in four years that she had ventured out to the cinema to see the Royal Film Show, the Queen thoroughly enjoyed herself, commending Yul Brynner – who happened to attend the screening – for his work with the United Nations as 'a special advisor on refugee problems'.[16] In Paris, a fascinating accommodation was made for the non-English speaking audiences who attended the stage version of *West Side Story*, as a cinema screen was raised above the stage in order to incorporate subtitles – a strategy that Baz Luhrmann would repeat for US audiences in his operatic re-telling of *Romeo and Juliet: La Boheme* (2002). The response to the performance – despite, as one reviewer notes, the dancers' almost falling in one 'slippery spot near the footlights' – was overwhelmingly positive.[17] So, too, despite rising Cold War tensions, the

---

[15] Jule Styne, quoted in Archer p. 16.

[16] 'Queen Goes to Film: Elizabeth Braves Snowstorm to See "West Side Story"', *The New York Times* 27 February 1962, p. 27.

[17] Milton Bracker, 'West Side Story Greeted in Paris', *The New York Times* 31 March 1961, p. 22.

film adaptation of *West Side Story* played to an enthusiastic crowd during its appearance in the Soviet Film Festival. But before the screening there was one caveat issued – by, oddly enough, *Nuremberg* director Stanley Kramer – who 'reminded the audience that "West Side Story" portrayed only one side of American city life', lest the crowd come away from the film assuming that New York, the holy city of American capitalism, was a violent place filled with guns, gangs, and immigrants (which, of course, it was).[18] Naturally the Soviets, known for the best ballet companies in the world (such as the Bolshoi and the Kirov), found the dance sequences particularly inspiring.

However, as indicated above, *West Side Story* did not fare well with Puerto Rican audiences, who felt stereotyped as either sexy spitfires or predatory punks. The principal argument raised by the film's major critics has to do with the 'authenticity' of the represen-tation of Puerto Ricans – both in terms of casting *and* acting. George Chakiris, for example, who was made to play the part of Bernardo in brownface, has been derided for his 'flawed accent and eccentric Spanish pronunciation . . . .';[19] the fact that the role won him an Oscar underscores the depth of *mis*understanding that has come to define *West Side Story* for Latinos. (That the casting of Natalie Wood in the part of Maria was particularly troubling goes without saying.) Historically underrepresented or, more often, mis-represented in films, Latinos are a multiracial people, whose status as such has been violently reduced on screen to a set of 'visual and aural devices . . . mobilised to signify the(ir) specificity . . . .'[20]

[18] '"West Side Story" is Applauded in Soviet Film Festival Showing', *The New York Times* 9 July 1963, p. 28.

[19] Negrón-Muntaner, p. 91.

[20] Ibid.

Chakiris's performance epitomises how these falsifying devices function, as a stylised accent and make-up come to reflect all that is quintessentially 'Puerto Rican'. Nevertheless, Puerto Ricans were not really surprised by the casting decisions, for their scarcity on screen was so egregious that, as late as 1995, when the film *My Family/Mi Familia* was produced, it was lauded as 'the first . . . English-language theatrical release targeted at Latinos where every single character is played by a Latino, not Marisa Tomei, not Lou Diamond Phillips, not Angelica Houston'.[21]

Another enduring problem for Latino audiences is the pronounced absence of 'Puerto Rican blacks' from the production, which, as one critic observes:

> makes the 'epidermal' differences secondary, even an aesthetic affectation. Brownface in this case is a way to get outside of 'white' skin – although not too far – and into the skin of another without risk. It is the analogy of tourism and ethnic dining, with the 'Latino' style and music connoting everything opposed to rigidity and repression: a boundless energy and irrepressible sexuality.[22]

Reporting on the 1962 Oscars – a big night for *West Side Story*, to say the least – Murray Schumach notes in his description of the gala that

> (o)ne attempt to mar the holiday atmosphere was averted by the police. They broke up an attempt to picket the ceremony by

21 Santiago Nieves and Frank Algarin 'Two Reviews: *My Family/Mi Familia* and the *Perez Family*', in *Latin Looks: Images of Latinas and Latinos in the U.S. Media* (Boulder, Colorado and Oxford: Westview Press, 1997), pp. 221–24, p. 221.

22 Negrón-Muntaner, p. 92.

members of the Hollywood Race Relations Bureau. This Negro group, which has been disavowed by the National Association for the Advancement of Colored People, said it was demonstrating to call attention to its claim that Negroes are not fairly portrayed in movies.[23]

Again, as with Crowther, Schumach misses the point: the protest outside was inspired by what was going on *inside*; the picketers were trying to convey that the 'universal' acclaim for *West Side Story* was not received as such by minority groups – adding to the generation gap a fundamental lack of racial understanding that the film itself addresses – a situation that would begin to be redressed by the then-burgeoning Civil Rights movement.

Another conspicuous absence from the film commentary of the period was any discussion of two of *West Side Story*'s more unusual characters, Baby John and Anybodys. In a sophisticated, contemporary reading of the film's sex and gender dynamics, Frances Negrón-Muntaner offers the following observation:

In *West Side Story*, the gangs are also themselves differently gendered and sexualized. While the Sharks are solidly heterosexual and self-contained as a single ethnic group, the Jets are constantly menaced by the specter of homosexuality and gender splits. In this sense, the narrative offers spaces of identification with the Jets not only because they are 'white', but because they are site of negotiation concerning gender and sexual identity, a possibility not available to the Sharks. This gender/sex negotiation is easily glossed over in race-centered discussions of the film, in part because it takes places on the

[23] Schumach, p. 47.

narrative's margins through the characters of Baby John and Anybodys.[24]

Indeed, in the midst of the debate over whether or not Puerto Ricans are fairly represented on screen, it is easy miss just *how negative* the treatment of Anybodys – a butch girl with short cropped hair who binds her chest and begs to be 'one of the boys' – really is. Whenever Anybodys tugs at someone for inclusion in the gang, she is met with typically ruthless rejoinders. For example, when she insists that she 'want(s) to fight' the Sharks, one of the Jets mutters wryly: 'How else is she going to get a guy to touch her?' Negrón-Muntaner astutely argues that 'While the Puerto Ricans suffer racism, they constitute a community composed of a specific socially recognized subjectivity'; by contrast, 'Anybodys, a woman without a proper name, has no community, and she suffers from a lack of recognition as a subject. She is an open subject – 'anybody' – sitting on the sexual/gender fence'.[25] What Negrón-Muntaner does not note is the fact that there is an additional kind of violence inscribed in Anybodys' name, for she is not the singular 'anybody' but, rather, the confused plurality conveyed by 'Anybodys' and, as such, she is 'anybody's' to claim – anybody other than her 'self' – as the film's unavowed 'other'.

The case that Negrón-Muntaner makes for Baby John is a bit harder to earn. He is the figure who gets 'bloodied' at the beginning of the film in the opening brawl, and Officer Shrank shows a keen interest in knowing exactly who 'bloodied' him, as if he had just been deflowered. Hence, there is no question that Baby John, through both his name and his quiet, private, and

[24] Negrón-Muntaner, p. 98.
[25] Ibid., p. 99.

occasionally frightened demeanor, is the most feminised male character in the film. This point leads Negrón-Muntaner to make the provocative claim that 'Anybodys and Baby John are the split subjectivities of the pre-Stonewall homosexual figure; bitchy and sweet, hostile and resassuring'.[26] However, this brilliant observation is followed by a slightly more outlandish one – that Baby John becomes the film's repository of 'a white Jewish gay subjectivity' – as the only figure into whom the filmmakers can cathect their own gay, Jewish, identities. While it is true that at one point in the film, Baby John flips through a Superman comic book and says 'Gee, I love him' (which causes the immediate homophobic reply 'So, marry him!'), Baby John is as interesting, if not more so, as a figure who, like 'Anybodys', represents a *vacated* subjectivity – in this case, a 'baby' devoid of the requisite manliness – rather than a character as socially and ethnically specific as Negrón-Muntaner suggests.

Yet perhaps the figure who is least understood is *West Side Story*'s principal director, Robert Wise, who was gracious enough to give Jerome Robbins the co-directing credit he so badly wanted, despite the perfectionism that eventually forced Robbins off the set. Fifty-seven year-old Wise, who had directed twenty eight films by the time he signed on to *West Side Story*, was a seasoned but under-acknowledged Hollywood director. As Eugene Archer observes in his review, Wise had directed horror films, sci-fi pics, Westerns, war films, suspense, sentimental drama, farce, 'big business' power struggles and, even, 'a dubbed Italian spectacle with Brigitte Bardot'.[27] Although Wise received an Oscar nomination for *I Want to Live!* (1958), a film critiquing capital punishment, it

[26] Ibid.
[27] Archer, p. X7.

wasn't until he was named Best Director for *West Side Story* that he became something of a household name. Still, Wise was destined to be overshadowed by the likes of his more famous collaborators; the soft-spoken man who had a flare for 'hard-hitting' realism remained the dark horse of the fabulous five, obscured by the long shadow cast by Robbins, Sondheim, Laurents, and Lehman. Moreover, the fact that, as he moved up through the ranks of the industry (he had been responsible for editing Orson Welles's *Citizen Kane*, still heralded today as the best film of all time), Wise is rarely mentioned even in retrospectives of his impressive body of work. But perhaps what most overshadowed Wise's achievement in *West Side Story* is the fact that 1961 was nothing less than an *annus mirabilis* – a year of wonders – for cinema. Indeed, among the other films nominated for Oscars were the aforementioned drama, *Judgment at Nuremberg*, as well as Ingemar Bergman's *Through a Glass Darkly*, Federico Fellini's *La Dolce Vita*, Elia Kazan's *Splendor in the Grass*, Vittorio De Sica's *Two Women* (for which Sophia Loren won the Oscar for Best Actress), Robert Rosson's *The Hustler*, starring the young Paul Newman, and *Breakfast at Tiffany's*, for which the song, 'Moon River' garnered the Academy Award. Perhaps, then, Oscar aside, it was enough for the inscrutable, deeply talented Robert Wise to be in such extraordinary company, the likes of which we shall never see again.

Zeffirelli's *Romeo and Juliet*: then and now

Little did Zeffirelli know at the time the extent to which 'Destiny' would shape the course of his life in the wake of releasing *Romeo and Juliet*. In an interesting interpolation – one that Zeffirelli cites as proof of his personal view about the role of fate – Lady Montague takes care of the wounded in the aftermath of the opening brawl. After the worldwide success of *Romeo and Juliet*, Zeffirelli himself would play the ministering angel to a jackknifed bus full of priests – some dead, some still capable of saving. Then, mere months later, Zeffirelli himself would be involved in a near-fatal accident in the very same place; as the car left the gas station, heading towards the dangerous curve, Zeffirelli recalls looking at the young male gas station attendant waving at him as though he were 'the Angel of Death'.[1] Oddly enough, were it not for another teenage boy, *Romeo and Juliet* would have met a similar fate, for halfway through the shooting, Zeffirelli had run out of his 'pathetic budget': '(t)he only thing I could do', recalls the director, 'was to throw myself at the feet of Charlie Bluhdorn, the head of Gulf and Western and therefore Paramount'.[2] During the screening of several key scenes, Zeffirelli noticed that Charlie was constantly talking

[1] Zeffirelli, *An Autobiography*, p. 232,
[2] Ibid., p. 228.

'about other matters' as 'the telephone rose and fell. My heart sank'. But suddenly, Zeffirelli explains, 'a thin, reedy voice struggled to make itself heard. "Will ya shad-up, Daddy?" Everyone fell silent, it was Bluhdorn's son Paul . . . . Bluhdorn was obviously impressed by his son's anger'.[3] When the financier heard from his own son's mouth that not only did the boy *like* the film, but also, he *understood* it, Bluhdorn doubled the film's budget to one and a half million dollars, enabling the show to go on. And on – and on – as Zeffirelli observes with great satisfaction, for the film, in grossing $50 million, made 'the highest ratio of investment to earnings in the history of the studio'.[4]

Nevertheless, for all its success at the box office and beyond, the release of Zeffirelli's *Romeo and Juliet* spawned a heated debate – not just among film critics writing in the sixties, but also between present-day scholars – as the place of this adaptation in the Shakespearean film canon remains the subject of dispute. Dividing the principal combatants into two 'rival households', Ace Pilkington observes that

> if the war between scholars and directors seems to be over, the peace terms have not yet been agreed, and there is a large no-man's-land into which film-makers wander at their peril. The principal combatants in this guerrilla conflict might perhaps be called the purists and the popularizers, and no modern director has a better claim to the dangerous title of popularizer-in-chief than Franco Zeffirelli.[5]

[3] Ibid., pp. 228–29.
[4] Ibid., p. 229.
[5] Pilkington, p. 164.

Indeed, among leftist critics at the time, Zeffirelli's *Romeo and Juliet* was 'simply cashing in on one of the "softer" versions of radicalism'; for as Russell Jackson explains, Zeffirelli and his cohort were accused of conflating the youth culture that the film celebrates with real innovation and social change.[6] Drawing a parallel between the Zeffirelli's 'Capulets and Montagues' and the British invasion's 'mods and rockers', Nina Hibbins' comment in a Communist publication, the *Daily Worker*, exemplifies this position, complaining that Zeffirelli's film failed to expose the underlying causes of the youth generation's angst: 'mods and rockers, or Jets and Sharks, are products of working class conditions in an advanced industrial age'.[7] In other words, in order to live up to its billing as 'the thing for young people to see',[8] Zeffirelli's film – set in an exclusively aristocratic society – could not possibly offer a meaningful investigation of the lived reality of social class antagonisms that fuelled so many of the youth movements of the sixties.

Yet, if, for some 'popularisers' Zeffirelli did not go far enough, then for the conservative 'purists' his *Romeo and Juliet* wandered too far afield from Shakespeare's sacrosanct verse. As Jackson points out, *Variety*'s comment on the release of the film in London says it all in its subheading: '"Inexperienced leads, or Franco Zeffirelli's brash casting experiment, hampers classic tale of love. Kids don't understand meaning of their lines. A tough sell"'.[9] On the subject of the proper articulation of these all-important lines, Harold Hobson epitomises the class snobbery that preoccupied the purists; citing

[6] Jackson, p. 219.

[7] Hibbins, quoted in Jackson, p. 217.

[8] Renata, 'The Screen: Zeffirelli's "Romeo and Juliet" Opens', *The New York Times* 9 October 1968, p. 41.

[9] Quoted in Jackson, p. 215.

Robert Stephens' noble portrayal of the Prince as the film's only redeeming feature, Hobson observes that the others – clearly lacking classical, 'Oxbridge' training, let alone an education in 'Received Pronunciation' (RP) – lazily 'trail around with them the flat vowels of red-brick universities'.[10] Even Renata Adler, who raved about the film following its opening in New York's Paris Theater, contends that the verse 'suffers a bit, sounding more like "West Side Story" than it ought to. In the classic speeches, one begins to worry about diction and wish the modern would recede and let Shakespeare play through'.[11]

Adler's reference to *West Side Story* is significant, as movie ads from 1968 indicate that this musical film was revived in theatres in order to capitalise on the popular success (not to be confused with critical acclaim) of Zeffirelli's film in America and around the world. In a *New York Times* ad from 4 October 1968, *Playboy* magazine brings both films together in an explicit pitch for Zeffirelli's adaptation: 'The entire film is a poem of youth, love, and violence . . . a Renaissance recapitulation of "West Side Story" played with pure 1968 passion!'[12] Indeed, the cultural relevance of Zeffirelli's film is suggested by *The New York Times* ad, which encourages audiences to attend the 'Swinging Youth Premiere': 'Come on down and meet OLIVIA HUSSEY and LEONARD WHITING, the fabulous teenage stars of "Romeo & Juliet" as well as your favorite deejays from WNEW-FM and a host of rock stars . . . IT'S YOUR NIGHT . . . COME DOWN AND MAKE IT YOUR SCENE'.[13] And in the end, it wasn't just teenage girls with their long, straight hair in centre-

[10] Hobson, quoted in Jackson, p. 219.

[11] Adler, p. 41.

[12] *Playboy Magazine* ad, *The New York Times* 4 October 1968, p. 39.

[13] Ibid.

partings – in imitation of Hussey's look – who left the cinema in tears. For as Kenneth Rothwell pointed out in 1973, even 'the harsher critics, the professional Shakespeareans, admitted they had wept despite themselves'.[14]

Ultimately, critics and scholars remain divided at best in their assessment of whether the film is, in fact, 'a poem' or a sacrilege. If Adler and Hobson critique the principals' enunciation of the lines, then others, like Kenneth Rothwell, defend the pair: 'Hussey and Whiting, while very young and inexperienced, have nevertheless been coached to within an inch of their lives to read selected passages with cogency and fidelity.'[15] In a directors' symposium, Zeffirelli himself confirms the rigor of the rehearsals to which he subjected the young actors:

> I've experienced the full range of actors and actresses playing in my films, from the two little 'green' actors playing Romeo and Juliet – he was a Cockney boy and she was fourteen – but I pulled out of them what I was looking for – youth, innocence, and passion. The words were conquered practically one by one, through the painstaking efforts of voice coaches and the actors themselves.[16]

The critical reception of the film's other major actors has similarly assumed a rather schizophrenic path. For many, Pat Heywood's robust Nurse was a revelation – at last sufficiently risqué, in both

 [14] Kenneth Rothwell, 'Hollywood and Some Versions of *Romeo and Juliet*: Toward a "Substantial Pageant"', *Literature/Film Quarterly* 1.4 (Fall 1973), p. 349.

[15] Rothwell, 'Hollywood', p. 350.

[16] Zeffirelli, 'Shakespeare in the Cinema: a film directors' symposium with Peter Brook, Sir Peter Hall, Richard Loncraine, Baz Luhrmann, Oliver Parker, Roman Polanski, and Franco Zeffirelli', in *Cineaste* 24.1 (1998), p. 50.

dialogue and demeanour, to bring the role to life – whereas for others, her portrayal 'seems too bawdy, cold and almost terrifying – in the way that characters in Disney movies suddenly become uncanny, and haunt children's dreams'.[17] The same contradiction affected reviews of Michael O'Shea's Friar Laurence, who is either a peace-loving academic – in Renata Adler's description – 'a modern, radical-understanding Dean',[18] or the far shadier character of the early Italian novellas. Indeed, many critics have commented on the excision of the Friar's final speech (and appearance) from Zeffirelli's film, a decision that leaves the audience questioning his moral fortitude at the very least, and, at the worst, his motives. Not even John McEnery's Mercutio has been spared a divided reception. Kenneth Rothwell contends that '(t)he only Mercutio who could possibly rival Barrymore's (from Cukor's 1936 film) is John McEnery's . . . (But) comparisons are misleading because the actors' conceptions of the role were so different: Barrymore was the master craftsman; McEnery, the exponent of an emerging youth culture and lifestyle'.[19] Chastely suggesting what this 'lifestyle' might be, Adler observes that 'a lot (is) made of the relationship between Romeo and Mercutio, beautifully played by John McEnery'.[20] Yet John Russell Taylor referred to McEnery's performance as '"an exercise in gutter camp"', while Anderegg more scathingly describes McEnery as 'an inveterate clown', whose individual scenes drag on to become 'merely another set piece, existing for its own sake'.[21]

More controversial than the acting is the music. For Rothwell, the score, has much to do with his singularly amusing observation that

[17] Adler, p. 41.
[18] Ibid.
[19] Rothwell, 'Hollywood', p. 346.
[20] Adler, p. 41.
[21] Taylor, quoted in Jackson, p. 219; Anderegg, p. 67.

'quite possibly Volpone in even his most orgiastic dreams could not have conceived of the box office fortune the film yielded',[22] for the 'saccharine strains of the pseudo-Elizabethan "What is a Youth?" took the cinematic public, especially the youth audience . . . by storm and overnight generated an unparalleled interest in Shakespearean film'. Page Cook sees the merits of the music even without considering the box-office returns, arguing that Nino Rota's score is not only 'cogent' and 'eloquent', but also 'a major contribution to film-music' in its own right.[23] Assuming quite the opposite tone, Michael Anderegg observes that '(p)articularly unfortunate is the inserted song, "What is a Youth?" a pseudo-Renaissance ballad . . . that accompanies the meeting of Romeo and Juliet, its banal lyrics and sentimental orchestration taking away from, rather than contributing to, the coming together of the lovers'.[24] Indeed, Zeffirelli is often criticised for the over-sentimentality and melodrama that characterises his films, which most critics attribute to his background as an acclaimed opera director. In this context, as Rothwell notes, Nino Rota's score alone makes Zeffirelli's *Romeo and Juliet* more akin to Paul Czinner's filmed ballet (1966) than to the 1954 adaptation by Renato Castellani, principally because 'it draws heavily on an operatic sensibility', resulting 'in a film unusually sensitive to the interplay between words and music'.[25] Deborah Cartmell describes the director's entire oeuvre as 'shar(ing) an unmistakable operatic conception',[26] while Anderegg adds: 'The Capulet ball demonstrates how much Zeffirelli is in love with spectacle . . . Zeffirelli's

---

[22] Rothwell, 'Hollywood', p. 349.

[23] Page Cook, 'The Sound Track', *Films in Review* 19 (Nov. 1968), p. 571.

[24] Anderegg, p. 67.

[25] Rothwell, 'Hollywood', p. 326.

[26] Cartmell, 'Shakespeare and Zeffirelli', in *The Cambridge Companion to Shakespeare on Film*, p. 213.

background in opera is here fully in evidence'.[27] According to Anderegg, the director's background in opera is both an asset and a detriment to his films, for Anderegg describes *Romeo and Juliet*'s mise-en-scène as 'rich, lush, (and) flamboyant'.[28] This last adjective hints at a disturbing trend in the criticism of Zeffirelli's work, namely, the tendency to interject judgements regarding the director's sexuality into analysis.

As Russell Jackson points out, even upon the film's release, critics like David Robinson observed that Zeffirelli '"uses young men as Busby Berkeley's musicals used girls. As far as the eye can see, Verona is full of Apollos with Denmark St. Hairdo's. These not very coded references to the director's sexuality would reappear later in the franker discourse of academic commentary"'.[29] As we have seen, whereas Peter S. Donaldson views the director's sexuality as an opportunity to constitute a bisexual cinematic gaze, others have more crudely described Zeffirelli's camera – at its best – as one-sidedly 'homosexual' or – at its worst – even 'sodomizing'.[30] However, the insinuations can be far more subtle; for example, one wonders whether or not Anderegg – had he been *unaware* of Zeffirelli's sexual orientation – would have employed the sexually-inflected expression 'Zeffirelli wants it both ways' to describe the director's simultaneous treatment of the feud as 'a seriocomic expression of mostly juvenile high spirits' and 'a deadly affair with grave consequences'.[31]

[27] Anderegg, p. 67.

[28] Ibid., p. 64.

[29] Robinson, quoted in Jackson, p. 218.

[30] William Van Watson, 'Zeffirelli, Shakespeare and the Homosexual Gaze', *Literature/Film Quarterly* 20 (1992), pp. 145–48.

[31] Anderegg, p. 66.

Unquestionably, codpieces *are* one of the uncredited stars of *Romeo and Juliet*, taking on a life of their own as each is made with colorful fabric and frills that draw heightened attention to the male actors' groin region; and yet, we are far more aware of the meticulously made costuming than what lies beneath it. Zeffirelli's controversial 1969 statement against nudity in Italian filmmaking is of particular interest in this context. Characterising Italian cinema in the late sixties as an unbearable wave of 'sexploitation' films, Zeffirelli, upon his release from the hospital (following the devastating car accident), indicated in no uncertain terms that he found *Teoroma* (Pier Paolo Pasolini 1968), *Bora Bora* (Ugo Liberatore 1968), and Fellini's *Satyricon* (1969) revolting, filling him with '"despair" for the future of the Italian cinema and its audience'.[32] For such comments, the director was expelled from the Italian Association of Cinema Authors, on the grounds that he spoke out against 'freedom of expression'.[33] Boldly, one of the famous 'offenders', Federico Fellini (along with Pietri Germi) defended Zeffirelli from the organisation's accusations; Pietri even resigned, despite being the Association's first president. Indeed, Zeffirelli was not the only director in hot water at the time; Fellini, though representing the other end of the spectrum in terms of his perspective on nudity, was charged with 'corrupting a minor' who was part of the notorious banquet scene in *Satyricon*.[34] Always hyperbolic and outrageous, Zeffirelli, on the heels of *Romeo and Juliet*'s success, commented that movies are now judged 'by how many nipples you have on the screen and how many Lesbians you can afford'.[35] One can't help but wonder

---

[32] Zeffirelli, quoted in Alfred Friedly, 'In Italy, Erotic Films Are Non Grata', *The New York Times* 14 Jul. 1969: p. 28.

[33] Friedly, p. 28.

[34] Ibid.

[35] Zeffirelli, quoted in Friendly, p. 28.

whether or not Zeffirelli would have changed his tune, had the trend tended more towards male nudity.

All that aside, it is important to acknowledge that, at least within the sphere of academic criticism, Zeffirelli's *Romeo and Juliet* has fared better in posterity than it did upon its initial release. Having won Oscars for costuming and cinematography, the film also earned nominations for Best Picture and Best Director – certainly a respectable showing at the 1969 Academy Awards. More importantly, it has stood the test of time as a film that is shown, often in comparison with Baz Luhrmann's adaptation, in classrooms around the world. Rehearsing the arguments that have been brought to bear on Zeffirelli's *Romeo and Juliet*, Kenneth Rothwell eloquently concludes:

> In the celluloid mosaic of a film, a director of a Shakespeare adaptation must juggle the demands of Shakespeareans who view picture and music as enemy to the word; cineastes who see word and music as hostile to the picture; and musicians who regard picture and word as distractions to the score. All these qualms might be dispelled, though, if more of us paid attention to André Bazin's attitude toward filmic adaptations of great plays: '. . . culture in general and literature in particular have nothing to lose from such an enterprise'.[36]

With a final appeal to the universal, Zeffirelli proves both Bazin (and Rothwell) correct, explaining that

[36] See Rothwell, 'Zeffirelli's *Romeo and Juliet*: Words into Picture and Music', p. 330; and Andre Bazin, *What is Cinema?* (Berkeley: University of California Press, 1967), p. 65.

With my films, I've tried to return Shakespeare to the popular audience he originally wrote for. Juliet Capulet and Romeo Montague in Verona expressed themselves more nobly, more fully, than young people do today. But what's more important is that the essence of man, what man is and what he needs, has not changed since the stone age. We cry and laugh at the same anguishes and the same jokes.[37]

Based on *Romeo and Juliet*'s $50 million in earnings, we can safely say that Zeffirelli got the *last* laugh.

[37] Zeffirelli, 'Director's Symposium', p. 55.

Romeo + *Juliet* takes the 'A' train

··

'Where is the audience willing to watch a classic play thrown in the path of a subway train?' wrote Jane Maslin of *The New York Times* on 1 November 1996.[1] The answer must have shocked her, since the response was, simply, *everywhere*. Indeed, Maslin's remark reminds us of the proverbial saying that one person's trash is another's treasure. Literally recovered from a trash can, Billy Strayhorn's 'Take the "A" Train' – referring to the famous subway line running from Brooklyn through Harlem and into Manhattan – became one of the most famous songs of all time. The analogy is instructive in light of Maslin's metaphor. Though trashed by most critics upon its release, Baz Lurhmann's *Romeo + Juliet* was treasured by audiences, breaking records as the first Shakespeare film ever to lead all films in box office receipts during its opening weekend.

Earlier, we heard from a range of critics that responded to the debut of Baz Lurhmann's *Romeo + Juliet* – most of them cynical towards and suspicious of the film's 'relentless, in your face MTV visual style'.[2] However, the constant references to the MTV 'aesthetic' in conjuction with *Romeo + Juliet* have proved irksome

[1] Jane Maslin, 'Soft! What Light? It's Flash, Romeo', *The New York Times* 1 November 1996: p. C1.
[2] Crowl, p. 119.

to scholars with a longer view of media history in mind. Marco Calavita refers to the MTV label as a 'film criticism fallacy'. While he notes that Hollywood film has taken cues from music videos in three fundamental respects – the use of popular songs, glossy atmospherics, and breakneck speed (achieved through 'manic editing') – Calavita also makes it clear that what hinders the interpretation of the film when the MTV trope becomes a reflex are false oppositions, which manifest themselves in 'hysterical judgments of what MTV and its audience represent'.[3] Anderegg, though ultimately more charitable towards Luhrmann's film, epitomises this tone when he observes that '(a)t first glance, Baz Luhrmann's *William Shakespeare's Romeo + Juliet* could be mistaken for yet another (mis)appropriation of Shakespeare's play for purposes of parody or even burlesque, a hip (hop?) retelling aimed at an irredeemably lowbrow audience of clueless teenagers living in an intellectually bankrupt culture'.[4] Indeed, as Calavita argues, the MTV style has become a kind of shorthand through which scholars and critics establish – and, in fact, seek to perpetuate – 'us'/'them' oppositions, which typically fracture along the predictable lines of 'Art versus commerce, adult culture versus youth culture, and ideas, humanity, narrative and coherence versus distraction, chaos, superficiality, and meaninglessness'.[5] In a persuasive argument, Calavita reminds readers that, ever since the 'New Wave' (which substantially pre-dated the 1982 birth of MTV), filmmakers have been experimenting with techniques that would prove highly influential with this televisual latecomer. Nevertheless, the 'staying power' of the MTV label has proven tenacious, largely

[3] Marco Calavita, '"MTV Aesthetics" at the Movies: Interrogating a Film Criticism Fallacy', *Journal of Film and Video* 59.3 (Fall 2007), p. 15.

[4] Anderegg, pp. 72–73.

[5] Calavita, p. 17.

because critics, as Calavita observes, 'want to set themselves and their preferred films apart from the juvenile, taste-challenged masses, but who often try to do so within a mainstream, corporate system, and according to the rules of good cinema from an imagined, Edenic past – before things got so fast and loud'.[6]

But fast and loud they were, and things were going to stay that way for the foreseeable future of Shakespeare on film. Unprepared for such a raucous crowd when he attended the debut of Luhrmann's film in the quiet town of Athens, Ohio, Crowl relates his surprise at the sheer number of high-pitched 'squeals, which sounded like weasel's in heat', every time Leo DiCaprio appeared on screen. Amusingly, at the point in the film when Juliet and Romeo are about to meet for the first time, Crowl recalls the girl behind him whispering: 'Don't touch him, you bitch'.[7] Indeed, even among scholars and critics, Claire Danes – rather than DiCaprio – received the lion's share of negative commentary. For example, Anderegg points out that 'Claire Danes consistently flattens her lines in such a way that nearly all emphases disappear. DiCaprio . . . finds ways – through pauses, taking deep breaths, halting his speech – to naturalize the rhythms while maintaining necessary emphases'.[8] Several critics objected not only to Danes's spoken language but also to her body language: 'in terms of desire and agency, Claire Danes's Juliet resides at the opposite end of the spectrum to Olivia Hussey's'; her Juliet 'is passive, rather than active, by comparison'.[9] Though in the minority, some critics have

6 Calavita, p. 28.

7 Crowl, p. 130.

8 Anderegg, pp. 76–77.

9 Lindsey Scott, '"Closed in a Dead Man's Tomb": Juliet, Space, and the Body in Franco Zeffirelli's and Baz Luhrmann's Films of *Romeo and Juliet*', Literature/Film Quarterly, Vol. 36 (2008), p. 137, p. 141.

seen Danes's calmer, steadier portrayal of Juliet as something of an asset. For example, changing his tune somewhat, Anderegg adds that the 'positive side to her performance' is that she 'clings to a plain, innocent sincerity throughout . . . .'[10] Indeed, scholars familiar with Danes's breakout role in the acclaimed television series *My So-Called Life* (1994–95) might recognise her approach to Juliet as an extension of her characterisation of 'Angela', the quiet but quirkily confident teen who is mature beyond her years, narrating, in voice-over, seventeen of the show's nineteen episodes. It was precisely Danes's 'girl-next-door' appeal which, paradoxically, caught Luhrmann's attention. Hence, I tend to think that Danes – not Luhrmann – interprets her film character as a refreshingly 'plain Jane' Juliet (after all, who can possibly hold a candle to DiCaprio's gorgeous, 'Ganymede'-like Romeo, whom Luhrmann's camera tracks like a hawk?).

Without question, DiCaprio is the object of Luhrmann's camera in ways that are not unlike Zeffirelli's approach to Leonard Whiting's Romeo. What is interesting (and troubling) is that, likely owing to Luhrmann's (hetero)sexuality, no one has claimed that his Romeo is the subject of a homoerotic or queer gaze. Rather, as Scott asserts, 'heterosexual love is "normalized" through the film's coded structures of seeing'.[11] Presumably, Scott is referring to the camera's tendency to align itself with Romeo's perspective on the action, so that he becomes less an object of the gaze and more the subject through whom the story is told. Elaborating on the film's hetero-sexually 'coded structures of seeing', he explains that, at the Capulet Ball, 'Luhrmann's film not only privileges Romeo's per-spective here (as opposed to Zeffirelli's treatment of a desiring

[10] Anderegg, p. 77.
[11] Scott, p. 143.

female gaze), but the drug-induced visions also imply a rejection of feminised or "weakened" masculinity'.[12] While this point is well taken, I remain puzzled by the total absence of criticism regarding the fetishisation of Romeo's slender, extremely feminised (indeed, almost androgynous) body. This is especially the case in the lovemaking scene, wherein it is DiCaprio's wounded body, as opposed to Juliet's supple frame, that is on display for the camera. The possibility that Romeo is more fragile than virile, perhaps even incapable of consummating the relationship, is suggested by the slow, strip-tease style revelation of his wounds; as Juliet helps him undress, he is shown wincing as his naked torso reacts in pain from his every movement. What is unique about Luhrmann's treatment of this scene, in which the sex (as in most versions) occurs off-screen, is the distinct impression that Romeo and Juliet's love 'is strikingly more tender and not so violently immediate and physical as that depicted in Zeffirelli's version'.[13]

One reason for the dearth of scholarship regarding the camera's potentially queer gaze in this film may stem from the fact that this type of commentary has been lavished exclusively on the figure of Mercutio, who plays a buff, black drag queen. Scholars remain divided as to whether or not this treatment of Mercutio is marginalising or, perhaps, a sincere multiculturalist gesture. Andorogg contends that while 'the more or less multiracial society of Luhrmann's film allows for considerable casting latitude, Mercutio's blackness marks him as beyond the pale in more ways than one', adding that, '(a)lthough he is not specifically depicted as "queer" as he is in Zeffirelli's film, he works himself into a state of

---

[12] Ibid.

[13] Jennifer L. Martin, 'Tights vs. Tattoos: Filmic Interpretations of *Romeo and Juliet*', *English Journal* (September 2002), p. 43.

hysteria with the Queen Mab speech, which suggests that the ambiguous sexuality of his "drag" get up is more than a costume – it expresses gender confusion and anxiety'.[14] In a way, Mercutio, with his black skin and white sequined dress, becomes, like Anybodys, a figure whose subjectivity is painfully vacated by his implicit failure to belong to a particular group – black/white, male/female, gay/straight – and, lest we forget, he is a kinsman to the *prince*, neither Montague nor Capulet. Interestingly, Richard Burt does not see the treatment of race in the film to be as stark: 'By not consistently opposing Montagues and Capulets racially either by color or accent, Luhrmann unsettles the idea that racial difference and racism drive their conflict'.[15] Assuming a different line of reasoning, Crowl finds Luhrmann's provocative casting decisions to be, ultimately, disingenuous:

> On the surface, the film looks like dream Shakespeare for the agenda of the National Education Association: Afro-Americans, Latinos, gays, and cross-dressers are all given place of promi-nence in Luhrmann's version of Shakespeare's universe. . . . But for all the film's inclusionary emphasis, it is still ultimately focused on two very white young stars – DiCaprio and Danes. Lurhmann, like Hollywood, can imagine a black, cross-dressing Mercutio, but not a black or Latino Romeo, nor a similarly ethnic Juliet.[16]

Crowl adds that in 'order for (the dark-skinned) Capulet to produce a daughter as pale as Claire Danes', the film must, essentially,

[14] Anderegg, p. 82.

[15] Richard Burt, 'Slammin' Shakespeare In Acc(id)ents Yet Unknown: Liveness, Cinem(edi)a, and Racial Dis-integration', *Shakespeare Quarterly* 53.2 (Summer 2002), p. 207.

[16] Crowl, p. 129.

overcompensate by making 'Diane Venora's Gloria Capulet blonde, white, and with an accent full of the deep American South',[17] an accent that conjures yet another cultural spectre that the film resists investigating: racial miscegination.

In point of fact, as in *West Side Story*, it is the representation of Latino culture that critics have been more inclined to take up in their arguments. Philippa Hawker offers the provocative observation that Luhrmann's 'depiction of Verona Beach and its inhabitants' attitudes to Latinity bears striking parallels with Shakespeare's Verona and Elizabethan assumptions about Spain and Italy'.[18] Jose Arroyo raises the stakes by suggesting that the film's representation of Latino culture sits comfortably with contemporary audiences as well, explaining that, with respect to Tybalt, 'the pride, temper and importance he attaches to family honour are far more under- standable to present-day viewers as Hispanic stereotypes than as the values of a Renaissance nobleman. Likewise, Juliet's refusal of her father becomes more transgressive when read through her ethnicity'.[19] For Richard Vela, the case is not as persuasive, for he claims that 'it is still difficult to show that Luhrmann's film deliberately explores ethnicity beyond what is necessary to demonstrate a fundamental difference between the two families'.[20]

Perhaps it's not so important to pin down Luhrmann's attitude toward Latinos or Mercutio's ambivalent sexuality in an anything- goes environment like 'Verona Beach', the implied geography of which has puzzled scores of scholars and critics. While some have asserted that the film is set in Florida or Miami, several others have

[17] Ibid.

[18] Hawker, p. 243.

[19] Jose Arroyo, 'Kiss kiss bang bang', *Film/Literature/Heritage*, edited by Ginette Vincendeau (London: British Film Institute, 2001), p. 123.

[20] Richard Vela, p. 92.

read the film as Cuban-American. But the west coast also comes into play when critics attempt to discern the real coordinates of Luhrmann's vertiginous setting, as still others have located the film in places ranging from Los Angeles to Mexico, when, in point of fact, *Romeo + Juliet* was shot in Mexico City and the coastal town of Vera Cruz (fittingly, 'cruz' means 'cross' in Spanish, complementing all the religious iconography that engulfs the mise-en-scène).[21] According to the director, he 'was attracted to Mexico City because he felt that it provided a landscape where corporate values had not yet absorbed or destroyed the ties of traditional religious piety'.[22] What Luhrmann doesn't say is that it was also much less expensive to shoot the film in Mexico than it would have been in the US. Nevertheless, the important point to take away is that 'place' in *Romeo + Juliet* is ambiguous in a way that is generally enabling – productive rather than reductive – as Barbara Hodgdon attests when she notes that the film 'takes place, not in a European culture, but in a multicultural borderland – a mythic geographical space open to variant readings . . . .'[23] Above all, however, Luhrmann's setting, in keeping with Jameson's assessment of the postmodern condition, is 'a place where nothing seems experienced in and of itself, where things are instead filtered through media'.[24]

Indeed, the debate that every critic has been quick to enter centers on Lurhmann's apparent substitution of visual, mass-media correlatives for Shakespeare's text. In an interview, Luhrmann explains:

---

[21] See Richard Vela's compendium of views of the film's location, p. 106, n. 4.

[22] Crowl, p. 123.

[23] Barbara Hodgdon, '*William Shakespeare's Romeo + Juliet*: Everything's Nice in America', *Shakespeare Survey* 52 (1999), p. 95.

[24] Hodgdon, p. 94.

> Our philosophy in adapting *Romeo and Juliet* for the screen was
> to reveal Shakespeare's lyrical, romantic, sweet, sexy, musical,
> violent, rude, rough, rowdy, rambunctious storytelling through his
> richly invented language. We were adamant that we should
> maintain the colour and taste of the actual words even to the
> extent of the 'thee' and 'thou'.[25]

He adds, however, that '(w)here we took significant liberty was in
the restructuring and cutting. We felt it was important to serve
Shakespeare's ultimate goal of strong storytelling'.[26] Perhaps this
explains the following self-contradictory statement from *Times* critic
Janet Maslin, who complains that the 'biggest inconsistency to Mr
Luhrmann's approach involves the language of the play, which is
treated as sacrosanct when everything else about the film reflects
radical revisionism. In such an otherwise irreverent context, this
amounts to undue pretension, since so much of the dialogue is lost
and upstaged anyhow'.[27] How can the language be treated as
'sacrosanct' and the dialogue 'lost'? What Maslin may be reacting
to is Luhrmann's own challenging repertoire of cinematic language, which can, at times, lose the viewer in the act of translating
words to images. Anderegg avows this sentiment when he
complains that in titling the film '"William Shakespeare's"' *Romeo +
Juliet*, 'the intimation of irony is hard to avoid', given 'the distinctive
stylistic pyrotechnics of Luhrmann's style and the rather drastic
cutting of the script . . . .'[28] Whereas Anderegg traces Luhrmann's
camerawork back to 1920s-style filmmaking, Luhrmann's technique
could be said to date back even further to the Vitagraph *Romeo*

[25] Luhrmann, 'Director's Symposium', p. 48.
[26] Ibid.
[27] Maslin, pp. C1, C2.
[28] Anderegg, p. 73.

and Juliet (1908) which, we recall, employed seventeen different camera angles in a mere 15 minutes.

Nevertheless, film critics (as opposed to scholars) have almost universally panned the film's apparent privileging of bravura camerawork over Shakespeare's language. Generally speaking, US critics have tended to heap praise only on the film's two major British actors: Peter Postlethwaite (Friar Laurence) and Miriam Margoyles (Nurse). And this is what makes Sir Alec Guinness's remarks so stunning: 'what a relief it is to listen to American accents dealing with Shakespeare. They sound so much more authentic than our overrefined suburban efforts'.[29] Indeed, in support of this unexpected remark, Luhrmann's extensive research on Shakespeare's language – using both Anthony Burgess's work in linguistics and advice from the likes of Sir Peter Hall – led Luhrmann to a surprising revelation, when '(i)t became clear that Received Pronunciation, that is, the round vowel sounds of Olivier and Gielgud or "Voice Beautiful" as it is known, is a relatively new fashion', and that the Elizabethan style was, in fact, 'closer to the sound of the American accent than "Voice Beautiful"'.[30] Nevertheless, even new habits die hard, as comments from critics like Geoffrey O'Brien attest: 'It is the skittish handling of the language, though, that reduces Luhrmann's film to little more than a stunt . . . any speech longer than a few lines just gets in the way, and the effect all too often is of sitting in on the tryouts of a high school drama club'.[31] Of course, this was before *High School Musical* and the new US television series *Glee* took the 'high school drama' world by storm – a phenomenon that Luhrmann's film undoubtedly

[29] Sir Alec Guinness, *A Positively Final Appearance* (New York: Viking, 1999), p. 16.

[30] Luhrmann, 'Director's Symposium', p. 49.

[31] Geoffrey O'Brien, 'The Ghost at the Feast', *New York Review of Books*, 6 February 1997, p. 13.

helped to inaugurate, particularly given the success of *Moulin Rouge!* But, for better and, at times, for worse, the critical consensus on both sides of the Atlantic is that '(i)n this film, worldliness trumps innocence; the real overcomes the ideal; speed is all, and lyricism, though it emerges from time to time, is almost entirely transferred to the mise-en-scène and the music'.[32]

As in *West Side Story* and Zeffirelli's *Romeo and Juliet*, music does indeed play a key role in *William Shakespeare's Romeo + Juliet*. Evenly split on this issue, scholars and critics have praised the soundtrack for complementing the spoken word, as well as condemned it for subsuming Shakespeare's language. Sam Crowl, for example, observes that '(t)he best favor Luhrmann does his actors . . . is to shut down the perpetual soundtrack buzz'.[33] Yet music historian Michael Bracewell is quick to counter this sentiment, exalting in *Romeo + Juliet*'s score:

> But surely among the best examples of recent film soundtracks are those for Baz Luhrmann's Shakespeare's *Romeo + Juliet* . . . and *Moulin Rouge!* Luhrmann makes a creative virtue out of the postmodern condition, treating cultural history as a dressing-up box, database and colouring book. He understands the cumulative power of popular culture and is able to remould that culture – its iconography from music hall to musical to rap – into a gorgeous visual and musical sculpture. Achieved with neither knowing irony nor self-regarding cleverness, the joyously exuberant scores to Luhrmann's movies are the current full stop in the continuing history of the form.[34]

[32] Anderegg, p. 83.

[33] Crowl, p. 131.

[34] Michael Bracewell, 'The Best Music in Film', *Sight and Sound XIV* (September 2004), p. 29.

Though few critics have been as generous as Bracewell, many have commented on the effectiveness of the Des'ree number, 'Kissing you', which comes to function in the film as Romeo and Juliet's personal love theme, much in the same way that Nino Rota's arrangement does in Zeffirelli's adaptation. Written by British artist Des'ree and Timothy Atack, the song begins, appropriately, with the following stanza:

> Pride can stand a thousand trials
> The strong will never fall
> But watching stars without you
> My soul cries.

The immediate association of the lovers with stars is at once romantic and tragic, and the ballad is exquisitely sung by the self-fashioned black Diva Des'ree during the Capulet Ball. Following Mercutio's raucous rendition of 'Young Hearts', the 'first pure, achingly beautiful notes' play as Romeo and Juliet's eyes meet through opposing sides of the aquarium.[35] Even the film's most outspoken critics have had difficulty criticising this sequence, for the song creates – in the words of Michael Nyman (scorer for Peter Greenaway) – 'a kind of aural scenography which is as important as the costumes . . . . (it is) a sound that creeps into you'.[36]

Indeed, whenever this song plays in the film – often just as an instrumental variation – it seems as though time itself stands still, and that the legend can be subsumed in its exquisite stillness. Particularly at the Capulet Ball and, later, during the balcony scene, 'Romeo and Juliet alone possess a stillness and serenity, which

---

[35] Pearce and Luhrmann, p. 47.
[36] Nyman, quoted in Bracewell, p. 28.

Luhrmann conveys . . . by filming their scenes in softer focus and longer sequences, by making their theme a lyrical torch song and by contrasting their love with the absence of love in Verona Beach and Sycamore Grove'.[37] Particularly poignant during their first meeting across the acquarium, this 'lyrical torch song' sung by Des'ree does indeed provide the first moment of stillness in the entire film. Dominated by close-ups and two-shots, the camera steadies and, as Crowl begrudgingly admits 'even Shakespeare's poetry is given leave to speak for itself . . . .'[38]

It would be remiss not to comment on how Luhrmann's heavy-handed use of religious symbolism has affected the film's critical reception. For Vela, Luhrmann uses the enormous (superimposed) Christ statue and the various figurations of the Virgin Mary to 'defin(e) fundamental oppositions': 'The Montague world is connected with images of Christ and the crucifixion. . . . The Capulet world is connected with images of the Blessed Virgin Mary'.[39] Jennifer Martin adds that, by the same token, 'Lurhmann's use of religious imagery also suggests that religious dictates represented by the preponderance of religious icons are inadequate in explaining the confusion of postmodern life'.[40] In fact, Crowl notes that not even Christ himself can control the chaos that looms below his outstretched arms, for 'the Christ figure seems hedged in by the corporate towers of the Montagues and Capulets that flank his statue; his reach seems remote from the furious activity swirling about, far beneath his gaze'.[41] Hence, Crowl sees the film moving

---

[37] Scott, pp. 142–43.
[38] Crowl, p. 123.
[39] Vela, p. 95.
[40] Martin, p. 43.
[41] Crowl, p. 133.

away from Christ and toward the cult of Mary, noting that 'Mary worship is a feature of the Mediterranean and of the Latin American Roman Catholic Church (it is also a strong presence in Australia) and provides a link between Luhrmann (a native Australian), Shakespeare's Italy, and the film's Hispanic flavor'.[42] Crowl's incisive remark leads him to the observation that colour symbolism plays a significant role in the later stages of the film:

> Blue and yellow – Mary's colors – come increasingly to be identified with Romeo and Juliet. The fish in the aquarium through which the lovers first spy each other are blue and yellow; the neon crosses that line the aisle leading to Juliet's shroud are outlined in blue interspersed with the flickering yellow lights of the candles; the Mary shrine in Juliet's bedroom is a similar mixture of blue and yellow; and the color of the liquid in the vials provided by the Friar and Crusty (the Apothecary) – who has hidden the poison in the false bottom of a Madonna lamp – completes the color pairing.[43]

Not surprisingly, then, it is in the Marian Church of the Sagrado Corazon (Sacred Heart) that Romeo and Juliet breathe their last, where the flicker of candles and the neon blue crosses reflect 'a wedding of sixteenth- and twentieth-century light sources . . . .',[44] even as the light of these young lives is eclipsed by their ensuing wedding in death. And it is here, James Loehlin observes, that 'the film proposes a wild Marian merger of the grieving mother and her innocent, sacrificial children in the iconography of the film's setting

42 Ibid.

43 Ibid.

44 Anderegg, p. 75.

of Romeo and Juliet's deaths'.[45] In a great act of hubris, Luhrmann suggests that Romeo and Juliet, now safely within the Virgin's care, replace Mary and Christ as the ultimate vision of the pietá.

It seems, then, that only in death do Luhrmann's Romeo and Juliet find that other 'elemental existence' that the film's water imagery so relentlessly implies,[46] at last quenching the flames that have burned from the gas station at the film's beginning to the faintly flickering candles at its end. Unlike *West Side Story*'s Maria, Luhrmann's Juliet is robbed of the opportunity to speak any final words to her Romeo; for a few brief moments, the soundtrack is quelled and, having just witnessed Romeo in his death-throes, Juliet lets out a cry that echoes through the walls of the great church, underscoring just how young and alone she is in this vast, terrifying place. She then kills herself with Romeo's gun and, as the music returns, Juliet dies 'in a blaze of religious and musical glory . . . .'[47] Truly operatic, the real – though not official – end of Luhrmann's film occurs when, '(a)fter the double suicide, the watery romantic isolation of the lovers returns for a poignant moment. The last phrases of Wagner's "Liebestod" from *Tristan und Isolde* play during an overhead shot of the bodies . . . . Juliet's violent suicide is washed over by the ecstatic love-death of Isolde, swooning in bliss over the body of her lover'.[48] But we are brought back down to the grim intonations of reality all to quickly; following 'a long fade to white', the film 'dissolves' into what Barbara Hodgdon describes as the '"social real"', namely, 'a white-sheeted body on a hospital

[45] James N. Loehlin, '"These Violent Delights Have Violent Ends": Baz Luhrmann's Millennial Shakespeare', in *Shakespeare, Film, Fin de Siècle*, edited by Mark Thornton Burnett and Ramona Wray (London: MacMillan, 2000), p. 126.

[46] Crowl, p. 122

[47] Loehlin, p. 126

[48] Ibid., p. 131.

trolley',[49] which becomes the backdrop of the prince's closing condemnation. Appropriately, Crowl concludes that, having 'recas(t) Shakespeare as a secular saint',[50] Luhrmann picks up where Zeffirelli left off, for if 'Zeffirelli and Branagh nudged the Shakespeare film from the art house to the Cineplex', then 'Baz Luhrmann's *Romeo + Juliet* made it feel as welcome there as his Romeo and Juliet are in the Virgin's shrine'.[51] But the price of admission – at least for the lovers – was much too high.

[49] Hodgdon, p. 126.

[50] Crowl, p. 119.

[51] Ibid., p. 134.

Afterlives: the never-ending story

Although it could be argued that *any* story of tragic love that centres on opposition qualifies as an 'afterlife' of the three *Romeo and Juliet* film adaptations explored here, I am restricting examples of afterlives to a handful of acknowledged or culturally significant incarnations of this legendary love story.

West Side Story (Wise and Robbins 1961)

In the two-disc, anniversary edition of *West Side Story*, the second disc is titled 'West Side Memories', and contains interviews with many of the surviving actors and collaborators, with the conspicuous exceptions of Leonard Bernstein and Jerome Robbins, both of whom had died by the time the documentary was produced. In addition to seeing the storyboards, Boris Levin's set miniatures, and hearing Natalie Wood's recording of 'Tonight' (which would be dubbed by Marni Dixon in the finished product), the audience receives a wealth of insight into the behind-the-scenes story of *West Side Story*. Even more interesting, however, are the different interpretations of the film's legacy that arise from the interviews. Arthur Laurents, the screenwriter, observes that the film revolves around 'murders, and attempted rape and all this bigotry and hatred', whereas lyricist Stephen Sondheim explains that

> Many people think *West Side Story* is about prejudice, and I suppose it is if you look at the text. But that's not what it's really

about – it's about the theater. It's about how to use music and lyrics and book to combine in a sort of new way – not that we tried to do it new – it's just that's the way it turned out.

Throughout the documentary, we hear from the actors who remembered – with respect and fondness – the painful perfectionism of Jerome Robbins, who was eventually banned from the production because his constantly changing choreography had led to massive, costly delays in the film's shooting schedule. One castmember recalls that 'Jerry came from the ballet school which was very, very strict. And I don't think he was really happy with a dancer until their feet bled'. Rita Moreno, who figures prominently in the documentary, added that Leonard Bernstein's musical tempos didn't make matters any easier: 'Then along comes Leonard Bernstein with his 5/4 time, 6/8 time, 25/6 time – it's very difficult to dance to that kind of music, because it doesn't make "dancer sense"'. Referring to Bernstein, Sondheim made an interesting observation that could easily be applied to Franco Zeffirelli:

> All Lenny cared about was that his work should be taken seriously. He had been so often slammed by the critics for doing popular and serious work. If you're 'popular' that's one thing and if you're 'serious' that's another thing, but you can't be both at the same time. In other words your work is weightless if it's popular – until you're dead, at which point, then it's ok. And Lenny was keenly sensitive to that.

Speaking of the collaborative directing between Robert Wise and Jerome Robbins, Rita Moreno expressed her excitement with the unusual combination: 'It was like two great chefs who were trying to make this cake. It was exciting'. Evidently, Robert Wise, who shot the film from cranes, helicopters, and hand-made trenches for ground-level shots, couldn't have too many angles, and Robbins couldn't have too many takes. Other undisclosed details we learn about the film include Sondheim's insistence that the 'Officer Krupke'/'Social disease' number be moved to *before* the fight, as the comic musical routine made little sense to him in its placement after the murders of Riff and Bernardo. Subsequently, the number was moved and a new one was added: 'Cool'. The latter routine was so physically demanding that one actor – Baby John – collapsed on the set (he had pneumonia throughout the shooting of this number). Once the actors received word that 'Cool' was officially 'a wrap', they were so relieved that they took off their 'knee pads and burned them in a pile in front of Jerry's office'. When *West Side Memories* touches on the principals, Tony and Maria, Natalie Wood in particular is praised for her acting: 'She really looked like she was just so in love with Richard Beymour and in reality they didn't get along at all'. As for Beymour's performance, Rita Moreno says, simply: 'The role of Tony is just a workhouse part. No one's going to love you for it'. Part way through the production, another significant change was made, as Arthur Laurents thought that the 'Two Hands'/'One Heart' number was 'too pristine' for Tony and Maria's blossoming sexual affections for one another; hence, the collaborators used 'Two Hands' for the marriage scene, and 'Tonight', which was then only a melody played during the overture, became a major set piece as the theme of the balcony scene. In order to usher the lovers into the tragedy, however, a major change to the *Romeo and Juliet* story was added by Arthur Laurents, who explains: 'The thing that I was most proud of was changing the motive for the message not getting through. In the original, suddenly there's a plague . . . but in my version it's bigotry, which is one of the themes of the piece'. With obvious pride, Laurents adds: 'Nobody picked that up in this country ever, whereas in England it was lauded, because they know Shakespeare'.

Barely worthy of mention alongside a film of *West Side Story*'s calibre is the 1987 spinoff *China Girl*, in which Tony (who is Italian rather than Polish) and Tye (a Chinese immigrant from Hong Kong) form the tragic pair. Directed by Abel Ferrara, the film is shot on location in the streets of New York's Chinatown and Little Italy. Its only 'quotation' of Shakespeare's play occurs when Tony is teased for being a 'Romeo', whereas the gang fights and balcony scene – set on a fire escape as in *West Side Story* – are clearly indebted to the 1961 film. Although there is a character named Mercury, who is hot-headed like Shakespeare's Mercutio, the two otherwise have nothing in common. In addition to the setting of the 'Ball scene' in a disco, the only other resonance with Shakespeare's play and *West Side Story* is the fact that there is a generational conflict; however, the tension between the older and younger generation is entirely transferred to the Chinese side. The old mob boss, for example, wants a subtle approach to his 'corporate takeover' of the Italian quarter whereas the young generation would rather violently extort those Chinese who own restaurants in Little Italy. In his insightful commentary on this otherwise forgettable film, Richard Burt explains a key difference between *China Girl* and *West Side Story*: 'whereas Natalie Wood used a fake accent and wore unconvincing make-up to sound and look like the Puerto Rican Maria, the actors in *China Girl* are cast to encode racial and ethnic "authenticity", and in addition to a kind of identity politics casting, race and ethnicity are established through food . . . .'[1] Indeed, Tony and his older brother

---

[1] Richard Burt, 'Shakespeare and Asia in postdiasporic cinemas: spin-offs and citations of the plays from Bollywood to Hollywood', in *Shakespeare, The Movie II: Popularizing the plays on film, TV, video, and DVD*, p. 284.

own a pizza parlor and the Chinese mafia operate out of their restaurant in Little Italy.

Situating the film in terms of cinematic history somewhat redeems *China Girl*, as Burt insightfully notes that the 'Chinatown setting and the rewriting of *Romeo and Juliet* as an interracial romance may be read as symptomatic of Ferrara's response to the explosion of Hong Kong cinema in the 1980s, his claim both for Italian canonical cinema and for the resurgence of Italian-American films by the likes of Francis Ford Coppola, Martin Scorsese, Brian de Palma, and Michael Cimino that had dominated the 1970s'.[2] But the relationship between Tony and Tye is passive and uncompelling, as well as completely devoid of any noticeable sexual chemistry. In fact, Tony does not kill, or plan to kill, either of the two 'Tybalt' characters who ambush his unarmed brother and stab him to death. Unlike the relative balance achieved in *West Side Story*, in *China Girl*, the Italians are represented as much more humane than the Chinese – the latter are depicted as ruthless killers, willing to expand their mini-empire by any means necessary. In fact, when the young Chinese intentionally explode the restaurant in which the older generation locates its headquarters, the Italians are actually shown helping the Chinese in the wake of the disaster. Meanwhile, the Chinese gang even goes so far as to deface and destroy a statue of the Virgin Mary in the midst of an Easter parade.

Burt contends that *China Girl* also quotes Zeffirelli's *Romeo and Juliet* when we see a shot of Tony – repeated one more time in the film – nonchalantly holding a flower and smiling as he walks. The only other obvious citation of Zeffirelli is Ferrara's decision to show much more of Tony's flesh than Sari Chang's Tye in the aubade scene. Although Tye/Juliet, as in both Zefirelli and Luhrmann's film, remains hidden by a sheet, Tony's backside is fully exposed as he lies on top

[2] Ibid., p. 284.

of Tye. On the film's curious ending, Burt concludes: 'Ferrara's interest in *Romeo and Juliet* and in Zeffirelli's film puts him on the side of a conciliatory relation to Chinese cinema', which explains why

> *China Girl* ends twice: in the first ending, the Chinese return to Hong Kong leaving Tye alone to remain with Tony while the Italian-American gang members inexplicably let them walk; in the second, Mercury returns, equally inexplicably, and shoots both Tony and Tye, whose corpse is then cradled by her older brother. Tony's relatives and friends are nowhere to be found.[3]

The film's availability is highly limited; it is out of print on VHS and has not been released on DVD.

In 1997 Paul Simon attempted to produce *The Capeman* on Broadway, the story of a young Puerto Rican gang member who killed two white men in 1959 (after which he served twenty years in prison). As Negrón-Muntaner describes it:

> *The Capeman* was a zoom-in to *West Side Story*'s Chino, escorted out of the playground by cops, it lacked good choreography, inspired lyrics, and tight dramatic structure. The failure of *The Capeman*, as a show, however, combined with the significant exposure of its talent, had a critical, if unintended effect: it gave life to Latino musical careers, while killing the assumption that only Puerto Rican gang members make it on Broadway.[4]

In fact, in 1997, Jennifer Lopez reported – while visiting Puerto Rico – that her dream would be to star in *West Side Story* for a Broadway revival.

 [3] Ibid., p. 286.
[4] Negrón-Muntaner, p. 103.

In 2000, Mansoor Kahn directed a Bollywood version of *West Side Story* titled *Josh*, which translates literally to 'Frenzy'. Set in Goa, *Josh* features two rival gangs and their leaders: Max is the head of the Eagle gang, which is forever at odds with the new kids in town, the Bichhu gang led by Prakash. The situation becomes further complicated when Prakash's brother, Rahul returns from Bombay and falls for Max's twin sister, Shirley. The violence escalates when the unsuspecting Rahul, rather than returning to the city to open a restaurant, stays in Goa to open up a bakery, and an all-out war breaks out. How the two lovers, who reject the violent ways of their respective families, manage to reconcile their differences – if not among the gangs themselves then at least between each other – constitutes the remainder of the film. As is typical of Bollywood films, music figures prominently in this adaptation of *West Side Story*.

Also in 2000, the *West Side Story*-inspired song, 'Maria Maria' (performed by Carlos Santana and The Project G & B) topped the charts at number 1, holding the coveted spot for ten weeks. The song deals with hard times Spanish Harlem; however, the final stanza indicates that this 'west side story' will have a happy ending. The first and last stanzas are referenced below:

Oh Maria Maria
She reminds me of a west side story
Growing up in Spanish Harlem
She's livin' the life just like a movie star . . .

Maria you know you're my lover
When the wind blows I can feel you
Through the weather
Even when we're apart it feels like we're together.

Although 'Maria Maria' finished at number 96 on Billboard's 'All-Time Hot 100 Songs', it came in at number 2 on Billboard's 'All-Time Hot 100 Latin Songs'. In the wake of the success of the song, Carlos Santana has collaborated with Chef Roberto Santibañez to open five restaurants named 'Maria Maria'.

The discrepancy between the mainstream and the Latin song charts is telling, and this leads to a discussion of *West Side Story*'s legacy for contemporary Latino audiences. Frances Negrón-Muntaner explains that there 'is no single American cultural product that haunts Puerto Rican identity discourses in the United States more intensely than the 1961 film, *West Side Story*'.[5] 'For many Puerto Rican spectators who identify with the narrative', she continues,

> *West Side Story* is a morality play about 'our' everyday problems: racism, poverty, and the destructiveness of violence. An example of this pedagogical reading is exemplified by Actor's Playhouse, a Miami-based theater group that . . . staged the musical to a group of 'at risk' young adults (who) were mostly Latinos.[6]

The goal of this particular production was to steer the audience away from gangs and to encourage them to use means other than violence to resolve problems. But what about those spectators who don't identify with the narrative? Negrón-Muntaner observes that it 'is the universal consensus by both critics and creators of *West Side Story* that the film is not in any way "about" Puerto Rican culture, migration, or community life . . . . Hence, if *West Side Story* was

[5] Ibid., p. 83.
[6] Ibid., p. 84.

never intended to be "real" and doesn't feel real to Puerto Rican spectators, what accounts for its reality effects?'[7] Answering her own question, Negrón-Muntaner explains that 'West Side Story has provided what no Puerto Rican-made film has been able to deliver to date: a deceptively simple, widely seen, and shared text dwelling on still critical issues like migration, class mobility, racism, and police brutality'.[8]

For critics like Stacy Wolf, the disturbing legacy of West Side Story has more to do with sexuality than race – specifically, compulsory heterosexuality – a convention that is inherent to the genre of musical film. That such an 'aggressively heterosexual' production remains so popular is disturbing to Wolf:

> Through Broadway revival and productions in touring companies, high schools, colleges and universities, community theaters, (West Side Story) (and other) musicals continue to be woven into the fabric of American culture, and they continue to draw audiences year after year . . . . In this way, in the apparently innocuous and undeniably pleasurable practices of song and dance, musicals literally reproduce and reperform heterosexuality.[9]

Yet an indication of the changing times – and interpretations – of West Side Story is epitomised by the 1996 re-recording of the original soundtrack, which is dominated by black and Latino vocalists. Moreover, writes Negrón-Muntaner, 'To listen to Selena sing "A Boy Like That" with its refrain of "stick to your own kind" is nothing but

[7] Ibid.
[8] Negrón-Muntaner, p. 87.
[9] Wolf, p. 360.

chilling', given that she would be violently murdered by a disturbed associate shortly after the recording in 1995. Yet, the curtain officially fell on *West Side Story*'s problematic treatment of race, gender, and sexuality in another song recorded on the same CD, as Negrón-Muntaner concludes: 'the black/brown/straight face finally comes down when Little Richard sings "I Feel Pretty", and it is clear that no other performer was meant to sing this song'.[10]

Romeo and Juliet (Zeffirelli 1968)

If, as Richard Burt attests, one of the afterlives of Zeffirelli's *Romeo and Juliet* may be found in Abel Ferrara's *China Girl*, then it would be hard not to include *Shakespeare in Love* (John Madden 1998) – a high period piece about 'the making of' *Romeo and Juliet* – in this same category. Nominated for thirteen Oscars and winning seven, including Best Picture, Best Actress (Gwyneth Paltrow), and Best Supporting Actress (Dame Judi Dench), *Shakespeare in Love* is second only to *West Side Story* as the most critically-acclaimed Shakespeare adaptation of all time. Referring to this film as 'Shakespearean', however, is something of a paradox, for historical accuracy has little place in this comedy. Yet as a semi-candid and openly parodic depiction of the Elizabethan literary marketplace, the film importantly demystifies the romantic misconception of Shakespeare as a solitary genius. Rather than representing him as an inspired prodigy who composed his plays in a single sitting while remaining impervious to the need for profit – what Shakespeare's contemporary Ben Jonson disparagingly referred to as 'the money-gett' – the film represents authorship as a hostile workplace environment in which plagiarism is not criminalised but playwrights are. Moreover, the act of writing itself, at least initially, is not divinely

[10] Negrón-Muntaner, p. 102.

inspired but crudely formulaic, forced to cater to the lowest common denominator, characterised in the film as 'Comedie – and a bit with a dog'. In short, screenwriters Marc Norman and Tom Stoppard initially take pains to de-romanticise authorship and reconstitute it as a purely economic transaction, setting the stage for the film's eventual reversal of this perspective.[11]

Appropriately, *Shakespeare in Love* begins by reinforcing the importance of 'the money-gett'. Money, however, is precisely what the famous theatrical entrepreneur Phillip Henslowe *cannot* get, for the film's opening scene shows him being tortured with hot coals, based on his failure to pay the debt he has incurred for financing his latest production. Hence, when the scene cuts away to an advertisement for *The Lamentable Tragedie of the Moneylender Reveng'd*, the line between life and art is blurred in a way that the film will take for theme. Just as art clearly imitates life in the title of Henslowe's latest drama, *Shakespeare in Love* proceeds to represent the creation of *Romeo and Juliet* as a veritable transcript of Will's ill-fated love affair with Viola de Lesseps who, like Juliet, is betrothed to another man against her will.

When the audience first encounters 'Will Shakespeare', however, he is in the throes of writer's block, introduced as a vulnerable young playwright whose 'will' – popular slang for 'penis' in the Renaissance – has failed him. 'It's as if my quill is broken', Will exclaims to the apothecary from whom he seeks a cure, 'as if the organ of the imagination has dried up. As if the proud tower of my genius has collapsed. . . . Nothing comes'. It does not take a master of Renaissance word-play to recognise that the 'organ' that is really suffering is Will's *other* 'quill' in this playful vision of early modern

---

[11] Mark Norman and Tom Stoppard, *Shakespeare in Love: Screenplay* (London: Faber and Faber, 1999).

erectile dysfunction. Appropriately, at this juncture, Viola de Lesseps enters the scene as the would-be actress who is barred from stage performance, in keeping with Renaissance England's strict playhouse decorum. Thus, disguised as her 'cousin' Thomas de Lesseps, Viola auditions for a part in Will's new play and lands the lead – Romeo – which she continues to perform unbeknownst to everyone but Will himself, until the young malcontent and future revenge tragedy playwright John Webster discovers the two making love backstage.

Central to the sexual motifs introduced at the beginning of the film, playmaking in *Shakespeare in Love* is synonymous with love-making, as the transcript of *Romeo and Juliet* emerges from sexual collaboration between Will and Viola. For example, when the two lovers 'rehearse' the balcony scene exchange while having sex, it is difficult to ascertain which lines are recited from memory and which are improvised, since Will's entreaty, 'stay but a little, I will come again', coincides with his orgasm. Curiously, although Viola is never given credit for her additions to *Romeo and Juliet*, rival playwright Christopher Marlowe is represented as providing Will with the play's title and plot, as Norman and Stoppard offer an amusingly accurate vision of Renaissance playwriting as a predominantly collaborative enterprise (between men) as well as a cutthroat creative environment that predates copyright and the protection offered by intellectual property laws.

Howsoever comical, the playwriting scenes described above provide an accessible point of departure for educating audiences about the conditions of authorial production in the Renaissance. For instance, the film's representation of the contingencies and collaborations that alternately plague and propel the creation of *Romeo and Juliet* offers an ideal segue into the discussion of 'Shakespeare's' play as a work that exists in multiple and, in the case of the First and Second Quartos, dramatically differently versions. In addition, the failure to credit Viola, who is shown inventing nearly half of the play's lines, leads to a discussion of the taboo against female authorship and playwriting in particular. Indeed, the film's depiction of Will changing the title of 'his' play from *Romeo and Ethyl, the Pirate's Daughter* to *Romeo and Juliet* alludes not only to the literary piracy that is thought by some to account for one extant version of the play but also, in its eventual erasure of 'Ethyl, the Pirate's Daughter', suggests Virginia Woolf's famous speculation that John Shakespeare *also* had a daughter, known, simply, as 'Shakespeare's sister'. Conceived of, fittingly, in *A Room of Her Own*, Woolf imagines that Shakespeare had a sister who shared the same extraordinary gift for writing as her brother; owing to cultural mores, however, she was forced to keep her talent a secret and, eventually, committed suicide by drowning, paying quiet homage to another of Shakespeare's 'sisters', Ophelia.[12]

Shakespeare in Love concludes tragicomically with the stubborn Queen Elizabeth's reluctant commendation of Will as a poet of 'true love' and the immediate shipment of Viola off to the Virginia tobacco plantation owned by her wicked husband, Lord Wessex (played by Colin Firth). The last frame reveals that a shipwreck has left her to wander the beach alone, perhaps even widowed, as Will – basking in the glory of his success and the bane of his love's departure – superimposes writing on this final, solitary image of Viola, reinventing her as the star of *Twelfth Night*. Although the timing of the blockbuster seemed to owe something to the success of Luhrmann's 1996 *Romeo + Juliet*, the truth is, Marc Norman had devised the script and sold it to Universal in 1989; and in 1992, after Tom Stoppard had added his knowledge of Elizabethan theatre to

---

[12] Virginia Woolf, *A Room of One's Own* (1929), (New York: Mariner Books, 2005).

the screenplay, the film was to star Julia Roberts and Daniel Day-Lewis. But the latter could not be moved to play the part and Roberts quit, causing Universal to lose $4.5 million in pre-production expenditures. It wasn't until 1996 that the orphaned screenplay was purchased by Harvey Weinstein at Miramax; that same year, Paltrow and Fiennes were cast as the leads and the show went on – in style – to sweep the 1999 Oscars.

Unquestionably, the most profound influence that Zeffirelli's 1968 *Romeo and Juliet* had was on the US soap opera market, as Nino Rota was brought in to score the love-theme for an afternoon drama which, in its own right, was based on *Romeo and Juliet: The Young and the Restless*. And what better title to capture the energy and angst of the very youth generation featured in Zeffirelli's 1968 film? First broadcast in 1973, the show is set in an imaginary, Italian-named location called Genoa City, Wisconsin. The plot initially revolved around the affluent Brooks family and the poor Foster family; after successive re-writings and even wholesale character replacements in the 1980s, the 'two households' and sworn enemies would change to the Abbots and the Newmans. However, *The Young and the Restless* is best known for the rivalry between Katherine Chancellor and Jill Foster Abbot, one of the longest-running feuds in the history of daytime drama. The show continues to receive the highest ratings of any US soap opera. Moreover, to this day 'Natalie's Theme', composed by Rota, features a singular, haunting melody that is recognisable by audiences all over the world. Referring to Nino Rota, the great Federico Fellini once observed: 'He had a geometric imagination, a heaven-sent musical gift . . . His was an interior world, to which reality had little hope of access'.[13] The same might be said of Franco Zeffirelli himself.

[13] Fellini, quoted in Bracewell, p. 27.

Released in April 2010 (Gary Winick), the much-anticipated romantic comedy *Letters to Juliet* is a fitting homage to Zeffirelli's greatest love: Italy. With breathtaking views of Verona and Soave, the film is part of the post Merchant/Ivory explosion of the 'Italian travelogue' genre that brought us films about flawed-but-romantic trips to or within Italy such as *Bread and Tulips* (Silvio Soldini 2000), *Italian For Beginners* (Lone Scherfig 2000) *Under the Tuscan Sun* (Audrey Wells 2003), *My House in Umbria* (Richard Loncraine 2003), *Di Passagio* (Jim Kicklighter 2009), and *The Twilight Moon Saga: New Moon* (Chris Weitz 2009) – the latter is actually a vampire spinoff of *Romeo and Juliet*, with exquisite shooting locations in Monte-pulciano. *Letters to Juliet* is the story of a twenty-something American girl (played by Amanda Seyfried) who goes to Verona, where she becomes one of 'Juliet's secretaries' – one of the many young women who find old love letters under what is presumably the *real*, 'historical' Juliet's balcony – and respond to them with advice. (Such a club does exist in Verona, to whom a postman delivers several hundred letters a week from forlorn lovers.) When the protagonist discovers a 1957 letter written by 'Claire' (Vanessa Redgrave) she decides to undertake a quest to find – and reunite – the two long-lost lovers. Meanwhile, she finds herself drifting away from her fiancé back in the States and toward Claire's grandson. Providing a fresh spin on *Romeo and Juliet*, this version focuses primarily on divided lovers from the older, rather than younger generation, and shows off its Italian setting in a style that would make Zeffirelli proud; for 'oh, to know (his) Italy' is to love it.

William Shakespeare's Romeo + Juliet (1996)

'In a wonderful twist of irony, Franco Zeffirelli's film . . . once attacked for its heady excess when released in 1968, now came to be regarded, in the face of Luhrmann's end-of-the-century dynamic assault, as the "classic" or "real" version'.[14] Indeed, the fact that Luhrmann's film inspired a wave of teen adaptations of various Shakespeare plays only fanned the flames as Hollywood was soon teeming with popular films such as *10 Things I Hate about You* (1999, *Shrew*), *Never Been Kissed* (1999, *As You Like It*), *O* (1999, *Othello*), *She's the Man* (2006, *Twelfth Night*) – to name only the most successful. But despite the extraordinary hype Luhrmann's film received and produced as a fin-de-siècle phenomenon, its association with teen homicide has gone largely unnoticed. As Michael Anderegg points out: 'The last words we hear at the end of *Romeo + Juliet* ("we hope your rules and wisdom choke you") are from Radiohead, not Shakespeare, and they affirm a gene-rational conflict that we have not actually experienced, except intermittently, in the course of the film itself'.[15] Indeed, an angst-ridden fifteen year-old who was evidently influenced by Luhrmann's film – or at least the soundtrack – went on a murderous rampage, first killing his parents and, the next morning, killing two students and injuring at least twenty-four others upon entering the Thurston High School cafeteria in Oregon; evidently, when the authorities entered the gunman's house, they discovered *Romeo + Juliet*'s soundtrack playing on repeat. Though no one but the killer could truly be held responsible for this tragedy, it is worth noting that the lyrics of several songs on the soundtrack seem to invite destructive behavior. The groaning, melancholy words of the band Garbage in '#1 Crush' repeat 'I would die for you'; Everclear's 'Local God' asks the listener to 'Be my Romeo . . . tell me all about your pain . . . . you look so fucking stupid'; One Inch Punch ominously intones: 'I will split you in half'; and, finally, Radiohead's 'Talk Show Host' is, in light of the

[14] Crowl, pp. 119–20.
[15] Anderegg, p. 80.

circumstances, perhaps the eeriest of all, beginning: 'You want me – Fuckin' come and find me. I've been waiting . . .' This *real life* 'afterlife' of Luhrmann's *Romeo + Juliet* staged at Thurston High all too closely resembles Shakespeare's play in that, when all was said and done, two teens were dead.

On a slightly more optimistic note, Luhrmann's film inspired some wonderful commentary based on another morbid issue: the implied death of drama, cinema, or public life itself in his image of 'Sycamore Grove'. Some envisioned Luhrmann's film as an allegory of media imperialism in which only the strong survive; for Sam Crowl, the film's two discrete scenes featuring a rival medium – the television – are subsumed by our awareness of the larger cinematic frame: 'Shakespeare's story creates the news, and Luhrmann's film frames it'.[16] Disagreeing, Michael Anderegg finds Luhrmann's adaptation to be more of an homage to the stage: 'For all its cinematic verve, Luhrmann's *Romeo + Juliet* is a highly theatrical film, its style clearly drawn from Luhrmann's work in operas as much as advertising and rock videos'.[17] But the haunting, reoccurring image of Sycamore Grove – the remains of a ruined cinema – seem to belie this reading. For example, Judith Buchanon explains that the film's 'elegiac symbolism' marks the passing, indeed, the death, of 'public performative arenas – both theatres and cinemas . . . left to crumble in spaces no longer fashionable, memorials to their own outmodishness'.[18] Peter S. Donaldson concludes that 'Luhrmann's film belongs to a pointedly *post-theatrical* approach to Shakespeare film adaptation', while Richard Vela ups the ante by describing Luhrmann's mise-en-scène not only as post-apocalyptic

---

[16] Crowl, p. 134.

[17] Anderegg, p. 74.

[18] Judith Buchanan, *Shakespeare on Film* (Harlow, England: Pearson Longman, 2005), p. 236.

but also as a 'post-Shakespearean world'.[19] Regardless of the specific medium for which Sycamore Grove mourns, perhaps the more important point is the sheer plurality of readings that the tableau has inspired. The fact that no two critics agree about the meaning of this architectural monument is, in many respects, *quintessentially* 'Shakespearean', reminding us that Romeo and Juliet is a 'text' that is eternally in contention with itself.

Referring to Sycamore Grove, Sam Crowl observes that 'this marginal space between the city (the land of the father) and the sea (the land of the unknown) is the territory of the young and restless'.[20] It is uncanny that two of Leonardo DiCaprio's subsequent films were *Titanic* (James Cameron 1996) and *The Beach* (Danny Boyle 2000) – although the latter has nothing to do with *Romeo and Juliet*, the former is certainly a spinoff, as the rival factions are constituted along class lines between an engaged debutante Rose Butaker (Kate Winslett) and an impoverished artist Jack Dawson (DiCaprio). Though Jack dies of hypothermia in an effort to save Rose once the ship capsizes, Rose lives on to tell their story, which is narrated in flashback.

A more conspicuous spinoff of Baz Lurhmann's *Romeo + Juliet* is *My Shakespeare* (2005), a documentary about a young, multi-cultural group of non-actors from a poor section of Northwest London who put on an experimental production of *Romeo and Juliet* at the Royal Academy of Dramatic Arts. Though billed as '*My Shakespeare: Romeo & Juliet for a New Generation, with Baz Luhrmann*', the title is deceiving in that Luhrmann is never once on the set – he is intermittently shown on a screen giving advice to the 'at risk' teen actors as well as the director (British actor Paterson

---

[19] Donaldson, p. 198 (emphasis his); Vela, p. 99.
[20] Crowl, p. 121.

Joseph) as the production's mentor. A computer screen containing images of Luhrmann's own *Romeo + Juliet* is frequently shown in the shots of his 'advising sessions'. In the end, the production featuring an Afghani Juliet and Black Romeo receives a standing ovation and the cast members are transformed by Shakespeare – inspired to go on and do something with their lives. It is Baz Luhrmann – at the time new a father himself – who delivers the moral directly to the 'older generation' as a kind of second epilogue:

> The big idea at the end of the play is that it took the loss of their children for the adult world to realize that it is their hatred that has brought this about. What the Montagues and Capulets learn at the end of the play is that the problem was with themselves, the problem wasn't the other person's hatred; it came about because of their own hatred, their inability to resolve it. And if you have that inability, then one day, you will wake up, and your children will be gone.

As in *Romeo and Juliet*, it may be up to the teens themselves to ensure that this moral is heard, as one cast-member enthusiastically exclaims of the production: 'It was really, really good. I'(ll) be tellin' my grandchildron about it'.

Considering the many afterlives that Luhrmann's film implicitly invoked and provoked when it took the screen by storm in 1996, Philippa Hawker summarises the cultural forces against which *William Shakespeare's Romeo + Juliet* continues to contend:

> the figures of Romeo and Juliet are already inscribed into contemporary high and popular culture, in contexts ranging from *West Side Story* to Ashton's ballet, from Bugs Bunny cartoons

to the Everclear song on the film's soundtrack. How many countless times has the balcony scene been the subject of parody and homage? How many overt references are there in popular songs to the figure of Romeo? (And, for that matter, isn't it interesting how the word has acquired a pejorative, dismissive meaning: a 'Romeo' is a gigolo, a Latin lover or unreliable disposition. Juliet, however, has disappeared from view, remembered by little more than the bridal accessory known as the Juliet cap.)[21]

But as we have seen with *Letters to Juliet*, Juliet has made some-thing of a comeback in recent years, battling – in Deepa Mehta's *Water* (2005) in particular – to be so much more than a mere 'accessory'.

Referring to the relationship between water and *Romeo and Juliet*, Anderegg builds on Crowl's suggestion that the lovers seek another 'elemental existence' by adding that 'water suggests a purity, a spiritual component to their love, which is absent in Zeffirelli's version'.[22] Deepa Mehta's *Water* offers a brilliant literalisation of this trope against the backdrop of the Romeo and Juliet story. Nominated for an Oscar in the category of Best Foreign Film in 2007, *Water* is the most profound afterlife of *William Shakespeare's Romeo + Juliet*, as the third and final film in Mehta's 'elemental trilogy', which began with *Fire* (1996) and was followed by *Earth* (1998).

In her effort to draw attention to the social status of widows (which, despite the film's setting in British-occupied India in 1938, is very much a comment on contemporary Hindu fundamentalism).

[21] Hawker, p. 9
[22] Anderegg, p. 45.

Significantly, Mehta's exquisite, controversial picture was delayed by the same cultural laws her film sought to debunk. Banned from filming in the Holy City of Benares (on the Ganges River) in 1999 by Hindu nationalists, Mehta was eventually able to recreate the look of both the Ashram (widow's home) and of the Ganges by relocating to Sri Lanka, where she completed the film *six* painstaking years later. Though no longer the cultural norm, Mehta's film explains that according to Hindi scriptures, a widow has only three choices in life: 1) to burn herself on their husband's funeral pyre; 2) to consent to marry her deceased husband's younger brother; or, 3) to live out her years in an Ashram, shunned by society. The film suggests that this conception of widows-as-pariahs has far too many followers in today's India – as *Water* concludes by estimating that

> There are over 34 million widows in India according to the 2001 Census.
> Many continue to live in conditions of social, economic and cultural deprivation as prescribed 200 years ago by the Sacred Texts of Manu.

Much of the story is captured through the eyes of Chuyia, an eight year-old girl who has been married off to a sickly, elder man, who dies before they have really even met. The bewildered girl doesn't understand why her family has sent her to a veritable prison, in which the residents are required to have their heads shaven, wear meager white wraps, and receive only one meal a day; they are also forbidden to communicate with the 'outside world', from which the Ganges essentially separates them. Chuyia is befriended by the gorgeous Kalyani, the only widow permitted to keep her hair long because of her otherworldly beauty – that is, until she agrees to marry Narayan, a member of the elite Brahmin caste and an ardent follower of Mahatma Gandhi. When Kalyani's plans are made known to the others, the leader of the Ashram cuts her hair off and imprisons her, until Shakuntala, a deeply religious widow who begins to question her faith as she sees the young Chuyia die a little every day, sets Kalyani free. Together, Kalyani and Narayan are rowed across the 'Ganges' that represents the vast cultural divide that conspires against their romance. Despite the fact that a new and very unpopular law has been passed to allow widows to remarry, Kalyani relents halfway across the river, ashamed of her new look and fearful of facing the judgment of Narayan's wealthy Brahmin father. After conducting an elaborate purification ritual in the sacred water of the Ganges, Kalyani walks into the reservoir until she disappears beneath the water; her shoes and clothing are discovered the next morning near the steps. Though this event marks the end of the *Romeo and Juliet* theme, Chuyia's story remains unresolved at this point.

After telling the Ashram leader that she wants to go home because she believes that the new law entitles her to return to her family, Chuyia is sent off in a rowboat on a trip across the Ganges. However, along the way, the boat stops at what Chuyia believes to be Narayan's home. Goaded on by the woman charged with taking the girl 'home', Chuyia enters the sophisticated dwelling expecting sweets and bread, announcing to the stranger behind the curtain, 'I'm here to play'. Subsequently, she is raped (offscreen) and, upon her return to the Ashram side of the Ganges, Chuyia is shown collapsed in a foetal position on the bow of the rowboat; Shakuntala immediately sweeps her up and cares for her, seeking to purify Chuyia in the river. Too dazed to speak or walk, Chuyia is then carried off by Shakuntala to a rally for Gandhi, in whose care she hopes to leave the abused child. When Gandhi's train leaves, and no one will respect her wishes to 'take the child' because of Shakuntara's status, the desperate mother-figure spies Narayan, to whom she gives Chuyia, knowing that he will ensure that her wish will be honoured. As the camera lingers on a painful shot-reverse-shot sequence of Shakuntara staring at Narayan and Chuyia as the train pulls further and further away, we are left wondering where Shakuntara will go from here, now that she has heard Gandhi's religious beliefs and has momentarily escaped the Ashram. In a close up of Shakuntara's profile – her head slightly turned toward us (in the direction of the departed train) – we see a completely ambivalent character, certain that she has done the right thing for Chuyia, but wondering what she should do for herself. *Water* is one of those rare versions of *Romeo and Juliet* in which other storylines and characters prove to be equally, if not more compelling, than the star-crossed lovers themselves.

Summing up the value of adapting *Romeo and Juliet*, Rita Moreno implicitly returns us to the primal scene of love versus the legend, when she muses: 'It's romantic tragedy, and there will always be the Hatfields and McCoys, and the Antons and Marias. Always, always. There are no forces that can stop that story from happening in that particular way'. In Moreno's vision, love – not the legend – conquers all. And, as we await subsequent versions, we are assured, just as Christian's yet-to-be-written adaptation in *Moulin Rouge!* affirms, that in cultures all around the world, *Romeo and Juliet* is not only about 'a love' but, also, a *story* 'that will last forever'.

Select bibliography

Adler, Renata. 'The Screen: Zeffirelli's "Romeo and Juliet" Opens', *The New York Times* 9 October, 1968: p. 41.

Alighieri, Dante. *The Divine Comedy: Volume Two: Purgatory*, trans. Mark Musa (New York and London: Penguin, 1985).

Aragon, Louis. 'La nuit de Moscou', in *Le roman inachevé* (Paris: Gallimard, 1956).

Archer, Eugene. 'Filmed Musicals are on Increase', *The New York Times* 30 September, 1961: p. 16.

Arias, David Lagunas. *Romani Studies* 5, Vol. 12, No. 1 (2000): pp. 5–55.

Arroyo, Jose. 'Kiss kiss bang bang', *Film/Literature/Heritage*, ed. Ginette Vincendeau (London: British Film Institute, 2001), pp. 120–25.

Ascham, Roger. 'The Schoolmaster, or Plain and Perfect Way of Teaching Children the Latin Tongue' (London, 1570), pp. 23–28; reprinted in *Romeo and Juliet: Texts and Contexts*. Ed. Dympna Callaghan (Boston: Bedford/St. Martin's, 2003), pp. 167–175.

Babcock, Robert. '*Romeo and Juliet*, 1, iv, 86: An Emendation', PQ 8 (1929), 407–8.

Ball, Robert Hamilton. *Shakespeare on Silent Film: A Strange Eventful History* (New York: Theatre Arts Books, 1968).

Bandello, Matteo. 'La sfortunata morte di dui infelicissimi amanti che l'uno di veleno e l'altro di dolore morirono, con vari accidenti', *Le Novelle* (c.1554), in *Romeo & Juliet: Original Text of Masuccio Salernitano, Luigi Da Porto, Matteo Bandello, William Shakespeare*. Ed. Adolph Caso, trans. Percy Pinkerton (Boston: Dante University of America Foundation, 1992), pp. 53–88.

Barthes, Roland. *S/Z*, translated by Richard Miller (New York: Hill and Wang, 1974).

Bazin, Andre. *What is Cinema?* (Berkeley: University of California Press, 1967).

Bernstein, Leonard. *Findings* (New York: Doubleday, 1993).

Blayney, Peter. 'The Publication of Playbooks'. *A New History of Early English Drama*, ed. John D. Cox and David Scott Kastan (New York: Columbia University Press, 1997): pp. 383–422.

Boaistuau, Pierre. *XVIII Histoires extraictes des oeuvres italiennes de Bandel, et mises en langue Françoise ...* (1559). Les six premières par Pierre Boisteau, surnommé Launay, natif de Bretaigne. Les douze suiuans par Franc, de Belle Forest, Comingeois (Lyon, 1578), pp. 37–77.

Boccaccio, Giovanni. *Il Decamerone di Messer Giovanni Boccacci* (c. 1350–53; rev. 1370–71). Ed. Pietro Fanfani (Florence: Successori Le Monnier, 1904).

Bracewell, Michael. 'The Best Music in Film', *Sight and Sound XIV* (September 2004): pp. 26–29.

Bracker, Milton. '*West Side Story* Greeted in Paris', *The New York Times* 31 March, 1961: p. 22.

Braudy, Leo. 'Afterword: Rethinking Remakes' in *Play it Again, Sam. Retakes on Remakes*. Eds. Andrew Horton and Stuart Y. McDougal (Berkeley: University of California Press, 1998): pp. 327–34.

Brooke, Arthur. *The Tragicall Historye of Romeus and Iuliet* (1562), in *Brooke's 'Romeus and Juliet' Being the Original of Shakespeare's 'Romeo and Juliet'*. Ed. J.J. Munro. London: Chatto and Windus, 1908.

Brooks, Peter. *Reading for the Plot: Design and Intention in Narrative* (Cambridge: Harvard UP, 1984).

Bronfen, Elisabeth, *The Knotted Subject. Hysteria and Its Discontents* (Princeton: Princeton University Press, 1998).

Buchanan, Judith. *Shakespeare on Film* (Harlow, England: Pearson Longman, 2005).

Bullough, Geoffrey. *Narrative and Dramatic Sources of Shakespeare*, Vol. 1 (8 Vols.) (New York: Columbia University Press, 1957–75).

Burt, Richard. 'Shakespeare and Asia in postdiasporic cinemas: spin-offs and citations of the plays from Bollywood to Hollywood', in *Shakespeare, The Movie II: Popularizing the plays on film, TV, video, and DVD*: pp. 265–303.

Burt, Richard. 'Slammin' Shakespeare In Acc(id)ents Yet Unknown: Liveness, Cinem(edi)a, and Racial Dis-integration', *Shakespeare Quarterly* 53.2 (Summer 2002): pp. 201–26.

Bush, Stephen W. *Motion Picture World*, 5 December, 1908, pp. 446–47.

Calavita, Marco. '"MTV Aesthetics" at the Movies: Interrogating a Film Criticism Fallacy', *Journal of Film and Video* 59.3 (Fall 2007), pp. 15–31.

Callaghan, Dympna. Ed. *Romeo and Juliet: Texts and Contexts* (Boston: Bedford/St. Martin's, 2003).

Cartmell, Deborah. 'Shakespeare and Zeffirelli', in *The Cambridge Companion to Shakespeare on Film*, pp. 216–25.

Charnes, Linda. *Notorious Identity: Materializing the Subject in Shakespeare* (Cambridge and London: Harvard University Press, 1993).

Charnes, Linda. '"What's Love Got to Do With It?" Reading the Liberal Humanist Romance in Shakespeare's *Antony and Cleopatra*', *Textual Practice* 6, no. 1 (1992): pp. 1–16.

Clizia. 'L'infelice Amore de' due fedelissimi amanti Giulia e Romeo scritto in ottava rima da Clizia, nobile Veronese ad Ardeo suo' (1553), in Alessandro Torri's *Giulietta e Romeo* (Pisa, 1831): pp. 149–93.

Comolli, Jean-Luc, and Jean Narboni. 'Cinema/Ideology/Criticism' (1969) in *Film Theory and Criticism*, edited by Gerald Mast, Marshall Cohen, and Leo Braudy, 4th ed. (New York and Oxford: Oxford University Press, 1992): pp. 682–89.

Conrad, Peter. *To be Continued: Four Stories and Their Survival* (Oxford: Clarendon Press, 1995).

Cook, Page. 'The Sound Track', *Films in Review* 19 (November, 1968): p. 571.

Corrigan, Timothy. *A Cinema Without Walls: Movies and Culture after Vietnam* (New Brunswick: Rutgers University Press, 1991).

Crowther, Bosley. 'Film at the Rivoli is Called Masterpiece', *The New York Times* 19 October, 1961: p. 39.

Crowther, Bosley. 'Musical Advance: The "West Side Story" Expands on Screen', *The New York Times*, 22 October, 1961: p. X1.

Dalton, Michael. *The Countrey Justice* (London, 1618).

Donaldson, Peter S. *Shakespearean Films/Shakespearean Directors* (Boston: Unwin Hyman, 1990).

Donawerth, Jane. *Shakespeare and the Sixteenth-Century Study of Language* (Urbana: University of Illinois Press, 1984).

Da Porto, Luigi. *Istoria novellamente ritrovata di due nobili amanti, con la lor pietosa morte, intervenuta già nella citta di Verona nel tempo del Signor Bartolommeo della Scala* (1530), in *Romeo & Juliet: Original Text of Masuccio Salernitano, Luigi Da Porto, Matteo Bandello, William Shakespeare*, edited by Adolph Caso, trans. Maurice Jonas (Boston: Dante University of America Foundation, 1992): pp. 23–52.

Edelman, Charles. *Brawl Ridiculous: Swordfighting in Shakespeare's Plays* (Manchester: Manchester University Press, 1992).

Elizabeth I. 'Proclamation Prohibiting Unlawful Assembly under Martial Law' (20 June 1591); reprinted in Callaghan: pp. 232–33.

Erne, Lukas. 'Shakespeare and the Publication of His Plays', *Shakespeare Quarterly* 53.1 (Spring 2002): pp. 1–20.

Fitter, Chris. '"The quarrel is between our masters and us their men": *Romeo and Juliet*, Dearth, and the London Riots', *English Literary Renaissance* 30 (2000): pp. 154–83.

Freud, Sigmund. 'The Uncanny' (1919), *Studies in Parapsychology* (New York: Collier Books, 1963).

Friedly, Alfred. 'In Italy, Erotic Films Are Non Grata', *The New York Times* 14 July, 1969: p. 28.

Friedman, Michael. 'Introduction: "to think o' th' teen that I have turned you to": The Scholarly Consideration of Teen Shakespeare films'. *Shakespeare Bulletin* 26.2 (Summer 2008): pp. 1–7.

Geertz, Clifford. *The Interpretation of Cultures* (New York: Basic Books, 1977).

Gibbons, Brian. Ed. *The Arden Shakespeare Romeo and Juliet*, 2nd ed. (London: Methuen, 1980; 1997).

Goldberg, Jonathan. '"What? In a names that which we call a Rose', The Desired Texts of *Romeo and Juliet*', *Crisis in Editing: Texts of the English Renaissance*. Ed. Randall McLeod (New York: AMS Press, 1988): pp. 173–202.

Greg, W.W. *Dramatic Documents from the Elizabethan Playhouses: Stage Plots, Actors' Parts, Prompt Books* (Oxford: Oxford University Press, 1931).

Greenblatt, Stephen *Shakespearean Negotiations* (Berkeley: University of California Press, 1988).

Guinness, Sir Alec. *A Positively Final Appearance* (New York: Viking, 1999).

Gurr, Andrew. *Playgoing in Shakespeare's London*, 2nd ed. (Cambridge: Cambridge University Press, 2002).

Hailey, R. Carter. 'The Dating Game: New Evidence for the Dates of Q4 *Romeo and Juliet* and Q4 *Hamlet*', *Shakespeare Quarterly* 58.3 (2007): pp. 367–87.

Hallet, Bryce, 'British Love *Romeo* and Leave *Titanic*', *Sydney Morning Herald*, 21 April, 1998: p. 7.

Hardt, Michael, and Antonio Negri. *Multitude: War and Democracy in the Age of Empire* (New York: Penguin, 2004).

Harris, Diana. 'Violent Delights, Violent Ends: Baz Luhrmann's *Romeo + Juliet*', presented at the Centenary Conference of Shakespeare and screen scholars in Malaga, Spain, 21–24 September, 1999.

Hawker, Philippa. 'DiCaprio, DiCaprio, Wherefore Art Thou, DiCaprio?' *Meanjin*, March 1997: pp. 6–15.

Herrick, Robert. 'To the Virgins, to Make Much of Time', in *The Norton Anthology of English Literature*, 8th ed., Vol. 1 (2 Vols.). Ed. Stephen Greenblatt (New York and London: W.W. Norton, 2006): pp. 1659–60.

Hodgdon, Barbara. '*William Shakespeare's Romeo + Juliet*: Everything's Nice in America', *Shakespeare Survey* 52 (1999): pp. 88–98.

Holmer, Joan Ozark. '"Draw, if you be men": Saviolo's Significance for *Romeo and Juliet*', *Shakespeare Quarterly* 45.2 (Summer 1994): pp. 163–89.

Hoppe, Harry R. *The Bad Quarto of 'Romeo and Juliet': A Bibliographical and Textual Study*, Cornell Studies in English, 36 (Ithaca: New York, 1948): pp. 12–15.

Jackson, Russell. *Shakespeare Films in the Making: Vision, Production and Reception* (Cambridge and New York: Cambridge University Press, 2007).

Jameson, Fredric. 'Postmodernism and Consumer Society', in *Movies and Mass Culture*. Ed. John Belton (New Brunswick: Rutgers University Press, 1996): pp. 185–202.

Jameson, Fredric. 'Postmodernism, or The Cultural Logic of Late Capitalism', in *Postmodernism: A Reader*. Ed. Thomas Docherty (New York: Columbia UP, 1993): pp. 62–92.

Johnson, Biran D. 'Souping up the Bard', *Macleans*, 11 November, 1996: pp. 74–5.

Jones, Welton. 'Triumph of tragic love ensures long life of "Romeo"', *The San Diego Tribune*, 12 April, 1998: p. E1.

Jonson, Ben. *Timber: Or, Discoveries Made upon Men and Matter* (1616), *The Collected Works of Ben Jonson*, Vol. 8 (11 Vols.). Ed. C.H. Herford, P. Simpson, and E. Simpson (Oxford: Clarendon Press, 1925–52).

Kasha, Al, and Joel Hirschorn. *Notes on Broadway: Conversations with the Great Songwriters* (Chicago: Contemporary, 1985).

Kermode, Frank. *Romeo and Juliet in The Riverside Shakespeare*, 2nd ed. Ed. G. Blakemore Evans (Boston and New York: Houghton Mifflin, 1997): pp. 1101–03.

Kuhl, E.P. '*Romeo and Juliet*, I, IV, 84F', *PQ* 9 (1930): pp. 307–8.

Lacan, Jacques. 'Seminar on "The Purloined Letter"', Trans. Jeffrey Mehlman, in *The Purloined Poe: Lacan, Derrida, and Psychoanalytic Reading*. Ed. John P. Muller and William J. Richardson (Baltimore: Johns Hopkins UP, 1988): pp. 28–54.

Lanier, Douglas. 'Drowning the Book: *Prospero's Books* and the Textual Shakespeare' in *Shakespeare, Theory, and Performance*. Ed. James C. Bulman (New York and London: Routledge, 1996): pp. 187–209.

Lanier, Douglas. 'Film Spin-Offs and Citations', in *Shakespeares after Shakespeare: An Encyclopedia of the Bard in Mass Media Culture*, Vol. 1 (2 Vols.) (Westport, Connecticut and London: Greenwood Press, 2007).

Lehman, Ernest. 'Letter', 40th Anniversary Edition of *West Side Story*, DVD booklet.

Lehman, Ernest. *Screenplay*, 40th Anniversary Edition of *West Side Story*, 2-DVD commemorative set (2002).

Lehmann, Courtney. *Shakespeare Remains: Theater to Film, Early Modern to Postmodern* (Ithaca and New York, 2002).

Lehmann, Courtney. 'What is a Film Adaptation? Or, Shakespeare *Du Jour*', *Shakespeares After Shakespeare: An Encyclopedia of the*

Bard in Mass Media and Popular Culture. Ed. Richard Burt. Vol. 1 (2 Vols.) (Westport, CT: Greenwood Press, 2007): pp. 74–80.

Levenson, Jill. Ed. *The Oxford Shakespeare Romeo and Juliet* (Oxford: Oxford University Press, 2008).

Loehlin, James N. '"These violent delights have violent ends", Baz Luhrmann's Millennial Shakespeare'. In *Shakespeare, Film, Fin de Siècle.* Ed. by Mark Thornton Burnett and Ramona Wray (London: MacMillan, 2000): pp. 121–136.

Lord, Albert B. *The Singer of Tales,* 2nd ed. Eds. Stephen Mitchell and Gregory Nagy (Cambridge, MA: Harvard University Press, 2000).

Luhrmann, Baz. 'An Interview with Baz Luhrmann', *Cinema Papers* (February 1997): pp. 12–14.

Luhrmann, Baz. 'Interview', *The Guardian,* 27 April, 2000, http://www.guardian.co.uk/film/2000/apr/27/guardianinterviewsat bfisouthbank1#article_continue (accessed 11/08/09).

Luhrmann, Baz. 'A Note from Baz Luhrmann', in *William Shakespeare's Romeo + Juliet. The Contemporary Film, The Classic Play* (New York: Bantam Doubleday Dell, 1996): pp. i–ii.

Luhrmann, Baz, and Craig Pearce. *Screenplay. William Shakespeare's Romeo + Juliet. The Contemporary Film, The Classic Play* (New York: Bantam Doubleday Dell, 1996): pp. 1–162.

Lyly, John, *Campaspe* (1583). Ed. G.K. Hunter (Manchester: Manchester University Press, 1991).

Macherey, Pierre. 'Creation and Production', in *Authorship from Plato to the Postmodern.* Ed. Sean Burke (Edinburgh: Edinburgh University Press, 1995): pp. 230–32.

Manning, Roger B. *Village Revolts: Social Protest and Popular Disturbances 1509–1640* (Oxford: Oxford University Press, 1988).

Marx, Karl, *Critique of Hegel's Philosophy of Right* (1843). Ed. Joseph O'Malley (Cambridge: Cambridge University Press, 1977).

Martin, Jennifer L. 'Tights vs. Tattoos: Filmic Interpretations of *Romeo and Juliet*', *English Journal* (September 2002): pp. 41–46.

Maslin, Janet. 'Soft! What Light? It's Flash, Romeo', *The New York Times,* 1 November, 1996: p. C1.

Mathews, Peter. 'Review of *William Shakespeare's Romeo + Juliet*', *Sight and Sound* 7.4 (April 1997): p. 55.

Milton, John. *Paradise Lost in John Milton: Complete Poems and Major Prose*. Ed. Merritt Y. Hughes (New York: Macmillan, 1957).

Moore, Olin H. *The Legend of Romeo and Juliet* (Columbus: Ohio State University Press, 1950).

Negrón-Muntaner, Frances. 'Feeling Pretty: *West Side Story* and Puerto Rican Identity Discourses', *Social Text* 63, 18.2 (Summer 2000): pp. 83–106.

Nieves, Santiago, and Frank Algarin. 'Two Reviews: *My Family/Mi Familia* and the Perez Family', in *Latin Looks: Images of Latinas and Latinos in the US Media* (Boulder, Colorado and Oxford: Westview Press, 1997): pp. 221–24.

Norman, Mark, and Tom Stoppard. *Shakespeare in Love: Screenplay* (London: Faber and Faber, 1999).

O'Brien, Geoffrey. 'The Ghost at the Feast', *New York Review of Books*, 6 February, 1997, p. 13.

Outhwaite, R.B. *Dearth, Public Policy and Social Disturbance in England, 1550–1800* (Cambridge, Cambridge University Press, 1991).

Ovid. *Metamorphoses* (8 AD). Trans. Charles Martin (New York: W.W. Norton, 2004).

Patavini, Rolandino. 'Cronica Marchie Trivixane' (c. 1262), *Rerum Italicarum Scriptores*. Ed. L.A. Muratori (Città di Castello: Tipi dell'editore S Lapi, 1905).

Pearlman, E. 'Staging *Romeo and Juliet*: Evidence from Brooke's *Romeus*', Theatre Survey 34 (May 1993): pp. 22–32.

Peck, Seymour. 'Again the Movies Sing and Dance', 2 July 1961: p. SM16.

Petersen, Lene. 'De-composition in Popular Elizabethan Playtexts: A Revalidation of the Multiple Versions of *Romeo and Juliet* and *Hamlet*', *Oral Tradition* 23.1 (March 2008): pp. 118–147.

Peyser, Joan. *Bernstein: A Biography* (New York: Beech Tree, 1987).

Pilkington, Ace. 'Zeffirelli's Shakespeare', in *Shakespeare and the Moving Image: the plays on film and television*. Eds. Anthony Davies and Stanley Wells (Cambridge: Cambridge University Press, 1994): pp. 163–79.

Playboy Magazine ad, *The New York Times*, 4 October, 1968: p. 39.

Pretenders. 'When Will I See You?', *Packed!*, 1981.

'Queen Goes to Film: Elizabeth Braves Snowstorm to See "West Side Story"', *The New York Times*, 27 February, 1962: p. 27.

Rolling Stones. 'Street Fighting Man', *Beggars Banquet*, 1968.

Rothwell, Kenneth. *A History of Shakespeare on Screen: A Century of Film and Television* (Cambridge: Cambridge University Press, 1999).

Rothwell, Kenneth. 'Hollywood and Some Versions of *Romeo and Juliet*: Toward a "Substantial Pageant"', *Literature/Film Quarterly* 1.4 (Fall 1973): pp. 343–51.

Rothwell, Kenneth. 'Zeffirelli's *Romeo and Juliet*: Words into Picture and Music', *Literature/Film Quarterly* (Fall 1977): pp. 326–331.

Rozen, Leah. 'Picks & Pans', *People Magazine*, 1 November, 1996: p. 21.

Sandoval, Alberto. 'West Side Story: A Puerto Rican Reaing of "America"', *Jump Cut* 39 (1994): pp. 59–66.

Saviolo, Vincentio. *His Practise* (London: printed by Thomas Scarlet, 1595).

Salernitano, Masuccio. 'The Thirty-Third-Novel,' from *Il Novellino* (1475), in *Romeo & Juliet: Original Text of Masuccio Salernitano, Luigi Da Porto, Matteo Bandello, William Shakespeare*, ed. Adolph Caso, trans. Maurice Jonas (Boston: Dante University of America Foundation, 1992): p. 15–22.

Schumach, Murray. '"West Side Story" Wins Oscar as Best Film', *The New York Times*, 10 April, 1962: p. 47.

Scott, Lindsey. '"Closed in a Dead Man's Tomb": Juliet, Space, and the Body in Franco Zeffirelli's and Baz Luhrmann's Films of *Romeo and Juliet*', *Literature/Film Quarterly*, Vol. 36 (2008): pp. 137–46.

Sevin, Adrien. 'Le Philocope de messire Iehan Boccace Florentin' (Paris, 1542), Cf. H. Hauvette, 'Une variante française de la légende de Roméo et Juliette', *Revue de littérature comparée* I, 3 (1921): pp. 329–37.

Sidney, Sir Philip. *Sir Philip Sidney: Selected Prose and Poetry*. Ed. Robert Kimbrough (Madison: University Press, 1983).

Siegel, Paul. *Shakespeare Quarterly* 12.4 (Autumn 1961): pp. 371–92.

'Shakespeare in the Cinema: a film directors' symposium with Peter Brook, Sir Peter Hall, Richard Loncraine, Baz Luhrmann, Oliver Parker, Roman Polanski, and Franco Zeffirelli', in *Cineaste* 24.1 (1998): pp. 48–55.

Spillers, Hortense. 'Mama's Baby, Papa's Maybe: An American Grammar Book', *Diacritics* (Summer 1987): pp. 65–81.

Stone, Lawrence. *The Crisis of the Aristocracy 1558–1641* (Oxford: Oxford University Press, 1965).

Swinburne, Henry. *A Treatise of Spousals*, Section IX: Of Ripe or Lawful Age for Marriage (1600), printed in 1686; reprinted in Callaghan: p. 288.

Tatspaugh, Patricia. In *The Cambridge Companion to Shakespeare on Film*, 1st ed. Ed. Russell Jackson (Cambridge: Cambridge University Press, 2000): pp. 135–59.

Tourneur, Cyril. *The Atheist's Tragedie* (1611). Ed. Irving Ribner (Cambridge, MA: Harvard University Press, 1964).

Travers, Peter. 'Just Two Kids in Love', *Rolling Stone*, 14 November, 1996: pp. 123–4.

U2. 'In the Name of Love'/'Pride', *The Unforgettable Fire*, 1994.

Van Watson, William. 'Zeffirelli, Shakespeare and the Homosexual Gaze', *Literature/Film Quarterly* 20 (1992): pp. 145–48.

Vázquez, Blanca. 'Puerto Ricans and the Media: A Personal Statement', *Centro* (Winter 1990–91): pp. 5–15.

Vela, Richard. 'Post-Apocalyptic Spaces in Baz Luhrmann's *William Shakespeare's Romeo + Juliet*, *Apocalyptic Shakespeare: Essays on Visions of Chaos and Revelation*' in Recent Film Adaptations. Ed. Melissa Croteau and Carolyn Jess-Cooke (Jefferson, NC: McFarland, 2009), pp. 90–109.

Watson, Robert N. and Stephen Dickey. 'Wherefore Art Thou Tereu? Juliet and the Legacy of Rape', *Renaissance Quarterly* 58 (2005): pp. 127–56.

Welles, Stanley, et. al. *The Complete Works: Original-Spelling Edition* (Oxford: Oxford University Press, 1986).

Welles, Stanley. Ed. *The Oxford Shakespeare: The Tragedies* Volume III (4 Vols.), (Oxford and New York: Oxford University Press, 1994).

Welsh, Jim. 'Postmodern Shakespeare: Strictly Romeo', *Literature-Film Quarterly* 25.2 (1996): pp. 152–3.

Werstine, Paul. 'Plays in Manuscript', *A New History of Early English Drama*. Ed. John D. Cox and David Scott Kastan (New York: Columbia University Press, 1997): pp. 481–498.

West Side Memories, DVD commemorating the 40th Anniversary of the original release of *West Side Story* (2002).

'"West Side Story" is Applauded in Soviet Film Festival Showing', *The New York Times,* 9 July, 1963: p. 28.

Williams, Raymond. *Marxism and Literature* (Oxford: Oxford University Press, 1977).

Wolf, Stacy. '"We'll Always Be Bosom Buddies": Female Duets and the Queering of Broadway Musical Theater', *GLQ: A Journal of Lesbian and Gay Studies* 12.3 (2006): pp. 351–76.

Woolf, Virginia. *A Room of One's Own* (1929), (New York: Mariner Books, 2005).

Worthen, W.B. 'Drama, Performance, Performativity'. *PMLA* (October 1998): pp. 1093–1107.

Zeffirelli, Franco. 'Filming Shakespeare', in *Staging Shakespeare: Seminars on Production Problems.* Ed. Glenn Looney (London and New York: Garland, 1990): pp. 239–71.

Zeffirelli, Franco. *Zeffirelli: An Autobiography* (New York: Weidenfeld and Nicolson, 1986).

Žižek, Slavoj. *Enjoy Your Symptom! Jacques Lacan in Hollywood and Out* (New York: Routledge, 1992).

index

··